New Directions in Book History

Series Editors
Shafquat Towheed
Faculty of Arts
Open University
Milton Keynes, UK

Jonathan Rose
Department of History
Drew University
Madison, NJ, USA

As a vital field of scholarship, book history has now reached a stage of maturity where its early work can be reassessed and built upon. That is the goal of New Directions in Book History. This series will publish monographs in English that employ advanced methods and open up new frontiers in research, written by younger, mid-career, and senior scholars. Its scope is global, extending to the Western and non-Western worlds and to all historical periods from antiquity to the twenty-first century, including studies of script, print, and post-print cultures. New Directions in Book History, then, will be broadly inclusive but always in the vanguard. It will experiment with inventive methodologies, explore unexplored archives, debate overlooked issues, challenge prevailing theories, study neglected subjects, and demonstrate the relevance of book history to other academic fields. Every title in this series will address the evolution of the historiography of the book, and every one will point to new directions in book scholarship. New Directions in Book History will be published in three formats: single-author monographs; edited collections of essays in single or multiple volumes; and shorter works produced through Palgrave's e-book (EPUB2) 'Pivot' stream. Book proposals should emphasize the innovative aspects of the work, and should be sent to either of the two series editors.

Editorial Board
Marcia Abreu, University of Campinas, Brazil
Cynthia Brokaw, Brown University, USA
Matt Cohen, University of Texas at Austin, USA
Archie Dick, University of Pretoria, South Africa
Martyn Lyons, University of New South Wales, Australia

More information about this series at
http://www.palgrave.com/gp/series/14749

Rasoul Aliakbari
Editor

Comparative Print Culture

A Study of Alternative Literary Modernities

Editor
Rasoul Aliakbari
Comparative Literature
University of Alberta
Edmonton, AB, Canada

New Directions in Book History
ISBN 978-3-030-36893-7   ISBN 978-3-030-36891-3   (eBook)
https://doi.org/10.1007/978-3-030-36891-3

© The Editor(s) (if applicable) and The Author(s), under exclusive licence to Springer Nature Switzerland AG 2020
This work is subject to copyright. All rights are solely and exclusively licensed by the Publisher, whether the whole or part of the material is concerned, specifically the rights of translation, reprinting, reuse of illustrations, recitation, broadcasting, reproduction on microfilms or in any other physical way, and transmission or information storage and retrieval, electronic adaptation, computer software, or by similar or dissimilar methodology now known or hereafter developed.
The use of general descriptive names, registered names, trademarks, service marks, etc. in this publication does not imply, even in the absence of a specific statement, that such names are exempt from the relevant protective laws and regulations and therefore free for general use.
The publisher, the authors and the editors are safe to assume that the advice and information in this book are believed to be true and accurate at the date of publication. Neither the publisher nor the authors or the editors give a warranty, expressed or implied, with respect to the material contained herein or for any errors or omissions that may have been made. The publisher remains neutral with regard to jurisdictional claims in published maps and institutional affiliations.

Cover illustration: Getty Images, Pixelchrome Inc.

This Palgrave Macmillan imprint is published by the registered company Springer Nature Switzerland AG.
The registered company address is: Gewerbestrasse 11, 6330 Cham, Switzerland

ACKNOWLEDGMENTS

Numerous individuals, associations, and institutions have been instrumental in the creation of this essay collection. The nucleus of the project took form during the panel "Print, Public Readership, and Alternative Literary Modernities" held as part of the Engaging Communities Comparatively conference of the Canadian Comparative Literature Association at the University of Calgary, Canada, in 2016. Henceforth, various versions of the theoretical foundations and sketches of case studies for this volume were presented, for example, at the 25th annual conference of the Society for the History of Authorship, Reading and Publishing at the University of Victoria, Canada, in 2017, and at the annual conference of the Bibliographical Society of Canada at the University of Regina, Canada, in 2018. While participants and organizers of these conferences supplied much-needed impetus and critique, the University of Alberta Libraries and MacEwan University Library offered the materials, both secondary and historical primary sources. As such, the current incarnation of this project owes much to all of these.

The contributors to this volume deserve special acknowledgment. The essayists have not only consistently demonstrated acumen and professionalism but also meticulously engaged with editorial commentary and responded promptly. Although there were otherwise excellent, compelling, and promising works submitted for this project, not all of them perfectly fit the main goals of the study, and thus some had to be put aside. Still, I would like to offer thanks to the declined authors, as it was by perusing their abstracts, short essays, and full chapters that I further delineated and consolidated the main thematics and investigative scaffolds of the project into its present configuration.

As well, many thanks are due to my colleagues and friends—too many to mention by name—who never spared from me their insights, suggestions, and experiences in person, over coffee or meals, or by phone or e-mail correspondence. Of all these, a few individuals merit special thanks for, among other things, their vision, generosity, and diligence. During the initial phases of the project, Dr. Gary Kelly (Distinguished Professor in English and Film Studies and Comparative Literature, University of Alberta, Canada) supplied crucial advice and encouragement to help lift the project off the ground. Midway through the work, Dr. Jonathan Rose (William R. Kenan Professor of History, Drew University, USA; former president of The Society for the History of Authorship, Reading and Publishing and current co-editor of *Book History*) provided a much-needed positive reflection on the project, further propelling it forward. As well, Dr. Robert Fraser (Emeritus Professor of the English Department, Open University, UK) closely examined the theoretical foundations of the volume, introduced essential resources, and, equally importantly, shared his optimistic vision, further advancing the work. In addition, Dr. Heather Murray (Professor in the English Department and the Book History and Print Culture Program, University of Toronto, Canada) engaged with the theoretical bases and cases studies of the work and returned significant constructive commentary. Ultimately, Dr. Cindy Chopoidalo (Assistant Editor, *Canadian Review of Comparative Literature*) copyedited the volume both conscientiously and punctually, significantly improving linguistic and stylistic consistency and accuracy throughout the work. All these individuals merit abundant thanks for their generous, timely, and much-required input.

Last but not least, special thanks should go to Shaun Vigil (former Senior Commissioning Editor for Cultural, Media, and Communication Studies, Palgrave Macmillan), Camille Davies (current Editor of Palgrave's Cultural, Media, and Communication Studies), and their Assistant Editor, Glenn Ramirez, for processing the proposal and manuscript in such a professional and timely fashion and for always being highly accessible for all queries. On a related note, acknowledgment must be made to the blind-reviewers of the volume's initial proposal as well as that of the full manuscript for their substantial feedback. The project, as it currently stands, owes its cogency of argumentation, diversity of thematics and terrains, and, most important, its internal cohesion to their rigorous assessment.

Edmonton, AB, Canada   Rasoul Aliakbari

CONTENTS

1   Comparative Print Culture and Alternative Literary Modernities: A Critical Introduction to Frameworks and Case Studies   1
Rasoul Aliakbari

2   Song Dynasty Classicism and the Eleventh Century "Print Modernity"   23
Daniel Fried

3   Alternative Imaginaries of the Modern Girl: A Comparative Examination of Canadian and Australian Magazines   41
Victoria Kuttainen and Jilly Lippmann

4   The Making of a National Hero: A Comparative Examination of Köroğlu the Bandit   61
Judith M. Wilks

5   Between Poetry and *Reportage*: Raúl González Tuñón, Journalism and Literary Modernization in 1930s Argentina   83
Geraldine Rogers

viii   CONTENTS

6   New Fiction as a Medium of Public Opinion: The
    Utopian/Dystopian Imagination in Revolutionary
    Periodicals in Late Qing China   105
    Shuk Man Leung

7   Nineteenth-Century African American Publications on
    Food and Housekeeping: Negotiating Alternative Forms
    of Modernity   123
    Hélène Le Dantec-Lowry

8   Progressing with a Vengeance: The Woman Reader/
    Writer in the African Press   143
    Corinne Sandwith

9   Fashioning the Self: Women and Transnational Print
    Networks in Colonial Punjab   165
    Arti Minocha

10 Crafting the Modern Word: Writing, Publishing, and
    Modernity in the Print Culture of Prewar Japan   185
    Andrew T. Kamei-Dyche

11 "Books for Men": Pornography and Literary Modernity
    in Late Nineteenth-Century Brazil   205
    Leonardo P. Mendes

12 Print Culture and the Reassertion of Indigenous
    Nationhood in Early-Mid-Twentieth-Century Canada   225
    Brendan Frederick R. Edwards

Index   245

Notes on Contributors

Rasoul Aliakbari PhD in Comparative Literature, specializes in print culture, world literature, book history, writing and communication studies, and digital humanities with a comparative focus encompassing Anglo-American, Middle Eastern, and North African contexts. He has received several awards and scholarships including the Queen Elizabeth II Scholarship and the State of Kuwait Award in Islamic Studies. His publications have appeared in *Journal of Fairy-Tale Studies* and other journals. He has taught English, Comparative Literature, Writing Studies, and Communication Studies at the University of Alberta, MacEwan University, NorQuest College, and Northern Alberta Institute of Technology, all in Canada.

Brendan Frederick R. Edwards, PhD in History, is the head of the Library and Archives of the Royal Ontario Museum, after teaching at universities abroad and in Canada. He is the author of *Paper Talk: A History of Libraries, Print Culture, and Aboriginal Peoples in Canada Before 1960* (2005) and a number of essays, including contributions to volumes 2 and 3 of the *History of the Book in Canada* (2005, 2007). Brendan is a collaborator on the SSHRC-funded project *The People and the Text: Indigenous Writing in Northern North America to 1992.*

Daniel Fried is Associate Professor of Chinese and Comparative Literature at the University of Alberta, Canada, and specializes in comparative and theoretical approaches to Chinese intellectual history. He is the past president of the Association of Chinese and Comparative Literature, and the founding chair of the MLA forum in Pre-Fourteenth-Century Chinese Literature. His latest book, *Dao and Sign in History,* examines the Daoist semiotic tradition in the ancient and early medieval periods in comparison with twentieth-century continental philosophy. His paper in this volume is related to his research for a new book on Song dynasty print culture.

Andrew T. Kamei-Dyche is an Associate Professor teaching Japanese History and Social Science in the School of Global Studies and Collaboration at Aoyama Gakuin University, Japan. He is a scholar of Japanese book history and print culture, specializing in late nineteenth- and early twentieth-century publishing. His particular interest is studying networks among publishers and intellectuals. His publications include English and Japanese articles on publishers, bookstores, and reading, and he is working on a full-length study of the publisher Iwanami Shoten.

Victoria Kuttainen is Associate Professor in English and Writing at James Cook University, Australia. Her teaching and research interests include postcolonialism, Australian and Canadian Literatures, American and English writers, print culture, the intersections of media and literature, genre, gender, and colonial modernity. Her books include *Unsettling Stories* (2010) and *The Transported Imagination: Australian Interwar Magazines and the Geographical Imaginaries of Colonial Modernity* (co-authored with Susann Liebich and Sarah Galletly, 2018).

Hélène Le Dantec-Lowry is Professor of American Studies at Université Sorbonne Nouvelle, France, where she also directs the Center for Research on North American History (CRAN). She is a specialist of the cultural and social history of African Americans and women in the nine-teenth- and twentieth-century United States, and she was editor-in-chief for history for the *French Journal of American Studies* from 2013 to 2019. Her recent publications include *Writing History from the Margins: African Americans and the Quest for Freedom* (2017) co-edited with Claire Parfait and Claire Bourhis-Mariotti, and an online anthology of African-American historians, available at http://www.shs.terra-hn-editions.org/Collection/?-Historiens-africains-americains- (2018).

Shuk Man Leung is an assistant professor in the School of Chinese and the School of Modern Languages and Cultures at the University of Hong Kong. Her specialization includes late Qing, modern and contemporary Chinese literature, Hong Kong literature and print culture in Greater China. She holds a PhD from the School of Oriental and African Studies, University of London, and has an HKSAR government-funded project on the Chinese Cultural Revolution discourse in Hong Kong print media. Her articles have appeared in *Cultural Studies, Comparative Literature Studies*, and *Journal of Modern Literature in Chinese*.

Jilly Lippmann is an academic editor, a tutor in English Literature, and a doctoral candidate at James Cook University, Australia. Her PhD research focuses on representations of women, particularly the Modern Girl, in late colonial modernity in mainstream print culture and Australian literature. She has also been a Research Assistant and a Learning Advisor and Course Facilitator for first-year bridging courses into academic studies. She has served on numerous boards including the Foundation for Australian Literary Studies.

Leonardo P. Mendes obtained his PhD in Literary Theory at the University of Texas at Austin, USA. He is Associate Professor of Literary Studies at Rio de Janeiro State University, in Brazil. He specializes in nineteenth-century Brazilian fiction, the naturalist novel, and pornography. His publications include *O retrato do imperador: negociação, sexualidade e romance naturalista no Brasil* (2000), and many articles in scholarly journals, such as "*Álbum de Caliban*: Coelho Neto e a literatura pornográfica na Primeira República" in *O eixo e a roda* (2017) and "Zola as Pornographic Point of reference in Late Nineteenth-Century Brazil" in *Excavatio* (2018).

Arti Minocha is an associate professor at the Department of English at Lady Shri Ram College, Delhi University, India. She has taught various courses in Indian literature, modern British literature, world literatures, and Afro-American literature. Her articles on Indian theatre, print culture, and South Asian women's histories have appeared in many publications. Her current research project seeks to reinscribe women into histories of print and literary cultures and language debates in colonial Punjab. She has been awarded scholarships by the Charles Wallace India Trust and King's College, London, for this project.

Geraldine Rogers is Professor of Literature at the National University of La Plata (UNLP) and a researcher at the National Council of Scientific Research (CONICET) of Argentina. She specializes in Argentinean literature and periodicals and has delivered postgraduate courses and lectures in Spain (University of Seville and University of Salamanca), Brazil, and Chile. She is the author of the book *Caras y Caretas: Cultura, política y espectáculo en los inicios del siglo XX* (2008) and many articles, such as, most recently, "Jorge Luis Borges in Argentina" (*Oxford Research Encyclopedia of Literature*, 2018).

Corinne Sandwith is Professor of English at the University of Pretoria, South Africa, and is the author of *World of Letters: Reading Communities and Cultural Debates in Early Apartheid South Africa* (2014) and co-editor with M.J. Daymond of *Africa South: Viewpoints, 1958–1961*. Her research interests include African print and reading cultures and the history of reading and cultural debate in early apartheid South Africa. Her recent work focuses on the social lives of books and print materials, exploring questions such as the production of African literature and the circulation and citation of texts in disparate reading contexts.

Judith M. Wilks holds a PhD in Near Eastern Languages and Civilizations from the University of Chicago. She has taught most recently at Northwestern University, where she was an instructor in Turkish, Persian, and Islamicate literature. Her research focuses on comparative cultures, especially the historical intersection between literary and political trends. She has published numerous translations from Persian, Turkish, and Tajik (*Stories from Iran: A Chicago Anthology*, 1991; *World Literature Today*, vol. 70, no. 3, 1996), and is currently working on a comparative study of gender roles in Turkish and Persian folk tales.

LIST OF FIGURES

Fig. 5.1 The first edition of *La rosa blindada*, with xylography by J.C. Castagnino   92

Fig. 5.2 Series Redescubrimiento de España. (Ibero-Amerikanisches Institut Preussischer Kulturbesitz, Berlin)   98

Fig. 5.3 Series Redescubrimiento de España. (Ibero-Amerikanisches Institut Preussischer Kulturbesitz, Berlin)   99

Fig. 7.1 Title page of Abby Fisher, *what Mrs. Fisher knows about old southern cooking, soups, pickles, preserves,* etc. (San Francisco: Women's Co-operative Printing Office, 1881). Primary source edition. Nabu Public Domain reprints, ICG Testing.com. 424741LV00021B/929/P   136

Fig. 8.1 Women's Page Supplement (Title Page), *Bantu World* May 1936. (Courtesy of University of Johannesburg Special Collections)   145

Fig. 8.2 Women's Page Supplement (Additional Page), *Bantu World* May 1936. (Courtesy of University of Johannesburg Special Collections)   158

Fig. 9.1 The facsimile of the original cover page of *Cosmopolitan Hinduani*   172

Fig. 10.1 Dust jacket illustration from volume one of *Wagahai wa Neko de aru*, depicting the cat as an anthropomorphic Egyptian deity toying with humanity. (Source: Nihon Kindai Bungakukan/Holp Shuppan 1976 replica)   197

Fig. 10.2 Cover of the Iwanami Shoten one-volume edition of *Kokoro* (1914). (Source: Nihon Kindai Bungakukan/Holp Shuppan 1972 replica)   198

CHAPTER 1

Comparative Print Culture and Alternative Literary Modernities: A Critical Introduction to Frameworks and Case Studies

Rasoul Aliakbari

This essay collection is simultaneously diverse and focused, covering many subject areas that are interrelated in significant ways. The volume features examinations of various contexts of print modernity: African-American intervention via print into the bourgeois class, popular journalism and avant-garde poetry in Argentina, women-oriented commercial periodicals in Australia and Canada, nation formation through literary print in Azerbaijan and Turkey, erotica as popular literary print in Brazil, Indigenous nationhood and print and reading cultures in Canada, revolutionary utopian literary periodicalism in China, women's assertion in print and subjectivity formation in India and South Africa, canonization and classicizing through print and designating a native Chinese modernity, and the contest through publishing over outlining modern subjecthood in Japan. Nonetheless, and despite its diversity, the project is grounded in a central framework: the study of alternative literary modernities through the lens of comparative print culture.

R. Aliakbari (✉)
Comparative Literature, University of Alberta, Edmonton, AB, Canada
e-mail: rasoul@ualberta.ca

© The Author(s) 2020
R. Aliakbari (ed.), *Comparative Print Culture*, New Directions in
Book History, https://doi.org/10.1007/978-3-030-36891-3_1

1

Although they may not be explicitly named in every chapter of this collection, a few scholarly strands inform this project. Comparative print culture, the scholarly framework of this project, derives from two major areas: comparative literature on the one hand, and print culture and book history studies, with gestures in the direction of comparison, on the other. Comparative print culture primarily derives from Gayatri Chakravorty Spivak's recommendation in *Death of a Discipline* of an inclusive comparative literature in conjunction with area studies. In her words, "the politics of production of knowledge in area studies (and also in anthropology and the other 'human sciences') can be touched by a new Comparative Literature, whose hallmark remains a care for language and idiom" (2003, 4–5). Enabled by a transformed area studies, comparative literature becomes further capable of crossing borders of various sorts, including media. Building on this transdisciplinary coordination, Spivak contends that Southern Hemisphere languages must be regarded as dynamic cultural media rather than cultural objects of study based on preconceived Anglo-American academic models.[1] According to her, comparative literature and area studies "*can* work together in the fostering not only of national literatures of the global South but also of the writing of countless indigenous languages in the world that were programmed to vanish when the maps were made" (2003, 15; emphasis in original). Informed by Spivak, rather than presenting a monolithic model for the study of non-European print cultures, this collection recognizes, documents, and examines diversities of various sorts from production to circulation to consumption in printed materials that lead to the shaping of distinct cultures and literatures of modernity. For example, in Chap. 2 of this volume, Daniel Fried seeks to offer an understanding of modernity not necessarily tethered to the Western European experience, but as the simultaneously local and universal consciousness of an irreversible rupture between past and present as delivered in print. Grounded in this conceptualization, he argues that, despite being nascent and partial, the first print-cultural modernity occurred in eleventh-century China, where print was associated with canonicity and classicism in order to drive a high level of consciousness

---

[1] Also, see her "Can the Subaltern Speak?" for a critique of postcolonialism as a regulation of the nuances and complexities of cultural practices in the South in conformity with fixed, reductive North American academic models of postcolonial study. Moreover, by sketching alternative sites of literary modernity and print culture, this anthology attempts to provide responses, albeit partial ones, to the demonstration in "Can the Subaltern Speak?" of the inaudibility of voices on the periphery.

of temporal break and periodization. For this, Fried examines the collection, standardization, and canonization, during the eleventh century, of the works of Han Yu and Liu Zongyuan, two literati from the late eighth and early ninth centuries. This chapter scrutinizes the classicizing, canonizing, and printing of Han Yu's and Liu Zongyuan's against the backdrop of the eleventh-century vibrant publishing industry and thus demonstrates the reinforced perception, during the latter era, of stylistic and technological rupture with the antiquarian past, hence the Song dynasty *modernity* as opposed to a Tang dynasty *archaism*. In other words, Fried's essay outlines an *endogenous*, rather than a colonial or postcolonial Europe-prompted and thus *indigenized*, literary print modernity, shedding light on the complexities of the cultural practices embedded in Chinese literary print culture as a distinct conception and materialization of literary print modernity.[2]

The framework of this anthology also builds upon scholarly conversations on diversifying and multiplying book history studies in under-studied areas, thus the use of the term *alternative* in reference to sites of examination outside of Europe. A critical understanding of the divergences and convergences in the technology, materials, and cultures of print from inside and outside of the European context is an essential component of this collection. Elizabeth Eisenstein, in her now-classic *The Printing Press as an Agent of Change* (1979), stresses a formerly down-played dimension of European modernization mainly between the fifteenth and seventeenth centuries. She foregrounds the centrality of the print for the diffusion of classical cultural goods and the resultant nascence, and proliferation, of modern Western cultural, religious, and scientific schemata. However, her argument revolves around the print as an instrument of *constancy, fixity, uniformity*, and *permanence*, hence the standardization, amplification, security, and universality flowing therefrom. The current essay collection joins more recent scholarly conversations in comprehending the print, unlike Eisenstein's, with such attributions as *dynamicity, mobility, evolution*, and *repurposing*, thus further challenging Eisenstein's conceptions of, and further diversifying, the print, not only as an apparatus, but also as a culture and discourse. As an example, in *Agent of Change* (2007), Sabrina Alcon Baron, Eric N. Lindquist, and Eleanor F. Shevlin have partly sought

---

[2] Even though his work does not concern China or print culture, Hamid Dabashi does outline an account of an *endogenous* modernity; see his *The World of Persian Literary Humanism*.

to accomplish the diversification goal, among other objectives. For example, as Kai-wing Chow points out, woodblock printing, a highly developed, economical, and efficient print tradition, was extensively practiced in China, Korea, and elsewhere in Asia, and in Europe, before and after moveable-type printing was introduced in Europe. Having demonstrated this, Chow further suggests that "the various 'cultural' explanations for the differential impact of printing in Europe and China need to be reconsidered and the history of printing rewritten from a truly comparative perspective" (2007, 192). As another instance, Geoffrey Roper contends that Eisenstein's theory of print-induced modernity is not thoroughly applicable to the Arab and Muslim contexts due to the specific historical circumstances of Arabic textual transmission and book culture: the relatively late (i.e. in the second half of the nineteenth century) normalization of print as a method of textual transmission, and the prevalence during the nineteenth and early twentieth centuries of lithography rather than typography to reproduce the calligraphic features of manuscripts (2007, 265–66). In addition, Vivek Bhandari contends in "Print and the Emergence of Multiple Publics in Nineteenth-Century Punjab" (2007) that periodicalists and other agents of print used this medium, often outside the purview of the colonial state and European sponsors, alongside oral and performative cultures such as festivals and literary gatherings, to shape multiple public spheres and diverse vernacular literary cultures in India.

Nonetheless, the editors of the afore-cited *Agent of Change* mostly tend to find cultural evidence for Eisenstein's theory, rather than contest it, in zones outside of Europe. As such, my proposition for diversification and counterspace with a view of non-European modernities is informed by Robert Fraser's rich and dense analytical postcolonial book histories more than it is by *Agent of Change*. In *Book History Through Postcolonial Eyes* (2008), Fraser attempts to provide "a comparative study with a fairly broad sweep" focused on Africa and South Asia (ix). Fraser delineates the onset of Indian and African print modernities as reliant, not only on European pioneers in India and in South Africa, but also on local masters in possession of various forms of linguistic and mechanical expertise. Beyond that, Fraser's work is invested in the examination of the production of multifarious, and at times simultaneous, materializations of the text in orality, script, and print, and brings to light alternative sites such as South Asia and Africa, and alterative expressive media such as Namboothiri Brahmins' chorus of the *Rig Veda* in India's state of Kerala and Egyptian papyri spells. Through these examinations, Fraser challenges homogeneous and Eurocentric notions of the operations of the cultures of print and other media, as conceptualized, for instance, by Elizabeth Eisenstein, Benedict Anderson, and Marshall McLuhan. Concomitantly, Fraser discusses readership and qualifies a Saidian reading of European literature, on the grounds that, for instance, Victorian writer H. Rider Haggard's *King Solomon's Mines* (1885)—an English adventure novel set in Africa—did not rank high in the surveys of actual reading preferences of the populace in Accra, Ghana, conducted in 1956. Beyond that, Haggard's fiction was recast for counter-hegemonic political logics in works such as South African Sol Plaatje's (1876–1932) political historical novel *Mhudi* of 1930 (Fraser 2008, 174–76).

Nevertheless, Fraser's work is mostly invested in the study of the production of diverse repertoires of expression and calls for further discussions on the equally important dimensions of literary-cultural modernity: circulation, readership, and thematic analyses. Specifically, his study suggests the desirability of explicitly justifying the *comparative* aspect in juxtaposing Indian and African book histories, of exploring the implications of the comparison, and of digging deeper into the material-cultural transactions and intellectual dialectics between India and South Africa in the shaping of their cultures of print and modernities of various sorts. Although this anthology does not purport to thoroughly fill all these lacunae, it does make attempts. For instance, in Chap. 3, Victoria Kuttainen and Jilly Lippmann explicitly justify their comparative outlook on Australia and Canada of the 1920s and 1930s as two settler colonial domains in which the figure of the Modern Girl has been excluded from both established and revisionist national literary histories, even though, as their chapter further demonstrates, interwar commercial periodicals in both countries evince a plethora of Modern Girl narratives addressed to audiences across the economic spectrum. Addressing the anxieties involved in the projects of constructing national literary canons in Australia and Canada, their essay selects commercial magazines—*The Home* (Australia, 1920–42) and *Mayfair* (Canada, 1927–36, 1937–59) as upmarket serials, and *The Australian Woman's Mirror* (Australia, 1924–61) and *The Western Home Monthly* (Canada, 1899–1932) as mass-market outlets—and analyzes their respective thematics, audiences, and cultural implications all centered on the Modern Girl narratives, featuring independent "flapper-like" women. The (con-)textual leap from Chaps. 2 to 3, and to the rest of the volume, might appear far; however, this is because of the shift, past Fried's essay, from the *native* conceptualization of the modern to its reconfiguration as *domesticated*. In other words, whereas Fried, concerned with China's eleventh-century literary print culture, sketches an *endogenous modernization*, Kuttainen and Lippmann outline the Australian and Canadian manifestations of the Modern Girl as the *indigenized alternative* of its European and American exemplars of female self-designation through consumerism and non-conformist social conduct. In a complex yet well-focused comparative textual and contextual examination of the aforementioned serials, Kuttainen and Lippmann locate the Modern Girl at the crossroads of commodity, culture, narrativization, social classes, and gender hierarchies. As such, Chap. 3 brings to light the versatile roles of women during the interwar period in these settler colonial dominions and demonstrates a female-oriented alternative literary modernity grounded in commercial print culture, as opposed to masculinist and elitist literary historiographies.

Furthermore, in *Books Without Borders: The Cross-national Dimension in Print Culture* (2008), Robert Fraser and Mary Hammond seek to address "'where the books belong' without tethering it to any single location: generic, geographical, methodological or disciplinary" (2). In other words, they aim to find out "[e]xactly how, at various periods and in various zones, have books moved around the world and what difference has this made to their size, their shape, their weight, their appearance, even their contents and manner of address" (Fraser and Hammond 2008, 9). Among several chapters in their collection, Roshni Mooneeram's "Shakespeare's Postcolonial Journey" is closer to the objectives of this anthology. Mooneeram explores the re-appropriation of Shakespeare's works, including *The Tempest*, in post-independence Mauritius for the cultivation of national counter-colonial literary and theatrical discourses and practices (2008, 188–89). Another chapter in Fraser's and Hammond's anthology, Patricia May B. Jurilla's "A New Demand for Old Texts," explains the high popularity of metrical romances in the Philippines in the early twentieth century, on the grounds of their adoption by vernacular publishers and periodicalists to shape a Filipino culture of modernity and counter-colonialism long after the introduction of romances during the Spanish colonial period (1565–1896):

> The American administration prohibited the advocacy of Philippine independence, forbade the display of Filipino flags, and established English as the official language of the nation. In the face of such policies, Philippine

nationalism manifested itself in the celebration of local languages and literatures. Filipino journalists, critics, and scholars praised and promoted the literary tradition of the nation, particularly literature in Tagalog. (Jurilla 2008, 141)

Addressing *repurposing* as a print-cultural mechanism in (post-)colonial sites of literary modernity, in Chap. 4 Judith M. Wilks explores the evolving reuses of Köroğlu stories—a Robin Hood-like figure in Turkic oral heroic traditions and enduringly popular from the Balkans to Afghanistan—past its European Romantic vogue, as a national champion in Turkey and Azerbaijan in the twentieth century. Wilks' argument is similar to Kuttainen's and Lippmann's in Chap. 3 for its elaborate but focused comparative study of textual and contextual terrains. Nonetheless, Wilks documents the reimagining of Köroğlu, as an outlaw and apt fighter in the original Turkic oral culture is Romanticized and partly cleansed in nineteenth-century Orientalist publications suiting the target European readers' bourgeois decorum before he is re-appropriated and adopted, during the twentieth century, in literary print and other media for nationalist and communist modernization projects, respectively, in Turkey and Azerbaijan. The hero undergoes a high degree of transformation from a bandit-hero to, eventually, a nationalist and socialist icon; however, East-West transculturation aside, Wilks' essay also ties in with Daniel Fried's in Chap. 2 in that both studies point to a *literary-cultural past* as simultaneously, and thus oxymoronically, classicized and revitalized for delivering *a modern present*. While not exclusively focused on print culture per se, Wilks is mindful of the reciprocal intellectual transactions between Azerbaijan and Turkey in their modernization phase, and conducts, at the intersection of politics, literature, academic scholarship, and language, a vivid comparative study of the various remediations and transmediations of Köroğlu by Ottoman and Azeri authors such as Mehmet Emin Yurdakul (1869–1944) and Uzeir Hajibeyli (1885–1948), respectively.

Compared to Wilks' essay, Geraldine Rogers' Chap. 5 offers an account of repurposing as embedded primarily in periodical culture. Rogers examines journalistic chronicling in 1930s Argentina as a *reworking* of its French exemplars catering to the *distinct* Argentinian literary, social, and political circumstances of the time. She grounds her critical and contextual investigation in the premise that Latin American modern cultures and systems of communication cannot be taken as replicas of their European counterparts, and despite their appearances as opposites, journalistic correspondence and poeticization are complementary modes of articulation, a set of distinctly Argentinian circumstances that she describes as "divergent" or "peripheral" modernity vis-à-vis Europe. Her essay delivers these premises specifically by discussing the career of Raúl González Tuñón (1905–74), one of Argentina's foremost chroniclers and avant-garde poets, and specifically his distinctive blending of poetry and periodicalism in "reportage" to turn it into an effective tool, given the publication of his works in Buenos Aires, for his social and political commentaries on the ramifications of modernizations of various sorts. In other words, Rogers' essay demonstrates the retooling of the popular French genre of chronicling for the constitution of a distinctive Argentinian vernacular of modern literariness, a political journalistic poetics, and as such aligns with the previous chapters and further advances *alternative modernities* as a framework for considering non-European literary print cultures.

Chapter 6, by Shuk Man Leung, integrates with Chaps. 3, 4, and 5 as it engages with the repurposing of Western models as a characteristic of the constitution of distinct non-European literary print cultures. Leung demonstrates how, in the late nineteenth and early twentieth centuries, Chinese New Fiction, a literary genre with a political function, was reworked from Western and Japanese sources. This chapter documents the political and literary revisionings of Western literary imaginaries in revolutionary periodicals of late Qing China designating the latter, for the burgeoning Chinese public sphere and citizenship, a modernizing sociopolitical counterpart alternative to the West. A representative indication of re-appropriation is the very utopia Leung discusses: though Sir Thomas More's classic 1516 work bears the same title, the utopia of late Qing Chinese New Fiction is different, suggesting advocacy on a national level for the decline of dynastic real-world sociopolitical systems and institutions and for the emergence of a prospective modern future. Further, Leung contextualizes the Chinese literary political utopian imaginations within the flourishing modern press of the time and examines how the concept was transmediated in the major turn-of-the-century revolutionary periodicals such as *Jiangsu Journal, Study Abroad and Translation Magazine,* and *The Alarming News from Russia.* Her essay examines these serials not only for their utopian narratives about the modernization of China but also for their circulation and readership. Another feature that distinguishes the Qing reworking of utopia from its Western exemplars is the intertextuality between the utopian fictional narratives themselves and the political editorials of the periodicals in which they appeared. In this sense, Leung's discussion of *an alternative literary print modernization* resonates with Geraldine Rogers' in the preceding chapter in that both account for distinctive non-European *political poetics* as transmediated through modern periodical cultures.

Furthermore, whereas Rogers briefly cites "peripheral" and "divergent" modernities for sketching Argentina's political and literary periodical culture of the 1930s, it is equally important to outline *multiple modernities*. This is even more significant since the discussion of modernity and its diverse manifestations across cultures is central to this project. As a recent offshoot of the theorizations of modernity, the term "multiple modernities" is increasingly popular in social sciences. Revisiting Karl Marx, Émile Durkheim, and Max Weber, and exposing some of the Eurocentric assumptions underlying their theories, Shmuel Eisenstadt, Jens Riedel, and Dominic Sachsenmaier define multiple modernities as follows:

> The core of multiple modernities lies in assuming the existence of culturally specific forms of modernity shaped by distinct cultural heritages and socio-political conditions. The forms will continue to differ in their value systems, institutions, and other factors. For example, structural differentiation is a typical feature in the institutions of modern societies, ranging from family patterns to socioeconomic institutions and mass communication. Differentiated structures, modes of openness, and ways of questioning the basic premise vary greatly, however, across cultures and historical periods. Unique forms of modernity are created by different activists and social movements that hold distinct views of what makes a society modern. In other words, even though distinctively modern structures, institutions, and cultural systems have spread around the globe, different equally modern societies have appropriated them in a variety of forms. They have done and continue to do so in reference to each other but particularly in reference to the European and later American dynamism of modernity. (2002, 1–2)

Although the concept of multiple modernities is a response mostly to the sweep of economic globalization and homogenization in the aftermath of the fall of the Soviet regime, its insights and framework are relatively applicable to time-spaces outside of the Cold War context. This is because Eisenstadt, Riedel, and Sachsenmaier seek to qualify the assumption in classic theories of modernity that the structural and cultural programs of European modernity, with its hegemonic and homogenizing tendencies, "would 'naturally' be absorbed by all modernizing societies, possibly with local variations" and would ultimately prevail in the whole world (2002, 4). More specifically, Eisenstadt defines multiple modernities as an opposition to the view that "the cultural program of modernity as it developed in modern Europe and the associated basic institutional constellations would ultimately prevail in all modernizing and modern societies" (2002, 27). On the other hand, Eisenstadt contends that modernity and westernization are not the same and explains the history of modernity as "a story of continual constitution and reconstitution of a multiplicity of cultural programs and cultural patterns of modernity" (2002, 27). In this regard, Sachsenmaier recommends that "for the purpose of establishing a new ethical universalism, concerted comparative efforts should establish the commonalities and differences between all kinds of cultures in value systems, sociopolitical orders, attitudes to modernity, and other problem zones" (2002, 62–63).[3]

Sachsenmaier's emphasis on the comparative approach and on outlining the multiplicity of modernities informs part of the framework of this project, as indicated regarding the previous chapters. This essay collection is further steered by the discussions of the titular *alternative modernities*, a term derived from the work of Dilip Parameshwar Gaonkar, who regards cultural modernization as a dichotomy between bourgeois order and avant-garde modernity, beginning with the Romantic movement and continuing in popular and commercial media. Surveying an extensive range of thinkers, including Karl Marx, Charles Baudelaire, Max Weber, and Walter Benjamin, Gaonkar suggests that modernity is not a finite moment but an ongoing project that has spread and is spreading across the globe after it was born in the West, and operates from the twin matrices of change and routine (2001, 1–7). In the (post-)Enlightenment era, "the modern is associated with the scientific superiority of the present over antiquity"

---

[3] For another study of multiple modernities, see Jenny Kwok Wah Lau's *Cinemas and Popular Media in Transcultural East Asia* (2002). This anthology explores East Asia's multiple modernities as locale-based reactions in which "each society mobilizes its own cultural resources, less for 'coping' with Westernization, as the West may view it, than for a double negotiation between social and cultural modernity" (9). Lau's work also highlights the transregional dialectics underlying the formation of cultures of modernity in the area, amongst other things (2002, 3), debunks the view of the formation of East Asian culture as a one-way response to the "West" (2002, 7), and demonstrates that the cinematic portrayals of women in traditional and popular cinema of Hong Kong are more progressive than their counterparts in artistic films (2002, 8–9).

(2001, 6), and modernity is "a leap in the open air of the present as history" (2001, 7).

Having laid these grounds, and by drawing on the writings of Arjun Appadurai and Paul Gilroy, Gaonkar contributes to further provincializing Western modernity and to designating alternatives outside Europe: "To think through and against means to think with a difference – a difference that would destabilize the universalist idioms, historicize the context, and pluralize the experiences of modernity" (2001, 15). In other words, "the proposition that societal modernization, once activated [as in Western Europe] moves inexorably towards establishing a certain type of mental outlook [...] and a certain type of institutional order [...] irrespective of the place is simply not true" (Gaonkar 2001, 16). It is within this framework of culture- and site-specific understanding that he explores the processes of "creative adaptation" involved in "other theaters of modernity." Examples in Gaonkar's work include the discourse and practice of Mexican citizenship as contingent on the specific and shifting local, national, and international historical, economic, and political circumstances of Mexico, rather than being a progressivist logic of expansion (2001, 16–18). As another example of alterity, the peoples of the African diaspora have similarly created their own versions and visions of pan-African modernity, despite the pervasive external forces of colonialism and slavery, using the languages, religions, and political ideals of the colonizers (Gaonkar 2001, 18).[4]

Alternativity as a counter-hegemonic and revisionist site is also a major frame of reference in this collection. This is evident in the chapters sketched above and in the rest of the volume. For example, in Chap. 7, Hélène Le Dantec-Lowry links modernity specifically to the nineteenth-century publication of African-American cookbooks and housekeeping guides against the backdrop of White dominance, demonstrating the formation of an alternative modern Black subjectivity facilitated by the emerging culture of print and its associated socioeconomic mobility toward the middle class. Le Dantec-Lowry's comparative study occurs at the crossroads of race, gender, politics, and economy, and includes thematic and contextual examinations of Robert Roberts' *House Servant's Directory or, A Monitor for Private Families* (Boston, 1827), Tunis G. Campbell's *Hotel Keepers, Head Waiters, and Housekeepers' Guide* (Boston, 1848), and Abby Fisher's

---

[4] For an account of the origins of the term *alternative modernity* in anthropology, see Kelly, "Alternative Modernities or an Alternative to 'Modernity'" (2002).

What Mrs. Fisher Knows About Old Southern Cooking, Soups, Pickles, Preserves (San Francisco, 1881). She further situates these publications within the expansion of print technology and increase in literacy rates in the nineteenth-century United States, describing the two earlier works as the first such guides ever published in the United States and the latter as an exceptional publication in the white-dominated South. Uncovering their authors' pro-Black stances, her essay highlights these materials as a significant corpus of African-American intellectual output alongside, for instance, Phillis Wheatley's poetry, slave narratives, and Black-oriented counter-hegemonic and revisionist American history books. For Le Dantec-Lowry, this commercial corpus of prescriptive literature was the site of struggle to cultivate, against White-dominated capitalist modernity, *a more inclusive* bourgeois modernity, hence the term *alternative modernity*. In other words, putting Roberts', Campbell's, and Fisher's difficulty in accessing publication and distribution networks in the larger context of the anti-Black racism of the nineteenth century, and pitting those against these authors' commercial and societal achievements through printing, Chap. 7 regards these emergent circumstances as a challenge to the prevailing racial and economic orders toward further mobilizing an *alternate modern* vision of blackness: one of agency, aptitude, and assertiveness.

As a further example of multiplication and of creating an alternative to hegemonic modernity, Chap. 8, by Corinne Sandwith, explores black women's participation in the public print culture of the 1930s in South Africa, and the possibilities and limitations of this participation in the formation of an alternative modernity consisting of communities of black female writers and readers against the contemporaneous backdrop of male- and white-dominated commercial newspapers and predominant European modes of feminine socializations. Sandwith notes that, while the white female journalist as contributor, letter-writer, and editor had become a commonplace phenomenon in South Africa's print culture by the late 1930s, the same cannot be said of African women, whose interventions were comparatively less. Nonetheless, the launch in 1932 of the front-runner, English-language "Woman's Page" in the weekly Johannesburg-based newspaper *Bantu World* created an exception within which the traditional and emerging forms of femininity were renegotiated and refashioned in reference to black women's modernization in such areas as marriage, sexuality, family, morality, education, and labor division. This chapter further highlights these journalistic writings as a precursor to the advancement of African women's written literature. Sandwith historicizes these contests and negotiations, which revolved around gender, race, and modernization, in the larger context of the commercialization and ideological containments of African newspapers, rapid urbanization, and Christian missionary writings, and examines the extent to which black female essayists and correspondents of the "Women's Page" such as Rossie Khabela, Johannah G. Phahlane, Dora Msomi, and Ellen Pumla Ngozwana reconstituted and redesignated Western modern femininity, ultimately making *Bantu World* a host to a resistant and *alternative African modernity* as distinct from the dominant European exemplars. As well, in this sense, Sandwith's essay specifically aligns with Victoria Kuttainen's and Jilly Lippmann's chapter, since both studies sketch alternative modes of constituting modernity as female centered and as grounded in the printed periodical culture.

Although the discussions of multiple and alternative modernities are integral to this volume, this project also, and more specifically, examines alternative, non-European sites and cultures of print in conjunction with discussions of *literariness*. With regard to literary modernity, Paul de Man has posited, in exploring the interplay between history and modernity, that modernity "exists in the form of a desire to wipe out whatever came earlier, in the hope of reaching at last a point that could be called a true present, a point of origin that marks a new departure" (1983, 148). De Man further notes that literary modernity in fact involves "dependence on similar assertions [of being a new departure] made by their literary predecessors; their claim to being a new beginning turns out to be the repetition of a claim that has already been made" (1983, 161). As such, he contends that literary modernity is not truly unprecedented but is a continued repetition in literary history. Moreover, Jurgen Habermas has discussed (literary) modernity as an unfinished project. Contending that during the French Enlightenment "the modern" became, rather than looking back at the ancient antiquity, belief in a teleology of progression (1985, 4), Habermas adds that "in sum, the project of modernity has not yet been fulfilled" (1985, 13).

Building on these articulations of literary history, literary comparativist Javed Majeed has redirected Habermas' and De Man's discussions to an examination of literary modernity in South Asia; specifically, how some South Asian writers in the colonial period consciously self-identified as *modern* in comparison and contrast to their *traditional* antecedents. For example, Majeed characterizes Faiz Ahmed Faiz's Urdu poetry as willfully departing from pre-modern self-reflexive poetics of ghazal into modern realism (2012, 264). He also regards Muhammad Iqbal's epic poem *Javed Nama* (1932) as a takeoff from the exemplar of Rumi's *Masnavi* by featuring linear narrative progression in an episodic plot. A common thread Majeed identifies among Tamil, Bengali, and Sindhi poets and prose authors is their self-conscious use of conventional and traditional forms, figures, and material in presenting innovative, experimental, and thus modern poetics, thus breaking away from traditional literariness and consciously designating themselves as modernist. In other words, according to Majeed, traditional South Asian literariness—including oral narratives, Sanskrit literature, and the Perso-Arabic tradition—is used to shape a literary modernity that is exemplified by the South Asian novel, whose protagonists are generally champions of modernism and social reform. One such example is Ratan Nath Sarshar's *Fasana-i Azad* (Majeed 2012, 269–70). One of Majeed's conclusions is that, given the multifarious traditional repertoire of written and oral devices, conventions, and thematics upon which South Asian novelists drew, their output should be assessed, not merely against European standards of realist novels, but as a genre-in-the-making, as aesthetics in progress (2012, 217). By examining their textual output, Majeed characterizes South Asian poets and novelists of the colonial period as agents of a literary modernization particular to South Asia. His work, along with those of his theoretical antecedents such as Habermas and de Man, points to literary modernity as an ongoing project and as a set of European, regional, and local confluences that are particular to specific times and places.

This view also informs some of the contributions to this anthology, as literary modernity is treated not only as departures specific to print-oriented time-spaces but also as confluences of international, regional, local, past, and/or present elements reworked by authors, publishers, printers, distributors, or readers. For instance, in Chap. 9, Arti Minocha revisits turn-of-the-century Punjab, India, to demonstrate the participation of women in print culture, despite their erasure from colonial and reform discourses in conventional literary and print historiographies. Her essay focuses on Susila Tahl Ram's novel *Cosmopolitan Hinduani*, written in English and published in Lahore in 1902, as an example of women's intervention in print-based literary modernity amidst religious and class struggles of the time. With a view of the contemporaneous thriving of multiple print publics, such as those of Sikhs, Hindus, and Muslims, Minocha regards the publication of Tahl Ram's novel as an onset of women's intervention in bourgeois subjectivity on both textual and contextual levels, involving transregional and transnational networks of ideal and material-cultural exchange. Minocha's project furthers some of the major objectives of this collection; she examines Tahl Ram's rescripting of modern Western liberalism by infusing it with domestic cultural, religious, and written and oral literary matter. Specifically, she elucidates the repurposing in Tahl Ram's characterization of "the new woman" as a distinctive cosmopolitan refutation of English, colonial Indian, and Indian reformist modes of subjectivity. As such, Minocha's essay also aligns with Kuttainen's and Lippmann's chapter in their respective reconstitutions of a print-based modern literariness centered on modern womanhood.

Similarly, in Chap. 10, Andrew T. Kamei-Dyche outlines the formation of an *alternative literary modernity*, albeit in the print culture of pre-war Japan. He explains the development of Japan's modern sensibilities with reference to Japanese writers such as Mori Ōgai (1862–1922), Natsume Sōseki (1867–1916), Higuchi Ichiyō (1872–96), and Hiratsuka Raichō (1886–1971), and Japanese publishers such as Iwanami Shoten, in spite of governmental and Western influences. In explaining Japan's print modernity, Kamei-Dyche takes into account the turn-of-the-century sweep of state-sponsored and West-simulating technological and cultural modernizations, against which he highlights the multifarious efforts of these literary and cultural agents to mark the contours, and substantiate the conception, of a distinctive modern Japanese literariness that undermined, problematized, complicated, and/or transcended Western and Japanese governmental formulations. Particularly, despite the state's attempts to promote Japan as a fully modernized society on a par with Western nation-states but also possessing a unique traditional heritage, in a monolithic and all-encompassing discourse, Kamei-Dyche further informs us that the writers' and publishers' alternate vision of Japanese modernity propounded a non-cohesive understanding of Japan's tradition, synthesized and enmeshed indigenous Japanese arts and thematics with Western ones, and questioned such totalizing and hegemonic binary categorizations as "Western" versus "Japanese" or "traditional" versus "modern," and, most important, those related to gender. Additionally, although Leung, in Chap. 6, and Kamei-Dyche, in Chap. 10, deal with different political and cultural circumstances pertaining to the respective modernizations of China and Japan, their projects portray the intelligentsia's attempts, within their respective booming print cultures and rises in literacy, to retool select modern Western and indigenous literary and cultural materials for reconfiguring the modern as an alternative to both hegemonic Western and top-to-bottom governmental models. However, whereas Chinese print modernity created a utopian optimism, the Japanese context points to critical realism, as these two chapters further demonstrate.[5]

In Chap. 11, Leonardo P. Mendes describes a similar situation of alternative print modernity involving the interfusion of Western and domestic templates. Yet, whereas Arti Minocha discusses realistic and serious fiction of relatively limited circulation in Chap. 9, Mendes brings to light commercialized literature of decadent character and wide readership in the late nineteenth century in Brazil. Surveying major disputes about what constitutes a Brazilian literary modernity, Mendes historicizes the phenomenon within public readers' growing access to erotic literature beginning in the 1880s and argues for the emergence of an alternative modernity beyond the scope of, and quantitatively more popular than, European and domestic novelism and realism in Brazil. Taking into account the rise of literacy and the expansion of printing technology and dissemination networks, especially in Rio de Janeiro and São Paulo, this chapter discusses how European humanist, libertine, and naturalist literatures were recast, remediated, and transmediated in order to generate relatively inexpensive pornographic printed materials of various formats—such as, for instance, *Covent Evenings*, *Voluptuousness: 14 Gallant Tales*, and *Album of Caliban*— which ultimately surpassed the European bourgeois novel in marking the contours of an emerging modern reading culture, amongst both women and men, at the turn of the century. While Kamei-Dyche, in Chap. 10, also touches upon literary canon formation as a site of contest for outlining a modern selfhood, Mendes' chapter resonates more so with Kuttainen's and Lippmann's Chap. 3, in which a *commercially popular, alternative* literary canon is pitted against novelism and nationalism, the latter two being centerpieces of mainstream literary historiographies.

Finally, Chap. 12, by Brendan Frederick R. Edwards, examines another example of the substantiation of an alternative modernity through literary and cultural print productions. Edwards delivers a comparative

---

[5] While this volume features contributions on China and Japan, it is worth highlighting the continuing paucity of scholarly material on the *early* print culture of East Asia. For instance, Japan enjoyed a vibrant woodblock printing culture in the Edo period, while, as another example, metal movable typography was employed in Korea during the fourteenth century. For more on these early print cultures, see Kornicki, *The Book in Japan* (2001); Berry, *Japan in Print* (2006); and Kamei-Dyche, "The History of Books and Print Culture in Japan" (2011); as well as Kim, "Literary Production, Circulating Libraries, and Private Publishing" (2004); and McKillop, "The History of the Book in Korea" (2013).

print-cultural examination of Euro-Canadian colonial settler literature and Indigenous Canadian literature, arguing that the latter, especially between 1915 and 1960, constitutes a counter-colonial literary alternative that articulated distinctive Indigenous communal selfhoods. Highlighting European alphabetical literacy, representation in printed literature, and access to publishing and dissemination networks as the major particles of literary print modernity, this chapter documents the marginalization of such Indigenous literary and cultural figures as Edward Ahenakew (1885–1961) and Charles A. Cooke (1870–1958) in comparison to their settler-Canadian counterparts such as Duncan Campbell Scott (1862–1947), and examines within that context the visions and accomplishments of the former for intervening in Canada's thriving print culture. Through textual thematic analysis, archival examination, and historical contextualization, Edwards shows how print culture was repurposed from a European tool of erasure against Indigenous communities to a means by which its Indigenous recipients could cultivate European alphabetical literacy, such as through missionary and government-run schools, and eventually to a vehicle for Indigenous individuals and communities to respond to colonial assimilation, to resist colonial settler stereotypes, and to craft their distinctive Indigenous visions of national subjectivity. Such attempts, nonetheless, were curtailed by Euro-Canadians' dominance over printing, circulation, and preservation. Edwards' study differs from Daniel Fried's in Chap. 2 in several ways, including temporal, spatial, and technological vectors. Their major contrast is that whereas Edwards' focus is a modern indigeneity in response to the colonial encroachment, Fried's work portrays an endogenous modernization, an indigenous modernity prior to European colonial contact. However, this discrepancy creates an integral relation between these chapters, and with the collection in general, as these studies outline indigenous literary print modernities that, given their formations, materials, and objectives, are manifestly *alternatives* to, rather than *replications* of, European models.

Sydney Shep reflects on such frameworks as transnationalism and postcoloniality in order to introduce a new model for book history (2014, 53). Nonetheless, her emphasis on the *book* as opposed to *printed matter*, the latter being the case in this volume, sounds exclusionary and betrays a *bookism* of sorts, which somewhat, though not exactly, resembles the aforementioned *novelism* and *nationalism* as mainstream, hierarchical, and exclusionary categorizations in designating literary canons. On the other hand, this volume does not work from Shep's assumption of the centrality of the book as an object or its "inherent" mobility and mutation (2014, 65); rather, the focus is on print, not merely as a technology, but, equally importantly, as a corpus, culture, and discourse, and as reused, recast, repurposed, remediated, or transmediated at the hands of cultural and literary agents, for the formation of divergent and distinctive but simultaneously interrelated modern subjectivities in the literary terrains and beyond. Additionally, whereas Shep assumes a somewhat glorifying outlook on the book as representing "the emancipation of knowledge" (2014, 55) that ultimately reaches the "edge of the civilized world" (2014, 57), this collection attempts to problematize a categorical assumption of European print culture, documents some of the print-based anti-colonial responses to this culture, and demonstrates the implications of print modernization, as politically charged pursuits, at the intersections of gender, economic class, national polity, and other markers.

Furthermore, though Robert Darnton proposes diagrams for the study of the book (2007, 503), this collection does not offer a strict model, but rather, an open framework pursuing a twofold goal: to explore the repurposings of print outside modern Europe as sites of alternative and counter-hegemonic (literary) modernities, hence further problematizing monolithic perceptions of the spread of European print culture, and to substantiate and further promote comparative approaches to the study of print (and not just of the book) as a technology and, more so, as a textual and human culture. That said, this collection does seek to carry out Darnton's emphasis on comparative history, which "is preached more often than practiced" (2007, 503). The essays in this anthology carry out comparatism in manifold ways—intra-, inter-, or trans-culturally, across temporal, spatial, linguistic, medial, generic, political, economic, and other borders. These essays are only representatives that seek to inspire further comparative print-cultural examination in sites that, given the limited space of an anthology, are not covered therein.

It is by building upon the above discussions, ranging from comparative and area literary studies, and postcolonial book history, to literary, multiple, and alternative modernities, that this volume presents *comparative print culture* for the study of *alternative literary modernities*. The designation of comparative print culture, as indicated in the descriptions of the essays, includes a wide range of scholarly practices that discover, examine, document, and/or historicize various occurrences of printed materials and their reproduction, circulation, and uses across genres, languages, media, and/or technologies, all within a comparative orientation. Comparative print culture for the study of alternative modernities documents, analyzes, and/or explains the repurposings of ideas and materials of European modernity across, through, and beyond various borders such as national polities, media, genres, languages, genders, economic classes, formats, and technologies that gesture toward the formation of, or substantiate, distinct subjectivities as modern and as grounded in the cultures and technologies of print. Particularly, and unlike national historiographies of print, comparative print culture transcends political borders to trace, analyze, and explain the circumstances of printed materials within and across national polities in order to develop fresh sites and models of comparison and understanding. Simultaneously, this anthology inquires into similarities and differences in the usages of print materials and technologies across borders of various sorts in order to further deconstruct the perceived universality of European print culture and to eventually illuminate alternative literary modernities based on examinations of various print-cultural productions. In other words, the project highlights the distinct ways in which various cultures of print, several of them originating in European colonialism, manifest the evolution, retooling, and redirection of European systems and cultures of print at the hands of publishers, periodicalists, reviewers, writers, readers, and others, forging their own versions of modernity and alterity outside Europe. Although the authors of the essays collected here may not mention these frames and figures explicitly, they do carry out the comparative designation in various areas and directions. As well, even though these essays investigate a seemingly varied array of topics, such as transregional and transnational dialectics, modern womanhood, remediation, transmediation, popularization, vernacularization, canonization, and nationalization, they eventually cohere with, and speak to, one another as grounded in the utilization and expansion of print culture for modern subjectivity formation outside Europe.

I opened this chapter by citing Spivak, whose insights I use to close my work: "A careful reading of literature coming out of 'the Third World,' with attention to language and idiom and respect for their grafting, will show that the inevitable themes of tradition and modernity, collectivity and individualism may be in play in many different ways" (2003, 66). While this observation is grounded in close textual readings, in this collection various texts are examined as embedded in their print-cultural contexts and as yielding insights into their distinct respective operations of literary modernity vis-à-vis European hegemony. In other words, this anthology, rather than presenting a monolithic frame, heeds Spivak's warning in "Can the Subaltern Speak?" of postcolonialism practiced as a universal and hegemonic scholarly model of exploring (post)colonial contexts at the expense of the multifarious voices that inhabit those peripheries and revisits the critique to highlight the multiplicity of frames and conceptions of modernity in the aforementioned cultures of print and literariness. In yet other words, this volume attempts to use the Subaltern in order to turn the so-called *Other* to *alternatives*.

WORKS CITED

Baron, Sabrina A., Eric N. Lindquist, and Eleanor F. Shevlin, eds. 2007. *Agent of Change: Print Culture Studies after Elizabeth L. Eisenstein*. Amherst: University of Massachusetts Press.

Berry, Mary Elizabeth. 2006. *Japan in Print: Information and Nation in the Early Modern Period*. Berkeley: University of California Press.

Bhandari, Vivek. 2007. Print and the Emergence of Multiple Publics in Nineteenth-Century Punjab. In *Agent of Change: Print Culture Studies After Elizabeth L. Eisenstein*, ed. Sabrina A. Baron, Eric N. Lindquist, and Eleanor F. Shevlin, 268–286. Amherst: University of Massachusetts Press.

Chow, Kai-Wing. 2007. Reinventing Gutenberg: Woodblock and Moveable-Type Printing in Europe and China. In *Agent of Change: Print Culture Studies After Elizabeth L. Eisenstein*, ed. Sabrina A. Baron, Eric N. Lindquist, and Eleanor F. Shevlin, 169–192. Amherst: University of Massachusetts Press.

Dabashi, Hamid. 2012. *The World of Persian Literary Humanism*. Cambridge, MA: Harvard University Press.

Darnton, Robert. 2007. 'What Is the History of Books?' Revisited. *Modern Intellectual History* 4 (3): 495–508.

De Man, Paul. 1983. *Blindness and Insight: Essays in the Rhetoric of Contemporary Criticism*. 2nd and Rev. ed., Introduced by Wald Godzich. Ann Arbor: University of Minnesota Press.

Eisenstadt, Shmuel N. 2002. Some Observations on Multiple Modernities: Multiple Modernities Defined. In *Reflections on Multiple Modernities: European, Chinese, and Other Interpretations*, ed. Dominic Sachsenmaier, Jens Riedel, and Shmuel N. Eisenstadt, 27–41. Leiden: Brill.

Eisenstadt, Shmuel N., Jens Riedel, and Dominic Sachsenmaier. 2002. The Context of the Multiple Modernities Paradigm. In *Reflections on Multiple Modernities: European, Chinese, and Other Interpretations*, ed. Dominic Sachsenmaier, Jens Riedel, and Shmuel N. Eisenstadt, 1–26. Leiden: Brill.

Eisenstein, Elizabeth L. 1979. *The Printing Press as an Agent of Change: Communications and Cultural Transformations in Early Modern Europe.* 2 vol. Cambridge, UK: Cambridge University Press.

Fraser, Robert. 2008. *Book History Through Postcolonial Eyes: Rewriting the Script.* London: Routledge.

Fraser, Robert, and Mary Hammond, eds. 2008. *Books Without Borders: The Cross-National Dimension in Print Culture.* London/New York: Palgrave.

Gaonkar, Dilip Parameshwar. 2001. On Alternative Modernities. In *Alternative Modernities,* ed. Dilip Parameshwar Gaonkar, 1–23. Durham: Duke University Press.

Habermas, Jurgen. 1985. Modernity—An Incomplete Project. In *Postmodern Culture,* edited and Introduced by Hal Foster, 3–15. London: Pluto Press.

Jurilla, Patricia May B. 2008. A New Demand for Old Texts: Philippine Metrical Romances in the Early Twentieth Century. In *Books without Borders: The Cross-National Dimension in Print Culture,* ed. Robert Fraser and Mary Hammond, 130–146. London/New York: Palgrave.

Kamei-Dyche, Andrew T. 2011. The History of Books and Print Culture in Japan: The State of the Discipline. *Book History* 14: 270–304.

Kelly, John D. 2002. Alternative Modernities or an Alternative to 'Modernity': Getting Out of the Modernist Sublime. In *Critically Modern: Alternatives, Alterities, Anthropologies,* ed. Bruce M. Knauft, 258–286. Bloomington: Indiana University Press.

Kim, Michael. 2004. Literary Production, Circulating Libraries, and Private Publishing: The Popular Reception of Vernacular Fiction Texts in the Late Chosŏn Dynasty. *Journal of Korean Studies* 9 (1): 1–31.

Kornicki, Peter F. 2001. *The Book in Japan: A Cultural History from the Beginnings to the Nineteenth Century.* Honolulu: University of Hawai'i Press.

Lau, Jenny Kwok Wah, ed. 2002. *Cinemas and Popular Media in Transcultural East Asia.* Philadelphia: Temple University Press.

Majeed, Javed. 2012. Literary Modernity in South Asia. In *India and the British Empire,* ed. Douglas M. Peers and Nandini Gooptu, 262–283. Oxford: Oxford UP.

McKillop, Beth. 2013. The History of the Book in Korea. In *The Book: A Global History,* ed. F. Michael, S.J. Suarez, and H.R. Woudhuysen, 593–604. Oxford: Oxford University Press.

Mooneeram, Roshni. 2008. Shakespeare's Postcolonial Journey. In *Books Without Borders: The Cross-National Dimension in Print Culture,* ed. Robert Fraser and Mary Hammond, 186–198. London/New York: Palgrave.

Roper, Geoffrey. 2007. The Printing Press and Change in the Arab World. In *Agent of Change: Print Culture Studies After Elizabeth L. Eisenstein,* ed. Sabrina A. Baron, Eric N. Lindquist, and Eleanor F. Shevlin, 250–267. Amherst: University of Massachusetts Press.

Sachsenmaier, Dominic. 2002. Multiple Modernities—The Concept and its Potentials: Multiple Modernities Beyond Academic Discourse. In *Reflections on Multiple Modernities: European, Chinese, and Other Interpretations*, ed. Dominic Sachsenmaier, Jens Riedel, and Shmuel N. Eisenstadt, 42–67. Leiden: Brill.

Sachsenmaier, Dominic, Jens Riedel, and Shmuel N. Eisenstadt, eds. 2002. *Reflections on Multiple Modernities: European, Chinese and Other Interpretations*. Leiden: Brill.

Shep, Sydney. 2014. Books in Global Perspectives. In *The Cambridge Companion to the History of the Book*, ed. Leslie Howsam, 53–70. Cambridge: Cambridge University Press.

Spivak, Gayatri C. 2003. *Death of a Discipline*. New York: Columbia University Press.

———. 2010. Can the Subaltern Speak? In *Can the Subaltern Speak: Reflections on the History of an Idea*, ed. Rosalind C. Morris, 21–80. New York: Columbia University Press.

CHAPTER 2

Song Dynasty Classicism and the Eleventh Century "Print Modernity"

Daniel Fried

1 Prologue: Ancient Moderns

What makes a print modernity, "modern"?

That word has a slipperiness which makes it difficult to use well: leave it as a simple shorthand for the early twentieth century, and it is safe. But certain discursive contexts and geographical frameworks easily push the "modern" back into the "early modern"; others bring it up right through the middle of the "postmodern" and drop it down into the "contemporary". The call to modernize this or that field of endeavor is a useful rhetorical tool in military affairs subcommittees, and academic governance councils. All the while, older assertions of the modern grow more faint, more quaint. Five centuries from now, James Joyce might still be thought of as a "modernist" writer—but he will not be a "modern" one, nor even one that can speak to "modernity".

Within the Chinese context, the notion of a "modernity" which came on all in a rush, one century ago, is deeply ingrained into popular con-

D. Fried (✉)
University of Alberta, Edmonton, AB, Canada
e-mail: dfried@ualberta.ca

© The Author(s) 2020
R. Aliakbari (ed.), *Comparative Print Culture*, New Directions in Book History, https://doi.org/10.1007/978-3-030-36891-3_2

23

sciousness, and within scholarship of modern literature, the last several decades have seen a wealth of inquiry into the ways in which periodical and book publishing shaped the experience of the modern for Chinese subjects. And yet the notion of a stark contrast between ancient and modern periods—mediated by loss or preservation of texts—is central to the oldest strands of Chinese intellectual history: in the *Analects*, Confucius laments the loss of ancient mores, and upholds ancient canonical texts and ritual practice against the decrepit practices of his contemporaries. The most canonical of China's ancient sages was, to his own mind, trapped in an age uncomfortably modern.

If we lose the moorings on "modernity", allow the concept to free-float away from any one period, would it have any purchase as a conceptual category that distinguished it from the basic vocabulary of time built into verbal tenses and building-block vocabulary? It could be used to designate a certain kind of consciousness of rupture between past and present. Expanding on common associations with the modernity of the early twentieth century, this vision of temporal rupture should be considered disorienting, mediated by drastic social or technological change, and irreversible. A "print modernity" might be provisionally defined as such a rupture either occasioned by print, or considered with respect to a print culture with which it is entwined.

If one could grant that much, one might argue that the first print modernity dates to eleventh-century China, and is tied to ways in which print captures and demarcates the classical, elevating the past in a way which creates a clear demarcation with the then-present. It is an admittedly odd way to use the concept of the modern, to attribute it to events one full millennium ago. But in thinking through how print culture relates to perceptions of periodization, and to the overwhelming newness of a given era, a little perspective is helpful, so that we are not blinded by the immediacy of the newest newness. If indeed this is a print "modernity", it is one very different than that described by Shuk Man Leung with regard to late Qing dynasty fiction later in this volume. The notions of a "public sphere", a collective national future which could be imagined in fiction, and even a polity conceivable as "China" in the sense that late Qing readers would have understood that word, were all absent from this period, fully eight and a half centuries earlier than that Leung describes.[1] However, like her articulation of a certain form of Chinese print modernity depen-

---

[1] For further details, see Shuk Man Leung's Chap. 6 in this collection.

dent on an act of historical imagination, this essay likewise focuses on ways in which the rapid development of a print culture facilitates a new, highly temporal consciousness on the part of participants in that culture.

When one realizes that print in this period was strongly associated with government sponsorship and orthodox status, and that the sudden explosion of texts was primarily a revolution in the accessibility of the canonical, it becomes clear that there is a temporal paradox at the heart of this age's experience of print. The old was new again, and the accessibility of the classical past was a part of what it meant to be modern, in the eleventh century. As the domain of print started to spread to more popular works in the twelfth and thirteenth centuries, that association of the modern with classical canonicity was later not so strong. However, as will be shown with regard to elite reception of the printed editions of neoclassical prose (*guwen*), the early association of print with canonicity drove a high level of consciousness of periodization and temporal break.

2   CHINA'S EARLY PRINT HISTORY
AND THE SONG DYNASTY

Eleventh-century China, during the Northern Song dynasty, might be identified as possessing the world's first print culture—albeit a nascent, partial one, co-existing with a still-vibrant manuscript culture. The technology of printing was considerably older: the first real widespread use of print was during the Tang dynasty, and early print projects dating to the seventh century eventually grew into the ninth century use of print to disseminate and standardize large libraries of Buddhist texts. Antecedents of the technology go back even earlier: it is likely that the dedicated carving of woodblocks for print was inspired by the much-older practice of taking paper rubbings from carved stone steles. Such practices had taken off starting in the second century AD, when the wide-spread development of commercializable paper-making techniques, and the development of elite styles of calligraphy caused the popular practice of searching out carved stone texts to copy by rubbings. For-purpose printing followed along in these tracks through its earliest centuries, conceived of as a nonce activity engaged in for the purpose of promulgating one specific text worthy of canonization or emulation.

Things begin to change in the late tenth century, after the new Song dynasty consolidated control over China, following decades of chaos and war. As a means of shoring up support for its rule among the large

Buddhist clerisy and laity, the Song emperors did sponsor more large-scale print projects of Buddhist sutras. However, the key development was the simultaneous printing of standard editions of the Confucian classics, in conjunction with the renovation of the examination system which tested mastery of those texts, and which was the gateway to government service. In theory, the examination system through previous dynasties had been meritocratic, but for practical purposes was only open to those families with the financial capital to pay for hand-transcribed copies of the classics, usually written on silk scrolls. The sudden availability of cheap textbooks meant that any families above the level of subsistence farming had reason to invest more in their sons' education; although little data is available on literacy rates, it seems that a sizeable percentage of the urban population must have been raised from basic literacy to much higher levels of literacy, producing for the first time a potential mass readership. At the same time, the large state-sponsorship for printing projects such as multiple editions of the Buddhist sutras and Confucian classics began to produce classes of artisans trained in proper printing techniques. Once a given state-sponsored print project came to an end, it is likely that many of these workers found they had an incentive to go into business for themselves as independent printer-booksellers—especially after a formal ban on private printing was lifted in the latter half of the eleventh century (Zhang 1989, 57–58).

Moreover, it was very easy for artisans to go into business for themselves because almost all printing was woodblock carving. Moveable type was invented in the early eleventh century, but barely used through the end of the dynasty. Hence, there was little capital investment needed upfront in a typeset and press—one simply had to pay for wood, paper, ink, and carving tools. And the actual labor of carving could often be done by low-wage, semi-literate workers, because blocks were usually carved through a hand-written sheet of calligraphy which was simply pasted on top of the block.[2]

These printer-booksellers seem to have printed their own student editions of the Confucian classics as a main product, but also had an incentive

---

[2] A convenient summary of the economics of woodblock printing during the Song dynasty, and which should be relatively accessible for non-specialists, can be found in Mun (2013), 4–5.

to find other new books which might be saleable. At the same time, the sudden increase in numbers of those taking the imperial exam meant much greater numbers of failed candidates with an incentive to try to make money off of their literary training, and who could in fact provide the new printing class with new titles to put on the market. These changes did not all happen immediately, but by the early eleventh century, it was clear that consciousness of print editions' availability was changing the way intellectuals thought about books, even if this could not yet qualify as a "print culture". Not only was the mass availability of books changing the way that people were consuming and composing texts, there was considerable self-consciousness among readers that the world of reading had changed dramatically in just a few decades' time. One of the more important developments in publishing which helped to create such consciousness was the creation of canonical editions of earlier writers, apparently inspired by the way in which print was standardizing editions of the Confucian classics and Buddhist sutras.

Among the first major print projects of individual authors in the early Song were collected editions of the works of two literati active in the mid-Tang, late 8th to early 9th centuries, Han Yu (韓愈, 768–824) and Liu Zongyuan (柳宗元, 773–819). Han and Liu were both important poets, but within standard Chinese literary history they are now both remembered as avatars of classical prose style, who had revived the much-earlier style of the Han dynasty by departing from the contemporary vernacular evolution of the language. (In comparative terms, one can think of the way in which Renaissance Latin was much closer to Livy or Horace than was Medieval Latin, partially because the much stronger relative position of European vernaculars freed Latin from the burden of being a living language.) During their own time, Han and Liu were well-regarded, but it was the Song dynasty which made their works, and their stylistic reforms, canonical, and this canonization happened through the effort to collect and print their works for the first time. In particular, this Song consolidation was pushed first by the tenth century statesman and literatus Liu Kai (柳開, 947–1000) followed by Mu Xiu (穆修, 979–1032); however, these would later run through many other editions during the dynasty, many edited by among the most famous Song writers (Yang 2002, 84).

28   D. FRIED

3   SONG NEO-CLASSICISM AND "MODERN" EDITIONS OF HAN AND LIU

All of the above summary is common knowledge to specialists in Chinese print history, and in Song dynasty literature. Generations of Chinese scholars have already done foundational work in establishing the lineages of certain editions, and the motivations underlying Northern Song classicist movements. For the most part, the sort of print culture studies which have become central to Western scholarly discussion in the past few decades have been pursued in English (and occasionally in other European languages). Even these have tended to focus on the later Ming and Qing dynasties, when print culture was much more highly developed, and had helped create robust markets in vernacular fiction and drama. However, there have also been a number of important recent studies, starting with Susan Cherniack's ground-breaking work on the relationship of issues of transmission and circulation of texts to larger trends in Song book culture. Sometimes scholars working on longer surveys, such as Joseph McDermott and Lucille Chia have included valuable sections on Song materials. But, in particular, Hilde de Weerdt has been extremely active in examining early Song printing, and while all of her various publications cannot be mentioned here, a recent edited volume by De Weerdt and Chia has brought together a wealth of different perspectives on how print touched on book collection, religion, medicine, and historiography in the Song and succeeding dynasties.

Across the various research of people who have worked on the Northern Song, there is an initial consensus forming about the highly partial character of print in the period. Some scholars in Song studies are uncomfortable claiming that this period possessed a true print culture, because manuscript culture remained central to intellectual life during this period—and indeed, long after. And there is a diversity of opinion as to whether the economics of print at this relatively early period can actually be said to have constituted a substantial change in the way that books affected relations between books and readers.[3] Manuscript and print collections interacted in various ways—with most collectors possessing works in both manuscript and print, and using both manuscript and print editions of

---

[3] Cynthia Brokaw has offered a helpful, if now slightly dated, summary of this debate; it can safely be said that work published in the last few years has not fully resolved the differences in perspective which she identified. See Brokaw (2007), 260–2.

works to edit and collate new editions, as well as for general reading, research, and composition of new works. Manuscript was a part of the print process: with woodblock printing, text for each plate had to first be hand-copied onto a paper which could be glued to the block for carving. And, most importantly to the present study, the distribution of print was uneven: geographically, socially, and generically. During the Northern Song dynasty, some kinds of works were printed—and others were not. Print was typically reserved for works assumed to merit public notice and mass distribution, and while commercial print shops did gain a foothold even in the early years of the dynasty, a much larger role was played by various government organs, both in the capital and at the provincial and local level.

One important topic which has not yet been given sufficient attention is why, in the midst of that partial print culture, Han and Liu were among the first individual authors to have their works printed, and the relation of that printing to the canonization of their style. As Douglas Skonicki (2014, 10–11) has demonstrated, in the first years of the dynasty the preference for the neoclassical style was at such a low point that practitioners such as Liu Kai discussed their work almost as if recipients of a secret lineage; and this attitude may have encouraged the printing of Han and Liu, a process which by disseminating the texts publicly destroyed purely private claims to their accessibility. There seems to have been an association of print technology with authority and canonicity. Print was mostly what one used to widely distribute important texts deemed worthy of imperial support—whether the sacred scriptures of Buddhism, or the secular Confucian classics. In this light, it makes sense that Han and Liu would become almost the first subjects for a "merely" literary print project: they were not just representatives of the recently-past dynasty whose literary accomplishments are revered. They were the representatives from that dynasty of the much-older classical style. And, unlike the actual classical works which were their model, such as the *Records of the Historian* of Sima Qian (司馬遷, 145 BCE-?), or especially the works of the Han essayist and rhapsodist Yang Xiong (楊雄53 BCE-18 CE), the output of Han and Liu did not circulate in standard collected editions previous to the Song: their texts were the kind of thing that ought to be canonized, and needed to be standardized.

The example of the canonization of Han and Liu well illustrates how a vibrant and living contemporary publication industry grows up against that past-centred initial impulse—and highlights the way in which print foregrounds temporality in ways that are highly productive, if also confusing, to the people involved. There is a contradiction here: we can see in the language surrounding the printings of Han and Liu a kind of reverence for classicism which, by contrast, also creates a sense of the modern. There is something of a parallel here to the 19th- and twentieth-century consolidation of Japan's classical past through print which is described by Andrew Kamei-Dyche later in this volume,[4] though of course Song dynasty authors are not trying to define a national essence within a context of globalized imperialist competition. Instead, this is a society trying to define its intellectual life only on the temporal access of successive eras and movements, without needing to consider geographies.

Although early Song China was by no means a "modernist" stylistic environment, there were some notable stylistic experiments, such as the development of the "Xi Kun" poetic style (西昆體) of Yang Yi (楊億, 974–1020) and Liu Yun (劉筠, 971–1031), which resemble twentieth century deformations of traditional language use. However, what is more important than asserting a nascent "modernism" is recognizing the clear sense of a "modernity" which burgeoned at the time. There was a perception of rupture between past and present manifested in classicism and antiquarian collecting on the one hand, and formal and generic innovation, such as in the development of the *ci* (詞), on the other. In the language surrounding the Han and Liu printings, we have a few hints that the presence of print played a role in creating that perception of rupture.

Although we currently possess only thirteen versions of Han's works datable to Song editions, according to Liu Zhenlun (2004, 232), citations and second-hand references provide evidence of at least 102 editions circulating during the Song. This is no doubt a vast underestimation of the total number of copies in circulation; while the claim of five hundred separate published commentaries on Han circulating during the dynasty may have been an exaggerated estimate, it would not be an outrageous one, given how Han's classicizing prose style was later to become a model for ambitious literati. Evidence for the circulation of Liu's work is much thinner—less scholarly work has been done to track editions of Liu, but it also seems that there was proportionately less in circulation. We do know that, unlike Han's work which had circulated somewhat broadly in different manuscript collections, Liu's writings survived mostly in one collection by Liu Yuxi (劉禹錫, 772–842). By the time of Mu Xiu's printed edition of

---

[4] For further details, see Andrew T. Kamei-Dyche's Chap. 10 in this collection.

2 SONG DYNASTY CLASSICISM AND THE ELEVENTH CENTURY... 31

Liu Zongyuan, he was clearly trying to address what he had seen as a problem with the unavailability of texts.[5]

Mu Xiu seems clearly to have been the pivotal figure in the dissemination of editions of Han and Liu: the *Collected Works of Mr. Changli* (昌黎先生集) and the *Collected Works of Mr. Liu, of the Tang Dynasty* (唐柳先生集).[6] He was certainly remembered as such in the historical record: his biography in the *History of the Song* (宋史) writes of him:

> From the time of the Five Dynasties, prose had deteriorated, but at the beginning of the dynasty, Liu Kai began to make ancient-style prose. After that, Yang Yi and Liu Yun emphasized musicality, matching words to the sound, and all the scholars of the age followed their fashion. At that time, Xiu alone was known for ancient-style prose, and then Su Shunqin and his brothers all rambled after him. All though Xiu died in poverty, all the nobles and great men at that time said that one couldn't speak about prose ability without mentioning Legate Mu.
>
> 自五代文敝,國初,柳開始為古文。 其後,楊億、劉筠尚聲偶之辭,天下學者靡然從之。 修於是時獨以古文稱,蘇舜欽兄弟多從之游。 修雖窮死,然一時士大夫稱能文者必曰穆參軍. (*juan* 441)

The final sentence, referencing Mu's poverty, is worth noting, even though it throws into greater confusion some of the circumstances under which Han and Liu's works were printed. Because we do know that these collections were circulating in print editions during the eleventh century, and because we also know that Mu Xiu was the editor of the collections, he is sometimes described as their publisher, as if he were simply a wealthy aficionado of the classical style, who paid to have these editions privately printed in order to promote his own aesthetic tastes. But his biography stresses Mu's upright poverty at several parts of his life; the means by which he was able to bring the collection into print is not clear.[7]

---

[5] "When I was young, and was fond of looking through these two writers' [Han and Liu] works, I was often ill to think that Liu's works were not completely to be seen in the world, but those pieces appearing among men were a scattered hundred or more." "予少嗜觀二家之文, 常病柳不全見於世, 出人間者殘落才百余篇" quoted in Tang (2010), 53.

[6] If these reported titles are indeed original to Mu's editions, it shows the relative disparity in public familiarity with the two authors in the early years of the Song. Han (who was, after all, a much more prominent public figure) is identified simply by his courtesy name (*zi*), while Liu has to be identified by his surname and period.

[7] It is almost certain that Mu Xiu did somehow see the collections printed himself, somehow; his own postscript to the edition of Liu mentions a "pressing" (按), and an only slighter

32   D. FRIED

Uncertainty over the conditions of publication is unfortunately the rule rather than the exception when one tries to track down the history of individual titles during the Song. This may be deeply frustrating to readers working with more modern versions of print modernity, to whom all kinds of data are available regarding editors, publishers, financial support, size of print runs, prices, publication dates, sizes of print runs, exact locations of booksellers and range of circulation of a given text. For eleventh-century texts, almost all of what we know about publication histories has to be pieced together from offhand comments about editions in prose or poetry about other subjects. Partially this is due to lost records—if booksellers or government printing organs were keeping detailed records, these were in casual manuscript copies which never stood a chance of surviving. The only relatively reliable information about print projects is for the very largest, such as imperially-sponsored printings of the Buddhist canon, which were important enough to be recorded in official histories. However, the lack of secondary data is also due to the economics of woodblock printing, which are quite different from those of moveable-type presses. With woodblock printing, there is no investment in a typeset around which one built a permanent printing business; instead, all investment was into one given edition of one work. This means that printers could enter and exit the industry more easily, and there were hence likely more part-time or marginal printers—especially in this early period, when most printing was done by government offices, print runs were occasional projects of offices primarily concerned with various aspects of governance, regional or national. And then again, there may never have been any data on print runs, because stored woodblocks easily lend themselves to on-demand printing.

However, we do know, from indirect records about editions, stray comments about publishing houses, and the Song dynasty legal codes, that the eleventh century seems to have been a turning point in the growth of the print industry and the subsequent availability of books. Legal strictures against private printing were not lifted until the 1070s, but printing had spread considerably before then, from central government organs to regional and even local offices, and by about the middle of the eleventh century, print shops had become relatively common, especially in southern China (Li 1991, 69–70). And the consciousness of that expansion in the

comment by Wei Tai (魏泰) explicitly refers to possession of a printed edition of the work. See He (2011), 132–33.

scope and availability of print is evident when one examines a reminiscence of Ouyang Xiu, a central figure in the intellectual and political life of the dynasty, whose early access to a Sichuan-printed edition of Han's work seems to have been an intellectual turning point in his own life, and also to the growth of neoclassical standards which Ouyang himself would later help establish.

4 Reception of Printed Neoclassicism: The Case of Ouyang Xiu

Given the general lack of good data on individual print editions during the Northern Song, and in particular the difficulty of knowing how or when Mu Xiu's collections of Han and Liu were printed, it is necessary to consider the effect of print through its reception by readers. In the current case, an excellent example of how the bifurcation of classicism and modern consciousness played out in actual reading and compositional practice can be seen in the preface written by Ouyang Xiu (歐陽修, 1007–1072) in his edition of Han's works. Ouyang is one of the most famous of Song dynasty writers and statesmen; he would later be ranked right alongside Han and Liu in the pantheon of classical prose stylists. Moreover, Ouyang was one of the leading players in a series of political dramas that played out during the eleventh century, and which tied issues of classical exegesis and intellectual historiography to debates over state-centred reform programs. The history of those debates is complex, and far beyond the scope of this chapter, but it can be noted that the nature of Ouyang's conservatism was not simple: he was a leader of a failed political reform effort in the 1040s, and opposed to a successful reform effort which was gearing up just before his death in the 1070s. He became perhaps the leading advocate for writing in neoclassical style, but was at times a skeptic and a revisionist in his approach to canonical works.[8] By the time of his birth, the first collections of Han and Liu had already appeared in print, but as he describes, they had not yet found widespread acceptance.

In the preface, Ouyang begins by describing his first encounter with Han's work—he was living in a poor household in a remote area, but when playing at the house of a much wealthier friend, found a pile of

---

[8] For example, Ouyang's suspicion of Wang Anshi's reforms was linked to his questioning the authenticity of the *Rites of Zhou*. See Song (2015), 48–49. For a more general summary of Ouyang's approach to classical studies, see Liu (1967), 85–99.

books in a corner, and started flipping through the collected prose of Han Yu—judging from the context and the specific title he cites, *Collected Prose of Mr. Han Changli* 《昌黎先生文集》 this seems to be a Sichuan-printed edition dating to the Five Dynasties (Wan 1980, 167). He asked permission to bring the book home, and was hooked: "I saw its language was deep and grand, and though I was still young, and could not grasp the meanings, only seeing how stirring and boundless it was, it was something I could love" (1056–7).[9] Ouyang then goes on to explain, "At that time, the whole world was studying the works of Yang [Yi] and Liu [Yun], which were called "Timely [i.e., modern] Prose," and those who mastered it passed the exams and got positions and fame, and were thereby honored by their contemporaries, and no one yet was talking about Han's prose."

Ouyang describes his own studies for the imperial examination, and how he found more works of Han while studying, and thought that this was a kind of perfection at which students should stop. But he had no time to study Han seriously until after he had finally passed the exams, landed a post, and settled down in Luoyang. "And the disciples of Yi Shilu were all there, so together with them I practiced writing old-style prose, so I took out my copy of *Han's Collected Works* from storage, and annotated it, and I also sought old texts from those who had them and edited them. After this, all the students in the world have gradually trended toward the ancient style, so that Han's prose has been circulating for over thirty years now. No one studies anything except Han—that's what you'd call 'flourishing'!"

Through all of that initial narrative, time is constantly foregrounded. In part, this concern with time is the memory of his life as a student, not having enough hours in the day to study both what he would have preferred, and also what he knew would be on the imperial examinations. Ronald Egan has argued that "the Sung [Song] version of the *ku-wen* [guwen] movement really began as a protest against the required use of the Current Style in the examinations" (1984, 13), and Egan reads this preface primarily as a recollection of Ouyang's youthful resentment at the modish and overwrought style of Yang Yi which had become institutionalized as the expected style for exam papers. The preface certainly is that, but also more than just a simple recollected complaint. This is a narrative of Ouyang's own maturation in literature, retold from the perspective of a successful

---

[9] The following quotations from this essay are all from the same page numbers. All translations are my own.

2 SONG DYNASTY CLASSICISM AND THE ELEVENTH CENTURY... 35

older man returning to a book which, in his youth, had seemed a forbidden ancient pleasure. And Ouyang takes the occasion to meditate on the nature of succession of styles: he talks about literary fads as temporally determined, but these determinations are slippery. First there is the ancient, then there is the modern, and then the modern is displaced by the ancient again. Not having the time to study what one likes is itself a way to measure the rupture between the classical and the modern: that which is valued by the present is the foolishness of the present; ancient truths aren't banned, they are just crowded out by the need to make a living. And, of course, time is connected to the transition into print: when one does have time, one can collect, annotate, and publish, reviving the lost and scattered scraps of the past.

However, after this narrative, Ouyang offers an even more central meditation on the relation of time to Han, and to his own experiences with reading and republishing the texts:

> Alas! The Way certainly is put into practice far-off, and stops nearby; people ignore what is bygone, and value that of the present. It isn't just the habitual preferences of the age which make it so, it is also the natural way of things. That is why Confucius and Mencius were alarmed at their own age, and modeled themselves on the archaic past. The writings of Mr. Han sank and were unseen for 200 years, but later have now greatly been put into circulation. And this is not a reevaluation by preferences, but that after a while something will become bright again, and cannot be obliterated, though it might be eclipsed for a while, until finally becoming limitlessly glorious, and this is the natural Way of things... This collection came out of Sichuan, and the lettering and carving, are somewhat more refined than the common edition circulating today, and has gotten rid of many errors [謬]. These 30 years, whenever I have heard of someone having a good copy, I have always sought it out and made corrections from it...Alas! The way of Mr. Han's prose,[10] is revered by all ages, and is something we have because it was passed down by all the world. As for me and this edition, I especially treasure it because of its being an antique.

It is worthwhile to note the view of literary history here is complex, cyclical, and relative. Ouyang does start with a traditional classicizing

---

[10] Taking 文之道 as a unitary phrase, contrary to the editor's punctuation choice (perhaps motivated by the Song interest in Han's status as a transmitter of orthodox Confucian thought as well as of neoclassical prose style.)

lament about the Way being common in the past, and a lost wisdom for the present. But then he contradicts himself with the rest of the explanation—noting correctly that this classicizing lament is one voiced by Confucius about his own period. A style is in favor, goes out of favor, comes back again—this is not due to particular preferences, but is a natural development of the Way.

One can find antecedents for this way of talking about literary history—most notably in the *Wenxin Diaolong* (文心雕龍) five centuries earlier. But what makes this passage more odd are Ouyang's seeming contradictions in describing the script/print transition. The process of seeking out good editions which he describes is clearly, in context, describing his search for old manuscript editions which may have better texts than those which were used for the earliest print editions. He uses those to correct the text, and that is his justification for publishing the new edition of which this essay is the preface. However, he accounts for the presence of these old manuscript copies by asserting that they are "revered by all ages" and "passed down by all the world"—claims which make no sense against the background of his just-finished explanation of why the true classical way can be eclipsed for hundreds of years before coming back into acclaim.

This contradiction appears as a confused outgrowth of what the new technology and social fact of print is doing to older conceptions of literary history in the eleventh century. There certainly had been changes of literary style previously, and a literary historiographical tradition which had learned to account for them, often in the same moralizing tones that Ouyang evinces of longing for a purer past. For that matter, there had also been plenty of consciousness of the way in which texts are corrupted by the problems of manuscript traditions. And these presuppositions reinforced each other: since the great Qin-dynasty bibliocaust, the issues of lost canonical truths and insufficient textual traditions have been linked.

What is manifested in Ouyang's contradictory thoughts on time and textuality is the need to accommodate such traditional discourses to a new situation in which texts can be fixed, universalized, and sold in mass quantities without bias toward the present. Indeed, on the contrary, the official imprimatur of the state, combined with the promise of healthy market demand, means that there is a bias toward the classical and canonical in the world of print. For the most part, this bias was evident in the rapid production of commentaries on the Confucian classics, since these formed the backbone of the imperial examination system. There is still considerable scholarly work which remains to be done on that material, but it seems likely that the rapid growth in numbers of classical commentaries during the Song is not due primarily to a new obsession with scholarship, but rather to the needs of a broadened student base looking for exam prep materials. To a lesser degree, the proliferation of editions of Han Yu is driven by the same imperative, especially after classical style prose gained acceptance: he provided a model style to imitate in exam essays. A "modernization" of the exam system in the Song dynasty, and the concomitant expansion of potential for upward mobility down into the urban bourgeoisie, was only possible through the much broader dissemination of classical studies which print enabled.

5   Postscript: Time and Text

Both through the exam system itself, and also through the ways in which print had the power to popularize a style, the classical was becoming that-which-is-profitable-for-this-age. During Ouyang's youth, the fad for Yang Yi and Liu Yun had produced a normal narrative of a popular modern style and older, neglected classical style. But the revived popularity of Han, partially through Ouyang's own efforts, were scrambling that calculus, and making the avatar of ancient style that which is most useful for pure modern self-interest. This contradiction and loss of clear temporal divisions does not settle anything; it heightens consciousness of unsettled temporal categories. And as such, it may be a contributing factor to the many ways throughout the rest of the dynasty in which innovation is thoroughly intertwined with antiquarianism. New genres such as the "remarks on poetry" (*shihua*) and newly-invigorated genres such as the florilegium (*leishu*) were clearly dependent on access to a broader range of texts, through the print market, from which they could find and compare materials. Connoisseurship of calligraphy—and the hunt for original editions—was stimulated by the fact that woodblock printing reproduced calligraphy, and was a factor dividing cheap from valuable editions. And visual catalogues of rare vessels, such as the *Xuanhe Illustrations of a Breadth of Ancient Objects* (*Xuanhe Bogu Tu*) would not have been possible to disseminate effectively without the ease of combining text and graphics in woodblock.

Insofar as eleventh century Chinese literati may have paradoxically needed a canon-heavy nascent print culture to feel modern, they are not unique: a somewhat slower and more decentralized process helped early modern European literati to align themselves with the classical past against what they saw as the gross inventions of medieval scholars. But this is not always a normal direction for print culture studies, which often try to expand beyond the canonical, and explain the fuller context of popular and casual printed texts in which canons were enmeshed. Without gainsaying such work, the experience of Song dynasty China suggests that the printing of ancient classics, and the use of print to canonize less-ancient neo-classical work, can be central to the process of bringing readers to confront the newness of their own period. Printed classics become the mirror by which moderns see themselves, as if by a *gestalt*, and in reverse.

BIBLIOGRAPHY

Brokaw, Cynthia. 2007. Book History in Premodern China: The State of the Discipline I. *Book History* 10: 253–290.

Cherniack, Susan. 1994. Book Culture and Textual Transmission in Sung China. *Harvard Journal of Asiatic Studies* 54 (1): 5–125. https://doi.org/10.2307/2719389.

Chia, Lucille. 2002. *Printing for Profit: The Commercial Publishers of Jiangyang, Fujian (11th–17th Centuries)*. Cambridge: Harvard University Asia Center.

Chia, Lucille, and Hilde De Weerdt. 2011. *Knowledge and Text Production in an Age of Print: China, 900–1400*. Leiden: Brill.

Egan, Ronald. 1984. *The Literary Works of Ou-Yang Hsiu (1007–72)*. Cambridge: Cambridge University Press.

He Jipeng 何寄澎. 2011. *Bei Song de Guwen Yundong* 北宋的古文运动 [The Neoclassical Movement of the Northern Song]. Shanghai: Shanghai Guji.

Li Zhihong 李致忠. 1991. "Songdai Keshu Shulue," 宋代刻书述略 [General Remarks on Song Printing] *Lidai Keshu Gaikuang* 历代刻书概况 [Survey of Printing Across Dynasties]. Beijing: Yinshua Gongye Chubanshe.

Liu, James T.C. 1967. *Ou-yang Hsiu: An Eleventh-Century Neo-Confucianist*. Stanford: Stanford University Press.

Liu Zhenlun 刘真伦. 2004. *Han Yu Ji Song-Yuan Chuanben Yanjiu* 韩愈集宋元传本研究 [Research on the Song and Yuan Collections of Han Yu]. Beijing: Chinese Academy of Social Sciences Press.

Liu Zongyuan 柳宗元. 1979. *Liu Zongyuan Ji* 柳宗元集 [Collected Works of Liu Zongyuan], Vol. 4. Beijing: Zhonghua Shuju.

McDermott, Joseph. 2006. *A Social History of the Chinese Book: Books and Literati Culture in Late Imperial China*. Hong Kong: Hong Kong University Press.

Mun, Seung-Hwan. 2013. Printing Press Without Copyright: A Historical Analysis of Printing and Publishing in Song China. *Chinese Journal of Communication* 6 (1): 1–25. https://doi.org/10.1080/17544750.2013.753497.

Ouyang Xiu 欧阳修. 2001. *Ouyang Xiu Quan Ji* 欧阳修全集 [Complete Works of Ouyang Xiu], ed. Li Yian 李逸安. Vol. 3. Beijing: Zhonghua Shuju.

Skonicki, Douglas. 2014. 'Guwen' Lineage Discourse in the Northern Song. *Journal of Song-Yuan Studies* 44: 1–32. http://www.jstor.org.login.ezproxy.library.ualberta.ca/stable/44511238.

Song, Jaeyoon. 2015. *Traces of Grand Peace: Classics and State Activism in Imperial China*. Cambridge: Harvard-Yenching Institute.

Tang Jianghao 汤江浩. 2010. Shilun Liu Zongyuan Sanwen zai Bei Song Shiqi de Jieshou Wenti 试论柳宗元散文在北宋时期的接受问题[Remarks Upon Issues in the Northern Song Reception of Liu Zongyuan's Essays]. *Journal of Fuzhou University* 95 (1): 53–57. CNKI.

Tuotuo 脱脱. 1977. *Song Shi* 宋史 [Song History]. Beijing: Zhonghua Shuju.

Wan Man 萬曼. 1980. *Tang Ji Xu Lu* 唐集叙錄 [Records of Tang Collections]. Beijing: Zhonghua Shuju.

Yang Guoan杨国安. 2002. Ouyang Xiu 'Han Changli Xiangsheng Ji' Jiaokan Lunlue, 欧阳修《韩昌黎先生集》校勘论略 [Remarks on the Editing of Ouyang Xiu's *Collected Prose of Mr. Han Changli*]. *Guji Zhengli Yanjiu Xuekan* 古籍整理研究学刊 [*Journal of Research on Ancient Text Compilation*] 66: 84–87. CNKI.

Zhang, Xiumin. 1989. *Zhongguo Yinshuashi* 中国印刷史 [History of Chinese Printing], 57–58. Shanghai: Renmin Chubanshe.

CHAPTER 3

Alternative Imaginaries of the Modern Girl: A Comparative Examination of Canadian and Australian Magazines

Victoria Kuttainen and Jilly Lippmann

1 Introduction

As Rita Felski pointed out in her landmark 1995 study, longstanding meta-narratives about modernism have neglected women's prominent role in modernity. This observation stimulated the large-scale revisioning Felski undertook in *The Gender of Modernity*, engendered by the following guiding questions:

> How would our understanding of modernity change if instead of taking male experience as paradigmatic, we were to look instead at texts written primarily by or about women? And what if feminine phenomena, often seen as having a secondary of marginal status, were given central importance in the analysis of the culture of modernity? (Felski 1995, 10)

Despite revisionist accounts of modernity that have emerged since Felski's study, many of which have been more sensitive to the logics of scarcity and

---

V. Kuttainen (✉) • J. Lippmann
James Cook University, Townsville, QLD, Australia
e-mail: victoria.kuttainen@jcu.edu.au; jilly.lippmann@jcu.edu.au

© The Author(s) 2020
R. Aliakbari (ed.), *Comparative Print Culture*, New Directions in Book History, https://doi.org/10.1007/978-3-030-36891-3_3

41

exclusion that historically underpinned modernist studies, scholars of modernism have continued to sideline marginalized subjects. Thus modernism has not only tended to continue to disregard the modernity of women but also, and perhaps still more intensively, modernist studies have disregarded whole nations as sites of alternative literary modernities, especially in settler colonies like Canada and Australia. Standard accounts of these national literatures tend to focus on narratives of either the pioneering and settlement phases of the colonial era or the development of their self-consciously national literatures in the aftermath of the Second World War. In fact, the shared origins of these settler dominions, as well as their "struggle to legitimate the national literature" and overcome "the colonial mentality" which continued well into the post-war years to "disparage [...] the local product" (McDougall and Whitlock 1987, 7), stimulated the first of many comparative approaches to their literatures. It is consequently unsurprising that settler colonial cultures and their literatures are often either perceived as *never* modern or *born* modern, as David Carter has observed of the Australian scene (2013, viii–ix). This misconception tends to contribute to and become reciprocally reinforced by a relative lack of critical attention to the crucial modernizing years in Canadian and Australian literary histories.

In addition to this chronological miscoding, both Canada and Australia are also typically and falsely coded as masculine societies. "It virtually goes without saying," Kay Schaffer notes, "that national identity and the Australian character are masculine constructions" (1988, 4). Carole Gerson has observed much the same of Canada, noting the "dominant view that the great Canadian narrative concerned man's contest with nature" (2016, 345). As a self-described "feminist literary archaeologist" (1991, 46), Gerson has challenged this view of Canadian literature as one largely constructed by influential male nationalist critics. Since the 1980s, Drusilla Modjeska (1981) and Carole Ferrier (1985) have also reinstated the place of a number of significant interwar female writers who had been previously overlooked in Australian literature. But, in Australia, Modjeska focused largely on writers of social realist novels while Ferrier emphasized women's political writing. Correspondingly, in Canada, Gerson's significant revisionist literary historical scholarship has tended to focus on women's poetry (1991) or on women's issues in social realist novels (in Sugars 2015). These studies may have restored some aspects of women's literary and cultural history at the cost of overlooking others.

One figure missing from these accounts of Canadian and Australian literatures is the Modern Girl, as these studies seem to have emphasized versions of the earlier figure of the New Woman instead. Such emphasis potentially reinforces a version of literary cultural history that tends to reinscribe the sometimes problematic association between women and nation-building (Henderson 2003).[1] Moreover, this emphasis tends to obscure the multifaceted role played by women in transnational modernity in these settler colonial contexts, in which the association between women, commodity culture, and modernity provoked remarkably complex reactions. In contrast to the earlier figure of the New Woman of the 1890s–1910s, the Modern Girl of the 1920s and 1930s was not particularly concerned with suffrage or nationhood but was more engaged with issues of personal agency in a newly conceived public sphere. Through her association with cinema, jazz, fashion, glamour, and relatively open new attitudes towards sexuality, she experimented with ways in which self-styling afforded her purchase of new forms of self-determination and social mobility. The Modern Girl Around the World Research Group has observed that "[w]hat identified Modern Girls was their use of specific commodities and their explicit eroticism" (Weinbaum et al. 2008, 245). The emergence of the Modern Girl occurred "quite literally around the world" (Weinbaum et al. 2008, 1) as "a global phenomenon of the 1920s and 30s" (Weinbaum et al. 2008, 4).

Because of her appearance around the world as a figure of transnational modernity, the absence of the Modern Girl from standard and even revisionist histories of Canadian and Australian literatures is particularly conspicuous (Smith et al. 2018). This literary lacuna is all the more striking in light of her omnipresence in the Canadian interwar magazines on which Nicholas (2015) draws for her historical study, and the Australian interwar magazines examined by Liz Conor (2004) and Jill Julius Matthews (2005) in their cultural histories. In standard accounts, the missing women of national literature can be explained by their active exclusion from the male-centred canon (Gerson 2016). However, accounting for the missing figure of the Modern Girl is somewhat more complex and is connected, as Faye Hammill (2003) has hinted, to the commercial nature and success of narratives associated with her. This suggests that one major barrier to her inclusion within these national literary histories is her problematic

---

[1] See also Corinne Sandwith's and Arti Minocha's chapters in this collection for further examinations of the relationship between women, print culture, and the formation of modern subjectivity in South Africa and India, respectively.

relationship not only with modernity but also with transnational commodity culture. The figure's association with unfettered consumerism may have been cause for anxiety amongst those who were in the process of constructing nascent projects of national literature in Canada and Australia.

In this chapter, we are therefore committed to uncovering a *female-oriented* literary modernity grounded in the "feminine phenomena" (Felski 1995, 10) of commercial periodical culture. Following the approach of Margaret Beetham, we turn to the magazine as "a genre which addressed the feminine" (1996, 1) in our attempt to understand the complex multi-authored periodical as embedded in commercial culture whilst not overly determined by it. We also follow Beetham in viewing the representation of women in magazines as neither simplistically repressive nor naïvely productive of female agency but in a way that "throws light on complex relationships enacted in magazines between readers, writers, and editors" (1996, 2). In comparatively examining the figure of the Modern Girl in select Australian and Canadian magazine stories of the interwar period, we seek to expand understanding of alternative literary modernities through widening considerations of cultural value beyond the securely literary domain on which the important revisionist work of women's literary histories in Canada and Australia has been focused.

This is part of a larger project of critical recuperation that turns to magazines to explore what Michelle Smith has identified as "intriguing gaps in our knowledge" (2012, 12) of these nations' literary histories due to "a tendency to shelve works that may have been seen as backward or embarrassing" (Smith 2012, 12) by retrospective projects of national canon formation. Arguably, the intriguing gap of the Modern Girl was less associated with anxiety about backwardness and more informed by anxiety associated with her future and outward orientation, which potentially threatened the coherence of the project of literary cultural nationalism. In the Canadian and Australian contexts, literary and cultural hierarchies remained unstable during the interwar period prior to national canon formation (Carter 2004, 180; Kuttainen et al. 2018) when high culture was generally still regarded as imported from Britain and mass culture was seen as almost entirely derived from America (Hammill 2007, 19). Due to her relation to transnational, modern consumer culture, the Modern Girl was a figure of intense cultural contestation in these contexts, regarded as "simultaneously the sign of all that was wrong with the direction society was taking and the promise of a brave new world" (Matthews 2005, 19). Recuperating her presence in magazine fiction therefore connects to a broader task of deepening understanding of how these alternative literary modernities in settler colonial domains positioned themselves in relation to various, shifting values and cultural cross-currents.

2 (CON)TEXTS IN COMPARISON

Following Rasoul Aliakbari (2016) in his pursuit of "heterogenization," and resisting the urge to consider national literatures in terms of what Michelle Smith has called "homogeneous lumps" (2012, 12), we examine how the Modern Girl was positioned and contested in Canadian and Australian magazines in relation to cultural hierarchies of taste that aligned differently in relation to different classes of readers. By comparing similar tiers of print culture (upmarket quality magazines versus mass-market magazines) across national contexts, we uncover a more precise understanding of Canadian and Australian attitudes towards the figure of the Modern Girl than a single nation-centred approach might afford. The magazines examined in this chapter include comparably expensive and lushly produced upmarket quality magazines, *The Home* (Sydney, 1920–1942) and *Mayfair* (Toronto, 1927–1936; Montreal, 1937–1959); they also include more affordable and slightly less expensively produced, mass-market publications, *The Australian Woman's Mirror* (Sydney, 1924–61) and *The Western Home Monthly* (Winnipeg, 1899–1932).

In each of these magazines, the Modern Girl was visibly present in illustrations for fiction, on covers of magazines, in advertising, and in general discourse, often as a subject of debate. To focus our analysis of her, we have taken a slice approach, considering publications from 1932, when all the magazines that are the subjects of our study were simultaneously in print. Our concern with fiction in these magazines is paramount, but we read these stories alongside the advertising and non-fiction writing in which it is enmeshed. In particular, our interest centres upon a type of story we term "The Modern Girl Story," loosely defined by its focus on a cheerfully independent flapper-like character.

2.1 The Home

Carter has described the audience of the Australian quality magazine *The Home* as one "possessed of good taste and the means to purchase it" (2013, 137). Advertisements for a range of luxury goods including international travel, high-class hotels, upmarket hair salons, and ready-to-wear fashions from exclusive shops indicate that the magazine addressed, responded to, and helped shape the "smart set" in Australian interwar society. They also suggest the growing influence of American commercial and beauty culture. For instance, in one full-page advert for the New Jersey-based company Johnson & Johnson, a photograph of trouser-wearing Modern Girl instructs young female readers to "Stay Cool" (*The Home*, January 1932, 5). In the May issue, the same company tutors readers to use their product line Modess, purpose-designed "To Meet the Requirements of the Modern Woman" (*The Home*, May 1932, 5). These elements suggest the increasing influence of certain aspects of modern American commercial culture, but in most other areas the magazine maintained its steady gaze on Europe and England.

Visual culture in the magazine was generally dominated by material from London or the cosmopolitan centres of Europe. Fashion advice looked to Paris, in items such as "Fashion Points from Paris" (March 1932, 34), "Paris Prescribes" (May 1932, 40), or "Paris Notes" (December 1932, 83). Arty photograph features called "Social Studies" (March 1932, 21) filled the magazine with elegantly posed silhouettes of society debutantes, counterpoints to the Hollywood starlets that were increasingly featured in other magazines of the day. While film entered the review pages occasionally, the focus tended to remain on the plot of the play rather than the star. European starlets such as Greta Garbo or British theatre darlings such as Dame Sybil Thorndike (August 1932, 34; October 1932, 25) were covered, but cameos of movie stars are notably restrained. Society women who appeared in feature articles were typically from the upper echelons of English high society (June 1932, 27). Cumulatively, this material suggests that iconography around the Modern Girl is tastefully curated in *The Home*, hinting at the increasing influence of American glamour, while still predominantly looking to England for cultural cues.

The magazine was restrained in its embrace of American glamour, and this restrained tone extended to its fiction. Whilst fiction took up a larger proportion of the magazine in earlier years, by 1932 it appeared to have been largely replaced by a new section entitled "Instructional Articles." These were clearly targeted at the formation of the young woman's social persona, offering instruction in contract bridge, gardening advice, recipes for fine food and tasteful home décor, ideas for entertaining, reviews of classical phonograph records, and fashion tips. Typically, only a single one- or two-page story appeared in each issue, and few of these focused on the Modern Girl. Those that did demonstrated a pervasively negative and censorious attitude, often satirical, in the vein of celebrated English writer Evelyn Waugh's 1930 novel *Vile Bodies*, the well-known send-up of the moral and intellectual vacuity of British Bright Young Things. Aiming at a married reader rather than a young single reader, and consistent with the magazine's aspirational and instructional tone, the stories of *The Home* in 1932 focused on married couples rather than single girls.

In one such, "Full Circle" by Roger Maitland, a travelling gossip columnist remarkably similar to Waugh's character Adam Fenwick-Symes tells the story of "a rotter and a blackguard" who had "brought to London his newly acquired wife, a beautiful and innocent country girl who obviously adored him and who less obviously dreaded the environment to which he brutally introduced her" (*The Home*, September 1932, 78). In another, "Man of Honour" by Patricia O'Rane, a marital affair is narrowly circumvented when the values of restraint and virtue overcome passion (*The Home*, July 1932, 26, 53). Similarly, Velia Ercole's "Fool's Chance" raises the subject of a possible divorce but proposes a lucky and conservative resolution. A husband trapped in an unhappy marriage in which the couple "talked always [...] artificially, allusively, sometimes cleverly as in a drawing-room comedy" suggests a divorce, only to be dismissed by his utterly modern and blasé wife because "there seems no pressing need at the moment" (*The Home*, October 1932, 42). The marriage becomes unbearably strained until a strange encounter in a hotel room helps the couple overcome their mutual antipathy and reconcile. These conservative stories seem to serve a didactic purpose that favours social propriety and stability over individual passion and self-actualization, which is typically portrayed as destructive.[2]

Thus in *The Home*, the Modern Girl is visible in advertisements and in tastefully displayed visual culture, but curated and framed in keeping with the magazine's understanding and impressions of good taste. The models for ladylike fashions and behaviour mostly looked to Europe and to England, though influences of American beauty culture began to inflect advertising. Revealingly, in fiction, *The Home* is marked more by the absence of the figure of the Modern Girl than by her presence, and where she does appear in fiction, the tone is didactic moralism or satire. She is depicted as a figure of

---

[2] It is noteworthy that, in *The Home*, stories that focus on single girls are even more critical in tone. See, for example, "The Cheat" by J. Plain (*The Home*, November 1932, 44) and "The Bright Young Things at Bridge, etc." by Dudley Gordon (May 1932, 42), both of which are satires of the Modern Girl.

glamour, but also one of potential danger. Where she is not merely the target of directed instruction on matters of social propriety and restraint, the Modern Girl appears as the butt of a joke shared among readers in the know.

2.2 Mayfair

The remit, readership, and status of *Mayfair*, which has been classified as "a lifestyle magazine" targeting an "elite" audience (Potvin 2001, 3), suggest that it was a quality taste-making Canadian monthly that addressed an equivalent audience to that of Australia's *The Home*. Like *The Home*, the circulation of Mayfair was directed at a relatively small readership of local elites, comprising less than "20,000 copies in circulation" at its height (Potvin 2001, 32). In 1932, each issue contained one story, almost all of which were written by Ellen Evelyn Mackie. Notably, Hammill and Smith rank Mackie as one of the many authors who sustained magazine fiction in interwar Canada who are now forgotten (2015b in Sugars, 359). Each of her contributions can be considered a "Modern Girl Story"; cumulatively this forms a substantial body of Modern Girl fiction in *Mayfair*. In contrast to the negative portrait of the Modern Girl in *The Home*, readers are clearly meant to relish in the freedoms and fashionable lifestyle of the equivalent character in these stories in *Mayfair*.

In these stories, the Modern Girl can be found striking various inviting poses. She is inevitably "aimlessly smoking" like Tannis Chown of "Stepping Out" (*Mayfair*, February 1932, 29); typically "slim and boyish" like Sally Mumford in "Leave it to a Woman" (*Mayfair*, April 1932, 30); and frequently a youthful member of the smart set, talking slang and swilling cocktails: "just a snitch of gin," says one in "As Luck Would Have It" (*Mayfair*, March 1932, 30). She is often "an acknowledged leader" in social situations, popular among women and able to command her "pick of the men" for potential suitors, as in "Good Fish on the Sea" (*Mayfair*, May 1932 30); routinely flirtatious, as in "Wings Over a Dude Ranch" (*Mayfair*, August 1932, 26); and at ease in perilous social situations, as in "The Goose Hangs High" (*Mayfair*, September 1932, 32). In general, she is also visually enticing, an object of attention and the agent of her own affairs: a seductive self-determining modern subject on the move, associated with travel like the aviatrix of "Wings Over a Dude Ranch" (*Mayfair*, August 1932, 26) or the ocean-crossing Pamela Lloyd aboard a "great liner" departing for home in Montreal from England (*Mayfair*, May 1932, 30). Her links to the strikingly modern mode of automobility epitomize this heady mix of visual enticement, seduction, and agility. One such example is the car-race scene in Ellen Mackie's "Cheese Pairings and Candle Ends" from October 1932, in which the head-turning Modern Girl Betty Crombie is introduced:

> The vociferous tooting of a horn. Gary started, and turned involuntarily, to meet the challenging eyes of a girl in a robin's egg blue roadster, directly behind. A wrench at his wheel, and the car swerved right. With a bound the girl's throbbing racer leaped forward and shot on ahead. A low, triumphant laugh was borne back on the morning breeze.
>
> She was a lyric of color, sports suit and beret of gay buttercup, with a demure knot of yellow hair.
>
> "Boy, oh boy, what a color-study!" reflected Gary, despite a certain pique at the girl's mocking laugh. "Yellow and robin's egg blue—" Then, with a strange throb, he remembered her eyes. Deep blue, like hot-house grapes. Who could she be? He stared at the flashing machine which forged ahead with challenging speed.
>
> The spirit of adventure seized him. (*Mayfair*, October 1932, 28)

Betty is literally paces ahead: modern, self-propelling, pleasure-loving, and fast. When Gary finally manages to pull alongside her, the single girl and male immediately engage in flirty banter, which the female leads: "Can you spare me a smoke?" she asks, adding, "Left my cigarettes behind. That's what comes of dashing off to race with strange men" (*Mayfair*, October 1932, 28).[3]

Just as the figure of the Modern Girl threatens to cross boundaries of all kinds within these stories in *Mayfair*, the stories themselves also constantly threaten to cross class boundaries. A mix of sophistication and light fun, the stories themselves blur lines between commercial and artistic codes and mix the registers of art and entertainment. The slick, polished feel of Mackie's well-constructed and often lightly satirical writing seems

---

[3] Notably, Mackie's Modern Girls also regularly threaten to step out of the unspoken boundaries of class and race. Infatuated with his air of cosmopolitan sophistication, Tannis Chown pursues a romantic relationship with Adolph, even though her Anglo-Celtic admirers "Nick" and "Drew" call him a "dago" (*Mayfair*, February 1932, 54). As a figure, the Modern Girl is fraught with risk; Mackie's stories in *Mayfair* indulge in the fantasy of frisson and freedom which she seductively offers, but the plot's stylized resolution tends to restore her to the safe bounds of social propriety.

to have more in common with the sophisticated commercial art that graces the magazine's covers than with advertising or cinema alone. Further, as with many Modern Girls, Mackie's creations have an intense cinematic quality to them with their red lips, bobbed hair, or other visual cues gesturing towards the "visually intensified modern scene" that, as Liz Conor has noted, characterized modernity (2004, 7), in which women were presented and learned to negotiate their subjectivity as embodied "spectacles" (2004, 7). In "Stepping Out," most of the action occurs within the space of the cosmopolitan hotel's salon, where Adolph "practically made you a new face while you waited" (*Mayfair*, February 1932, 29): "The fashionable set lined up" for "the 'bridge face', the 'cocktail face,' the 'nightclub face' [...]" (*Mayfair*, February 1932, 29) appear elsewhere in the pages of the magazine, in its regular mixture of photographs of film actresses, advertisements, and fashion illustrations.

The Modern Girl fiction in *Mayfair* thus bore witness to modes of fusion and hybridity. She embodied the tensions between culture and commerce that were at the very heart of transnational modernity in these settler colonial domains. Whilst some of the advertisements *Mayfair* carried, for Simpsons or Calay, for instance, represented Canadian firms, this material was overwhelmingly American in origin. As Potvin explains, accepting these American advertisements was for *Mayfair* "a matter of economic survival" in an unprotected publishing environment immersed in a deluge of British and American imports (19). Although Potvin notes that American advertising was accepted as a necessary evil, he also concedes that much of the fashion advice in the magazine began by the end of 1932 to look to "New York as the preferred centre of style and fashion" (Potvin 2001, 10).

The Modern Girl thus sits at the crossroads of these various influences in this magazine. On the one hand, she conveys the ascendancy of American commercial culture, and on the other, she appears as an alluring beacon of tasteful sophistication and modern style. Similarly, Mackie's own writing style was sleek and polished, marked by some aspects of slick genre fiction, but also conveying a knowing, sophisticated tone. Reading across the page from the stories, the illustrated advertisements often ran seamlessly into the fiction in ways that complemented the illustrated stories and again blurred the boundaries between commerce and art, or commodity culture and fiction.

2.3 The Western Home Monthly

In contrast to the relatively small circulations of these quality magazines, Canada's *The Western Home Monthly* was a mass magazine. Carrying a range of advertisements for inexpensive beauty treatments and kitchen, cooking, or cleaning products, it was also a household magazine, addressing both men and women of several generations (Hammill and Smith 2015a, 355). Having established an audience of readers amongst Winnipeg and the largely rural prairie provinces of Canada whilst also seeking to grow its readership, its editorials covered a range of issues of importance to the region, nation, and the Empire. In addition to discussions of politics and Christian virtue, it also dispensed relatively progressive advice for women and men on marriage and legal matters, such as "Matrimony and the Matter of Money" by Emily F. Murphy (April 1932, 12–13). Unlike *The Home* and *Mayfair*, short fiction was its staple. It offered three to five illustrated stories in each issue, as well as the occasional serial. Many of these were genre stories featuring crime, detection, or man's contest against nature, but Modern Girl stories also appeared. In contrast to the way in which the Modern Girl was carefully curated in the high-class magazines *Mayfair* and *The Home*, however, these stories suggested mixed attitudes and a heterogeneous readership.

Montreal-based writer Anita Gabrielle Lavack's story "A Girl Needs a Trousseau" announces itself as a Modern Girl story through its signal word "Girl" and its focus on her commercial desires. The story's illustration, featuring a buxom young woman with bobbed hair dancing with her suitor, also underscores its topic (January 1932, 6). In Lavack's story, a single working girl with designs upon a Montreal scion crosses class lines and successfully works her street smarts upon the society set. Taking a cue from another family who managed to "buy off" a chorus girl who was threatening to marry their wealthy son, a high-society matriarch employs a junior company man to carry out a scheme to break off the relationship. In a plot involving hijinks, mistaken identity, and a clever twist, the wealthy son follows through on his intention to marry below his class, and the company man engaged to break off the relationship ends up falling for her friend too. To top it off, the girls cleverly repurpose money set aside as a reward for the company man, to purchase a trousseau for the bride, the matriarch's new daughter-in-law.[4] In contrast to the plots of *Mayfair* and *The Home*, the Modern Girl in this story manages to expand the boundaries of social propriety and mirthfully change the hearts and minds of the society set.

In other stories, the Modern Girl appeared as a love interest with the potential to derail the plans of the hard-working male protagonist. In these sorts of tales in *The Western Home Monthly*, the Modern Girl is a foreign element, typically associated with American big-city influences. In "The Lipstick Sort" by British genre fiction author Florence S. Howard-Burleigh, for instance, Miss Sandra Merridew is characterized as "one of the most thoroughly spoiled of the younger and brighter set" and "[m]ade up, of course, as they all are nowadays to a travesty of the normal human colouring, but so attractive" (May 1932, 9). The owner of the garage at which she parks her car dismisses her "with venom in his voice" as "that two-bit chunk of lipstick and powder, with the Isotta-Fraschini that she can't drive" (9). In addition to her lifestyle characterized by glamour and mobility, she is associated with American values and with promiscuity ("The Lipstick Sort," May 1932, 9). In the serial "Out of the Woods" by John Middleton Ellis, the Modern Girl is similarly positioned as an American temptress. The hard-working Canadian lumberjack and family man Con is lured by Clem, a mysterious stranger from New York who swindles the family out of their timber fortune. Down on his luck, Con is forced south to New York City, where he trains as a prize fighter. It is here that he first encounters "early morning throngs of hard-faced flappers [...] as they rushed to their work" (May 1932, 50). Before long, he falls under the influence of Kitty Fallon, who turns his attention away from the wholesome girl-next-door character he has left behind in Quebec, and introduces him to the world of mobsters, racketeers, and rum-running.

In yet another, "Cinderella Meets the Prince," by Alberta C. Trimble (August 1932, 14–15, 26–28) a didactic plot directs the young male suitor away from the allures of the American city and back to the heart of the small-town girl. Alvin Deane, a young man of marriageable age from small-town New England, leaves his cloistered life, where he feels the girls are cheap imitations of high-class city girls they have seen in magazines, in

---

[4] "The Run Across" (January 1932, 12, 13, 47) is another such Modern Girl story in *The Western Home Monthly* in which female resourcefulness and independence is celebrated. Its author, Louis Arthur Cunningham, was, like Lavack, one of Canada's most prolific writers of interwar magazine fiction who has been largely forgotten.

search of the real thing. At first overawed by the proliferation of "millions of short skirts and neat ankles" on the New York streets (15), the young man soon finds city girls to be "tawdry" and "blasé" (27). Downcast, contrite, and resolved to return to his hometown, Alvin gives up on his quest to find the girl of his dreams. At the last stroke of the clock before his departure, however, Alvin meets a girl, Kay Cardiff, who lives up to his fantasies. In a plot twist, she is revealed to hail from his hometown and is equally homesick for it and for its good men. These stories thus offer a cautious warning about the allures of the Modern Girl and her associated trappings of commercialized American modernity signified by big city life.

In part, the mixed attitudes towards the Modern Girl encountered in this periodical may be explained by its heterogeneous audience. The mixed nature of the stories also suggests that the magazine was at the crossroads of American and Canadian influences and was marked both by the trappings of modernity and by antimodernist impulses. Many of the stories were illustrated with lush, two-tone images of what Shannon Jaleen Grove (2014) identifies as the iconography of "wilderness adventure and that of pretty girls" (13). These signified, Grove explains, "the rivalry of the opposing political sentiments known as 'nationalism' and 'continentalism'" that positioned the mass-market Canadian magazine as a cultural battleground (13).

2.4 The Australian Woman's Mirror

In strictly economic terms, *The Australian Woman's Mirror* targeted a similar range of readership to *Western Home Monthly* in ways that suggest is can be considered its equivalent. A weekly magazine *Bulletin* (Sydney, 1924–61), it was an affordable publication that appealed to the aspirational working class. It was issued on newsprint-grade paper and presented a mix of serialized novels, short stories, and advice for housewives and single working women. With advertisements for inexpensive beauty treatments such as cold creams and soaps, as well as for foodstuffs and home products such as "Silver Star Rice Starch" or "Fairy Dyes," it offered free dress patterns, recipes, children's pages, book recommendations, and photo features focusing on attractive film stars and their latest movies. It also sometimes printed articles defending the role of women in the workplace and occasionally offered advice for women seeking a divorce or wishing to buy property.

In contrast to *The Western Home Monthly*, however, *The Mirror* did not address a mixed audience of men and women readers. Rather, as the counterpart to the predominantly masculine and nationalist *Bulletin* (Sydney, 1880–2008), from which it emerged as an offshoot, it attempted to compete with the new magazines imported from Britain and America that offered something more appealing to the growing segment of the female buying public. Even the title *The Mirror* suggested a space of intimacy and reflection, a refuge for feminine dreams of wish-fulfilment or escape from the masculine public sphere. Its first editorial proclaimed that "[v]ast changes have taken place in [women's lives] during recent years; and the daily and weekly newspapers written chiefly by men for men no longer fully answer their needs. 'The Woman's Mirror' proposes to serve those needs" (23 Oct 1924, 2). Another of its selling points was its female-oriented fiction in which "[e]very feminine interest and activity will be served in the best way" (2). Serialized fiction, short stories, literary anecdotes, poems, and book reviews were its staple, comprising over half the magazine's content, in which the Modern Girl often featured. In contrast to *The Western Home Monthly*, the Modern Girl was predominantly featured as the protagonist.

In one such serial, "Sanctuary" by Margaret Boyd (1 Dec, 1931, 4), a number of single women negotiate the establishment of their careers in work and romance at the height of the Depression in Sydney. One of them is an aspiring actress who hopes to achieve fame in the Hollywood talkies. Their status as Modern Girls is coded by their fashionable dress, their use of cigarettes, their career aspirations, and their relative freedom regarding sexuality. Yet, while the girls and their friends readily cross established lines of social propriety, they know that they still must appear to operate within these boundaries. The last instalment shows how Janie finally dismisses her French lover's influence in her life and accepts her dependable male friend's marriage proposal. Ultimately, sanctuary is found in stability and security, rather than in romance and risk.

Many of the Modern Girl stories in this magazine are likewise ultimately didactic even as they also offered working women dreams of romance and escape. "Romance" by Nina Lowe (12 July 1932, 8) provides a clear example, as the protagonist is a hard-working farm girl who reads too many romance novels. She is ardently pursued by Bill, whom she dismisses for the dream of "one experience that would stir her to the depths; one great twang upon her heart strings; one romantic glow of crimson to light the world," something like the situation in "a book she had read and was re-reading – the story of an Arab who discovered a lady lost in the desert with a collection of Paris model gowns" (8). It is only when a Syrian beggar appears at the farm "in the midst of her romancing" (51) and threatens her sexually that her oasis disappears. Like the stories in *The Western Home Monthly*, this tale warns not only of the sexual but also the racial dangers of crossing the unspoken boundaries of social respectability. It suggests that Modern Girls are perilously at risk if they mistake their romantic fantasies for reality, which remains at once threatening and dependable. Like Tannis Chown's Anglo-Celtic suitors, the boy next door is ordinary instead of exotic, but he provides a safe harbour in a world fraught with risk.

As in *The Home*, satirical pieces in *The Mirror* send up the Modern Girl. In one, "A Flapper Tragedy: A Short Story of a Modern Young Miss" (2 Feb. 1932, 8, 35, 36), the Modern Girl is depicted as vacuous, consumeristic, poorly mannered, and vain. The story's "tragedy" involves the flapper wearing inappropriately fashionable attire to school, where she experiences public shame and admonishment by the head mistress, who chides her in Latin: "*varium et mutabile semper femina*" (36) (women are ever fickle and changeable). This type of didactic tale warns female readers of the vain pursuits of fashion, even as it clashed with some of the non-fiction pieces advertising fashion and offering stylish advice, featured in the multi-authored, multi-genre magazine.

In the 26 January 1932 issue, for example, the article "Things Are Changing For Girls, by One Of Them," is bookended by attractive illustrations of women: one of them is a distinctly Modern Girl poised fashionably next to her Victorian mother, who is clearly portrayed as outdated. The article laments the disappearance of men who "not so very long ago […] courted us girls, invited us to the theatre and paid us attention in little thoughtful ways" (18). "Nowadays," the Modern Girl author warns, "I have found that there are really two types of men—the man who looks at women from only the sexual standpoint and the other type whom women interest and amuse as companions, and who, if he loves, gives all his love to the one woman, and the rest of the world is to him sexless" (18). She adds, "The first type of man means 'rocks ahead,' absolute trouble for any woman who could care for him. There are plenty of these men, no limit to their number, married and single" (18). Rather than warning against the Modern Girl, this article warns women about the Modern Man and even modern marriages. It cautions, "In trying to give men what they want, they [Modern Girls] are trying to be what they are not. It is pathetic in a way; it is unfair to the girl" (18). The Modern Girl, its author insinuates, should not play the game but stand on her own two feet and keep enjoying the things she likes, such as "dances, theatres and restaurants" (18), for example.

Not only does the magazine feature advice for the Modern Girl on matters such as men, but it also gives career advice. One such, "In a Detective's Office: The Thrills of a Girl's Unusual Vocation" by Private Secretary (19 Apr 1932, 11, 47) outlines the exciting rewards of a vocation with some risk attached and outlines the dividends paid in the investment of effort and time to build such a career. The article is accompanied by a photograph of a "Miss Storey, a woman detective from the North of England," who "employs only women" (11). Styled clearly as a Modern Girl, she poses boldly in the middle of the photograph wearing a cloche hat and a luxurious fur coat. Another such, "The McDonagh Girls: Talkie Production as a Vocation for Women" by Viola C. West (12 July 1932, 9, 45), outlines the career paths of three ordinary hard-working girls who achieved roles in Hollywood films. Both of these articles reward the aspirational dreams of young working women and direct their gaze to Hollywood glamour and London fashion in ways that are reinforced by the fashion advice and advertisements of the magazine, which also feature the Modern Girl.

Directed into both the domestic sphere and to the working class girl who could be expected to earn her own money, *The Australian Woman's Mirror* navigated the new identities on offer to Modern Girls in agile ways. Whilst providing dreams of escape and fantasy from domestic drudgery, the stories generally served didactic purposes. They warned young women of the social, sexual, and even racial risks of trading the dreamy images of the Modern Girl that suffused magazine illustrations, photos, and films for cruel realities. On the other hand, the magazine seemed to offer aspirational fantasies of new glamorous careers and encouraged the Modern Girl to become financially and emotionally independent.

3   Conclusions

Jill Julius Matthews has argued that "modernity refused" a tidy "segregation" between art and advertising, "promiscuously mingling culture and commerce, the beautiful and the vulgar" (2005, 19). In her work on Australian modernity, Matthews points out:

> Representing that fusion most visibly were modern women. Traditional symbols and embodiments of beauty, young women now engaged in selling and buying and came to symbolise commercial pleasures. The modern girl, the girl of today, the flapper, was both the subject and the metaphor at the heart of the international discourse of modernity [...]. (Matthews 2005, 19)

The Modern Girl challenges established and revisionist accounts of Canadian and Australian literatures and, in her boundary-pushing and code-crossing behaviour, even threatens the very coherence of orthodox approaches to national literature that have prevailed in these contexts since the formation of their national canons and survived challenges from feminist revisionism in the 1970s and 1980s. Whilst Canadian and Australian literary studies have largely ignored the figure of the Modern Girl until recently, it is all too apparent that she was a stock figure in Canadian and Australian magazines and regularly appeared in their fiction, even as a figure of contestation.

Despite critical orthodoxies that have placed the mainstream magazine and the novel in opposition, loosely categorizing the one as commercial and the other as literary, magazines of many kinds maintained strong links with literary culture, publishing short stories and serialized novels of varying quality by a range of writers, and often including book reviews and other aspects of book chat. As Hammill and Smith have written of the Canadian magazines they examined, "[s]everal of the magazines relied heavily on literary content" (qtd. in Sugars 2015b, 358). These texts also captured a broad audience. Rather than dismissing these literary artefacts because of their popularity, Hammill and Smith argue that this aspect is part of what makes studying mainstream magazines "important" (359). We have turned to them not only because they allow us to put the Modern Girl back in the picture of the literary and cultural histories of these nations but also because magazines can tell literary and cultural historians about their target demographic and help identify the differentiated tastes of readers.

Our comparative reading across four magazines of two classes, quality and mass, has revealed that the Modern Girl was coded differently according to readership, and that her associations with transnational modernity, with Hollywood images and London fashion in particular, were framed in distinct ways which varied with the different remit and audience of each periodical. The way in which she risked crossing established and unstated codes of cultural respectability and good taste meant that different tiers of society were positioned in relation to her in distinct ways.

It would seem that, on the whole, mass magazines were more positive towards the Modern Girl than were upmarket magazines, though she offered a fantasy of alternative lives to all classes of readers and can be found in the work of alternative writers, whose names were once well known by readers but who have been subsequently forgotten. Presumably, a risk of carrying this ambiguous class of fiction in an elite taste-making magazine was its uncertain status, and unclear affiliation with aspects of feminine modernity considered gauche, crass, or low class. Just as the plots of these stories often worked to contain the troublesome and transgressive Modern Girl by restoring her to the domestic sphere, these magazines similarly allowed readers to indulge in the fantasy offered by the Modern Girl while also seeking out ways to contain her potentially transgressive and dangerous qualities.

Our essay has aimed to challenge homogeneous approaches to national literature that focus on the coherence of the domestic narrative of nation at the cost of overlooking these sorts of messy and risky entanglements with transnational modernity. As such, we have sought to release the Modern Girl from this domestic containment. Moreover, our comparative examination demonstrates the repurposings of European and American cultural templates in Canadian and Australian contexts, at the so-called edges of transnational modernity. Our pursuit of the Modern Girl outlines an alternative designation of literary modernity as *female-oriented*, rather than masculinist, and as grounded in heterogeneous commercial periodical culture as opposed to canonical novelism.

Works Cited

Aliakbari, Rasoul. 2016. The *Arabian Nights* in the English Popular Press and the Heterogenization of Nationhood: A Print Cultural Approach to Benedict Anderson's *Imagined Communities*. *Canadian Review of Comparative Literature/Revue Canadienne de Littérature Comparée* 43 (3): 439–460. https://muse.jhu.edu.

Beetham, Margaret. 1996. *A Magazine of Her Own: Domesticity and Desire in the Woman's Magazine, 1800–1914.* New York: Routledge.

Carter, David. 2004. The Mystery of the Missing Middlebrow or the Course of Good Taste. In *Imagining Australia: Literature and Culture in the New New World*, ed. Judith Ryan and Chris Wallace-Crabbe, 173–201. Cambridge: Harvard University Press.

———. 2013. *Always Almost Modern: Australian Print Cultures and Modernity.* Melbourne: Australian Scholarly Publishing.

Conor, Liz. 2004. *The Spectacular Modern Woman: Feminine Visibility in the 1920s.* Bloomington: Indiana University Press.

Felski, Rita. 1995. *The Gender of Modernity.* Cambridge: Harvard University Press.

Ferrier, Carole. 1985. *Gender, Politics and Fiction: Twentieth Century Australian Women's Novels.* St Lucia: University of Queensland Press.

Gerson, Carole. 1991. The Canon Between the Wars: Field-Notes of a Feminist Literary Archeologist. In *Canadian Canons: Essays in Literary Value*, ed. Robert Lecker, 46–56. Toronto: University of Toronto Press.

———. 2016. Mid-century Modernity and Fiction by Women, 1920–1950. In *The Oxford Handbook of Canadian Literature*, ed. Cynthia Sugars, 337–351. Oxford: Oxford University Press.

Grove, Shannon Jaleen. 2014. A Cultural Trade? Canadian Magazine Illustrators at Home and in the United States, 1880–1960. PhD Diss., Stony Brook University.

Hammill, Faye. 2003. *The Sensations of the 1920s: Martha Ostenso's* Wild Geese and Mazo de la Roche's Jalna. *Studies in Canadian Literature/Ètudes en literature Canadienne (SCL/ÉLC)* 28 (2): 74–97.

———. 2007. *Women, Celebrity, and Literary Culture Between the Wars*. Austin: University of Texas.

Hammill, Faye, and Michelle Smith. 2015a. *Magazines, Travel, and Middlebrow Culture: Canadian Periodicals in English and French, 1925–1960*. Liverpool: Liverpool University Press.

———. 2015b. Mainstream Magazines: Home and Mobility. In *The Oxford Handbook of Canadian Literature*, ed. Cynthia Sugars, 352–368. Oxford: Oxford University Press.

Henderson, Jennifer. 2003. *Settler Feminism and Race Making in Canada*. Toronto: University of Toronto Press.

Jessup, Lynda. 2001. Antimodernism and Artistic Experience: An Introduction. In *Antimodernism and Artistic Experience: Policing the Boundaries of Modernity*, ed. Lynda Jessup, 3–10. Toronto: University of Toronto Press.

Kuttainen, Victoria, Susann Liebich, and Sarah Galletly. 2018. *The Transported Imagination: Australian Interwar Magazines and the Geographical Imaginaries of Colonial Modernity*. Amherst: Cambria.

Matthews, Jill Julius. 2005. *Dance Hall & Picture Palace: Sydney's Romance with Modernity*. Sydney: Currency Press.

McDougall, Russell, and Gillian Whitlock. 1987. Introduction. In *Australian/Canadian Literatures in English: Comparative Perspectives*, ed. Russell McDougall and Gillian Whitlock, 1–32. North Ryde: Methuen Australia.

Modjeska, Dusilla. 1981. *Exiles at Home: Australian Women Writers 1925–1945*. Sydney: Sirius Books.

Nicholas, Jane. 2015. *The Modern Girl: Feminine Modernities, the Body, and Commodities in the 1920s*. Toronto: University of Toronto Press.

Potvin, John. 2001. Fashioning Masculinity in *Mayfair Magazine*: The Aesthetics of the Male Body, 1927–1936. Master's Thesis, Carleton University.

Schaffer, Kay. 1988. *Women and the Bush: Forces and Desire in the Australian Cultural Tradition*. Cambridge: Cambridge University Press.

Smith, Michelle. 2012, Autumn. Mainstream Magazines, Middlebrow Fiction, and Leslie Gordon Barnard's *The Winter Road*. *Studies in Canadian Literature/ Ètudes en literature Canadienne (SCL/ÉLC)* 37 (1): 7–30.

Smith, Michelle, Clare Bradford, and Kristine Moruzi. 2018. *From Colonial to Modern: Transnational Girlhood in Canadian, Australian, and New Zealand Children's Literature (1840–1940)*. Toronto: University of Toronto Press.

Summers, Anne. 2016. *Damned Whores and God's Police*. Sydney: University of New South Wales Press.

Weinbaum, Alys, et al. 2008. The Modern Girl around the World: Consumption, Modernity, and Globalization: Introduction. In *The Modern Girl around the World: Consumption, Modernity, and Globalization*, ed. Alys Weinbaum et al. Durham: Duke University Press.

CHAPTER 4

The Making of a National Hero: A Comparative Examination of Köroğlu the Bandit

Judith M. Wilks

1 Introduction

Dating from at least the late sixteenth century and extending over an area stretching from the Balkans to Afghanistan, the Köroğlu *destan*[1] is one of the most enduring and widespread of the Turkic oral heroic traditions. Over time, the hero's character has undergone many transformations and has been viewed in a number of ways. From the portrayal of Köroğlu in the earliest recorded versions of the story as a violent, amoral scoundrel, it would seem that audiences of that time simply took a juvenile delight in the bandit-hero's ability to do great mischief with impunity. But over the course of the past century and a half, a different image has come to prevail: that of Köroğlu as a national hero, whether a champion of the oppressed masses, a defender from foreign invaders, or both. This very positive view

[1] For our present purposes, and in agreement with Karl Reichl's assessment of the genre issue in oral heroic traditions, we can consider the term *destan* as roughly equivalent to "folk epic" or "orally transmitted heroic tale."

J. M. Wilks (✉)
Northwestern University, Evanston, IL, USA

© The Author(s) 2020
R. Aliakbari (ed.), *Comparative Print Culture*, New Directions in Book History, https://doi.org/10.1007/978-3-030-36891-3_4

of Köroğlu has been featured in nationalistic publications and works of art from the early twentieth century onward. The hero has appeared in poems, novels, plays, films, and operas, and there are even statues erected in his honor in Bolu and in Baku. Nationalistic sentiment toward Köroğlu runs so high that rival claims to national possession of the Köroğlu *destan* by various Turkic groups have clouded scholarly discussion on its development.

In the context of this collection, this chapter compares repurposings of Köroğlu from the mid-nineteenth to the late twentieth century and points out how the recordings and publications of these bandit stories led to their eventual use in the construction of a new national identity in the modern nations of Turkey and Azerbaijan.[2] These publications are contextualized within political developments that created a demand for a new national hero, intellectual trends that coincided with this demand, literary figures who were willing to support the nationalist movement in their own countries when they themselves were not leading it, and a background of local folkloric motifs that were often incorporated into versions of the *destan* and affected how the hero was perceived. Tracing these developments in the transmission of this bandit legend provides a glimpse of how its publication played out both in the well-established literary circles of Paris and in two emerging literary modernities, those of Turkey and Azerbaijan. In the case of these two countries, as in other instances mentioned in Rasoul Aliakbari's introductory chapter in this volume, especially Patricia May B. Jurilla's observations regarding the Philippines, and those of Javed Majeed regarding South Asia,[3] folklore collection and an increased awareness of the common language played an important role in the formation of a national identity, tapping into a common store of legend and tradition to solidify communal sentiments. The Köroğlu cycle featured prominently in this process.

2 Contexts

2.1 Who Is Köroğlu?

Köroğlu is a bandit-hero similar in many ways to the English Robin Hood. There are whole episodes of their legends that parallel each other quite closely. Both bandits turn to a life of crime after some injustice is done to

---

[2] Throughout this chapter, unless otherwise noted, "Azerbaijan" will denote that part of the historical region which later became the Soviet Republic of Azerbaijan, not the Iranian province of the same name, despite the close cultural ties between the two areas.

[3] See Chap. 1 of this volume.

4 THE MAKING OF A NATIONAL HERO: A COMPARATIVE EXAMINATION... 63

them; each of them has a band of followers (the Merry Men in the case of Robin Hood, and the *deliler* in the case of Köroğlu); both use disguises frequently; both usually elude capture by the authorities, but are captured in one episode; and there are anti-clerical elements in both groups of stories. In general, it would not be too far off the mark to think of Köroğlu as a musically inclined Robin Hood with a horse.

It should be acknowledged, however, that this Robin Hood-like description of the hero applies only to the western versions of the story. The story of Köroğlu is shared not only by nearly all Turkic peoples from the Balkans to Central Asia, but also by some non-Turkic neighboring communities, such as the Armenians, Georgians, Kurds, Tajiks, and Afghans. There are, of course, differences among these many versions, the most important of these being the name of the hero and his occupation. In the western versions, he is a bandit leader very similar to Robin Hood, and his name is Köroğlu, meaning "son of the blind man." In the eastern versions, the hero is a legitimate ruler, either a tribal chieftain or a Sultan, and his name is Güroğlı (or Göroğlı), meaning "son of the grave," as he was born in his mother's grave. Although other differences both large and small exist among the various versions, in general, they can be separated into these two major groups, the western and the eastern traditions, with the Caspian Sea as a rough boundary between them. It is the western versions, specifically the Turkish and the Azeri, that are the concern of this chapter.

2.2 The Historical Identity of Köroğlu

There are basically two main historical prototypes of Köroğlu, and these two may or may not be the same person. More than a dozen documents in the *Mühimme Defterleri* (Sümer 9–46) suggest that Köroğlu Ruşen was a member of a group of bandits in the vicinity of Bolu in northwest Anatolia in the late sixteenth century. He later moved on to Ankara, but nothing is known of his ultimate fate. Nothing in these documents would lead one to believe that Köroğlu's motives were altruistic; it is stated that whole villages were abandoned out of fear of his band. The other possible prototype is a poet named Köroğlu who is known to have served in the Ottoman army under Özdemiroğlu Osman Pasha in the conquest of Tabriz. (Boratav, *İslam Ansiklopedisi* 913). The dates involved for these two prototypes are not irreconcilable, and bandits did

64   J. M. WILKS

sometimes serve in the army, so the question of whether they are one and the same person remains unresolved.[4]

Problems arise if one accepts one or both of these historical persons as the prototype for Köroğlu the national hero. If the hero of the *destan* was really the rapacious bandit of the Bolu region, the common people of Anatolia should have no reason to regard him as their champion. Likewise, if he truly was the poet who was on the side of the Ottomans in the bitterly fought battle for Tabriz, he should be no hero to the Azeris. Nevertheless, he came to be considered a hero in both these areas and among other Turkic groups as well.

2.3   The Earliest Recorded Versions of Köroğlu

All the earliest recordings of Köroğlu songs and/or stories are from countries in the Caucasus, primarily from Azerbaijan, in various languages and alphabets. In these early versions, the hero's character is not out of keeping with that implied by the historical evidence. He is described as an excellent fighter, a trait that remains consistent over time in all the versions of his story. It is his motives and his methods of fighting that undergo considerable transformations.

In the earliest known collection of the songs (only the songs, not the complete stories) of Köroğlu, that of the Armenian merchant Ilyas Mushegean dating from 1721, Köroğlu boasts of his battle prowess. Interestingly, this collection does refer to the use of firearms,[5] though in some later versions Köroğlu regards firearms as unmanly. In 1804, the Azeri poet Andalib Karacadağı published a collection of songs and other folkloric material that included 20 songs of Köroğlu. This work, the first

---

[4] Ra'is Niya discusses the views of many scholars on this matter, 143–45. Boratav is among the most prominent scholars who are of the opinion that the two were probably the same person. There are two scholars who voice doubts concerning this in *Sultan Baba ve Köroğlu*: Müjgân Cünbür, "Köroğlu'nda Kahramanlık ve Birlik Ruhu" 48, 53; and İsmail Görkem, "Köroğlu'nun Şiirlerinde Kahramanlık Unsurları", 61.

[5] Tahmasıp (1969, 471), the third stanza: "Tüfengçi çaxmağın çaxar" (tr: "The gunman fires his gun"), corresponding to a song in the Chodźko MS, f. 110: "Merd igit çaxmaqı çaxar gülle değen yeri yaxır" (tr.: "The manly hero fires his gun, the place where the bullet hits burns"). The Mushegean collection itself is now in the state archives in Yerevan. It is a 326-page codex consisting of selections from the classical and folk poetry of Azerbaijan, including 13 of Köroğlu's songs in Azeri Turkish written in Armenian script. Tahmasip included 7 of these 13 songs in this volume.

4 THE MAKING OF A NATIONAL HERO: A COMPARATIVE EXAMINATION... 65

of its kind written in Azeri with the express purpose of preserving Azeri folklore, is now in St. Petersburg. However, 19 of the 20 songs contained in Karacadağı's collection have been published by M. Tahmasıp in *Azarbaijan Dastanları* (1969), which includes, in addition to some of the aforementioned Mushegean songs, samples of other Köroğlu songs written in Arabic, Armenian, and Georgian scripts.

Stories of the adventures of the bandit Köroğlu—who may or may not be the same person as the poet, as has been discussed—were first published in 1830 in a Tbilisi newspaper. Ten years later, A. Shopin published a more extensive and detailed version, "The Tatar Legend of Keroqlu," in a Russian journal in St. Petersburg.[6] Shopin admits that he heard this legend from someone whose national origins were unknown, but an Armenian translator was used for the Russian article. In the opinion of Ra'is Niya, Shopin must have meddled with the version considerably, as it bears little resemblance to other Köroğlu stories. In Shopin's version, Köroğlu converts to Christianity for the sake of a beautiful Georgian girl, and ends up killing all his comrades and then himself because his resentful friends have murdered his beloved. Nevertheless, Shopin's version was the most complete Köroğlu version published until then (Tahmasıp 1969, 303–05).

A much more complete picture of the hero's character can be found in the first known prosimetric version of the *destan*, which included both songs and stories of Köroğlu. This collection was put together in the 1830s in Tabriz (Iranian Azerbaijan) by Polish diplomat and scholar Alexander Chodźko. It has subsequently been translated several times and is an important source for the study of Turkic folklore. In this manuscript (Bibliothèque Nationale, Supplément Persane #994), entitled the *Koroğli-nâma* and commonly referred to as the Paris manuscript, Köroğlu is indeed a bold and clever fighter, but he is also crude, clownish, and largely amoral; what human sympathy he does show is entirely impulsive. His less-than-admirable deeds in this version include shooting an opponent in the back in anger after being defeated in a fair fight, kidnapping a young boy named Ayvaz for questionable motives, and eating so excessively that he grows too fat to

---

[6] I include the sources for these two Georgian publications as cited in Bayat's bibliography. The Russian titles are thus transcribed with Turkish approximations of their pronunciation: "Drevnya Orguca, Zamok Razboynika Uruşana-Koroglı, yego İstoriya, Raskaz ob Erivanskom Sardare," *Tifliskie Vedomosti*, No. 68, 1830. The second work mentioned, compiled by Shopin, is listed as follows: Şopen, İ., "Koroglı. Tatarskaya Legenda," *Mayak Sovremennogo Proveşçeniya i Obrazovonnosti. Trudı Uçyonıh i Literaturovedov Ruskih i İnostrannıh, g. 1–2*, St. Petersburg, 1840.

66   J. M. WILKS

escape from the pit in which he is imprisoned. His buffoonery and gluttony are vividly portrayed, as in the pages-long description of a shepherd looking on in disgust as Köroğlu greedily gulps down a huge bowl of stale bread and sour milk, with clumps of the moldy bread catching in his mustache (MS ff. 15–17a). It is hard to imagine why any group of people in the present age would want to claim such a character as the embodiment of their finest qualities as a nation. The *Koroğli-nâma* is not unique in depicting Köroğlu in this way; other, slightly later, versions also stress his violent nature. For example, Radloff's 1872 version depicts Köroğlu as a very cruel character (Boratav 1931, 33–34).

However, when Chodźko later translated the Persian manuscript into English under the auspices of the Committee of the Oriental Translation Fund, the hero's character underwent a considerable change. With his readers' sensitivities in mind, Chodźko omitted from his English version almost all the obscenity, all the allusions to homosexuality, and much of the buffoonery in the Persian original. The Persian manuscript is liberally peppered with obscene epithets throughout; most frequently used are *son-of-a-whore*, *wife-panderer*, *son-of-a-bitch*, and other creative insults implying canine parentage. None of these appear in the English translation; Chodźko tones these down to something much milder, such as *scoundrel* or *rascal*, so that much of the vulgar flavor and humor of the original are lost. On the whole, Chodźko makes Köroğlu more acceptable to bourgeois nineteenth-century European standards of behavior and language.

It is clear from the comments Chodźko makes in his preface and introduction that he was very much aware of the need to take his audience's sensibilities into account. He mentions other authors who did the same: Ferdowsi (author of the *Shahnameh*) sought to please his patron, Mahmud of Ghazne (Chodźko 1971, introduction 5–6), and the *aşıks* who recited the poems of Köroğlu also adjusted their recitations as they gauged their audiences' reactions (Chodźko 1971, introduction 13). According to Chodźko, one of the strengths of his work is the insight it offers into the "Oriental" character, which, he says, must be genuine, since his sources were oral (Chodźko 1971, preface vii). His remarks on the "Oriental" character very much reflect the thinking of his time: they are strongly Eurocentric and rather misogynistic, and show a heavy influence of Romanticism. The only overt clue he provides as to who exactly he perceives his audience to be occurs in his favorable comparison of European Christian women with "Oriental" women (Chodźko 1971, introduction 10–11). No further specification of his intended readership is provided,

4 THE MAKING OF A NATIONAL HERO: A COMPARATIVE EXAMINATION... 67

but it is clear that he was aiming at a genteel European Christian audience, and so the hero's original rough nature is adjusted accordingly. Some softening of the hero's character is also apparent in other versions of the Köroğlu tales that appeared later in the nineteenth century, such as the Armenian version of Aghayean, published in Istanbul in 1893. In this version, Köroğlu makes some attempt to justify his deeds on moral grounds, alluding to the New Testament (!); he is also kind to his comrades and courteous to ladies.[7] This is one instance of how the hero's religious affiliation varies from version to version, depending on the intended audience or readership, in order to gain sympathy for the hero. Many such instances exist. Similarly, in the travelog of Baron von Haxthausen (1857), Köroğlu is somewhat more high-minded, with his retirement brought about by the advent of firearms. When someone explains to him what guns are and how they are used, he declares that the age of manliness is over and vows to fight no more (Boratav 1931, 44). This motif has appeared in many versions that followed, but it is most likely a romantic addition to the story. Firearms are mentioned in the earliest Köroğlu songs from the Ilyas Mushegean collection of 1721, as well as in Chodźko's *Koroğli-nāma*, in which Köroğlu sings and boasts about firearms, and even uses a gun himself once to kill a pasha who is fleeing out of sword's reach (MS f. 114; Chodźko 1971, 258).

The inaccuracies, omissions, and distortions present in Chodźko's English translation of the *Kuroğli-nāma* may be partly responsible for the popularity Köroğlu enjoyed in Europe. Chodźko published his translation, under the rather cumbersome title *Specimens of the Popular Poetry of Persia as Found in the Adventures and Improvisations of Kurroglou, the Bandit-Minstrel of Northern Persia* (hereafter abbreviated to *Specimens*), in London in 1842, but he was living in Paris at the time, as were many other Polish exiles. Through a mutual friend in the Polish émigré community, Adam Mickiewicz, Chodźko's translation found its way into the hands of George Sand. Sand was very enthusiastic about Köroğlu; she admired his bandit lifestyle, wild freedom, closeness to nature, lack of restrictions, and defiance of authority. She attempted to publish a French

---

[7] Boratav provides a synopsis of the three tales in this version in *Köroğlu Destanı* (62–64), but for the details, I am indebted to Professor Peter Cowe for his English translation. Boratav notes (*Köroğlu Destanı* 230, note 4) that other Armenian versions were being published in Istanbul in Turkish using the Armenian alphabet as early as 1875; their storyline closely resembles that of the other Istanbul versions, with the addition of some extra poems.

68   J. M. WILKS

translation of the English version in serial fashion in the *Revue Indépendante* beginning in January 1843, but only the first episode was ever completed because Sand encountered difficulties of various kinds, and Köroğlu last appeared in the *Revue Indépendante* in April 1843. Her interest in Köroğlu continued, however, and she included a summary of his adventures at the back of two of her own novels, *Le Meunier d'Angibault* in 1846, and *Piccinino* in 1855. She also managed to publish her translated excerpts, with illustrations by her son Maurice, in 1853,[8] and her translations of some songs of Köroğlu in the *Revue de l'Orient* (Ra'is Niyā 1988, 308). There was also one other French translation of Chodźko's *Specimens*, as well as a German one and a Russian one, all within a few years of its publication (Calmard 1983, 502–04). The Russian translation of Chodźko's *Specimens*, by S.S. Penn, was later used extensively by Azeri and other Soviet academicians in their research on Köroğlu, despite its imperfections (Ra'is Niyā 1988, 308).

Even the American poet Henry Wadsworth Longfellow, a frequent traveler to Europe who was acquainted with George Sand, was familiar with Chodźko's Köroğlu. Longfellow was moved to write a poem about a great leap of Köroğlu's horse (Canby 1967, 109–11). Undoubtedly, he used Chodźko's English translation as the basis for this poem, as he replicates Chodźko's error regarding the color of the horse: he calls it a bay, whereas the horse's very name in Turkish (Kırat) means "Gray Horse." Longfellow also translated other poems, unrelated to Köroğlu, from the back of Chodźko's volume.

It seems, therefore, that Köroğlu was fairly well known among the late nineteenth-century European intelligentsia, even if in a somewhat distorted and gentrified form. Paris seems to have been the center of his popularity, and there were many young Ottoman and Azeri intellectuals living there in those years, whether as students or exiles. It no doubt surprised them to find a familiar character from their home cultures achieving such recognition in the literary circles of Paris. Köroğlu in general, and Chodźko's *Specimens* in particular, also found echoes in the countries of the Caucasus, especially Azerbaijan and Georgia (Ra'is Niyā 1988, 251–55), where it formed the basis for further collection efforts and academic studies, in the native languages and also in Russian (Ra'is Niyā 1988, 308).

---

[8] On Sand's interest in social banditry, see Georgeon (1991, 259–69), especially 267.

2.4 The Influence of European Romanticism on the Köroğlu Story

As previously mentioned, Chodźko was living in Romantic-Age Paris when he published his English translation of the Köroğlu collection. In attempting to understand Köroğlu's appeal to the intellectuals of that time and place, it might be useful to identify briefly a few distinct strands in the complex phenomenon of Romanticism that are most relevant to its influence on the Köroğlu *destan* and on folk literature in general.[9] Romanticism involved the glorification of a distant, irretrievable past and saw folk literature as a bridge to that distant age, or in the words of the sociologist Ruth Finnegan (1979), to the "natural and primeval depths, as distinct from the externally-imposed, mechanical and rationalist forms of the contemporary world" (34). Folk literature was assumed to be of spontaneous origin, transmitted in a continuous and unchanging form through the generations, and serving as a reinforcement of communal identity in the past and the present. Many early collectors of folk literature, including Chodźko, sought to record folk narratives such as the Köroğlu stories as a means of glorifying the past. Perhaps some of the distortions in the process were the result of this preconceived notion of a glorified past; the hero's character needed to be polished to conform to that notion. This new interest in the

---

[9] Some of the strands of Romantic-Age thinking discussed here could also be applied in the case of the indigenous peoples in Canada, as discussed in Brendan F.R. Edwards' chapter in the present volume. The romantic notion of the "noble savage" and the romantic notion of the "social bandit" are not unrelated. Some parallels can be drawn between the situations in Canada on the one hand and in Turkey and Azerbaijan on the other. In both cases, characters were romanticized by a group in order to further the political ends of that group (settler culture in the case of Canada, returned émigré intellectuals in Turkey and Azerbaijan, with nationalist leanings). In both instances, the romanticization may not have been deliberate or conscious, as this trend was quite widespread at the time. Nevertheless, a romanticized view of a past culture could be made to serve a political purpose. The cases are dissimilar in some ways as well. For example, print culture was not new to either Turkey or Azerbaijan, and there was no distinct colonial relationship between western Europe and Turkey. In the case of Azerbaijan, Russia's dominance in the region did result in the subjugation of Azeri culture. However, in both the Canadian and the Turkish-Azeri cases, print was used to assert and strengthen "new" national identities. And if one broadens the Turkish-Azeri area to include the greater Middle East, the tendency of romantic Orientalists to relegate the native culture to an irretrievable *past* age (as was done in Canada) has been of tremendous consequence in modern Middle Eastern geopolitics, as discussed by Edward Said in *Orientalism* and elsewhere.

culture and language of the common people had profound implications for the development of nationalism as well (Hobsbawm 1992, 103).

Furthermore, there was a lively interest in "the Orient" during the Romantic Age, as Edward Said, for instance, has pointed out in *Orientalism*. Turkish culture in particular was very fashionable; George Sand sometimes dressed in what was considered a Turkish style, smoked a *narghileh*, and used Turkish elements in the décor of her residence in the Rue Pigalle (Georgeon 1991, 265). It follows, therefore, that "Oriental" stories such as that of Köroğlu had a special exotic appeal at that time.

There were also many revolutions happening in Europe in the mid-nineteenth century, some of them, as in the cases of Hungary and Poland, nationalistic in tone. Bandits, who were seen as typifying the opposition of the common people to the established powers, came to be romanticized. The idea of "social banditry," of robbing the rich to give to the poor, was first applied to long-standing bandit stories such as Robin Hood in this period (Holt 1982, 136, 165, 183–86), in spite of the complete lack of historical evidence to support this. George Sand also found the notion of social banditry appealing; her novel *Piccinino* deals with this theme (Georgeon 1991, 267–68).

The many Turks and Azeris who were living in Paris in the mid- to late nineteenth century could not help but be influenced by these ideas, as they began to develop a new self-awareness inspired by the newly emerging European study of Turcology (Lewis 1982, 345–51). One can even trace in the writings of some of them, such as Ahmet Ağaoğlu, an evolution of their identities (Shissler 2003, 7–8, 44; Altstadt 1992, 69). Many became ardent nationalists, and when they returned to their respective countries, they were able to share their new ideas with like-minded intellectuals, including those who had not themselves spent time in France.

Many of the leaders of nationalist thought and movements in both countries knew each other personally, and there was much reciprocal influence. In the case of Turkey, early nationalist thinker Ibrahim Şinasi left his literary journal *Tasvir-i Efkâr* to Namık Kemal when he left for Paris, and when Namık Kemal in turn left for Paris in 1867, he left the journal in the care of Recaizade Mahmut Ekrem (Akyüz 1964, 477). All three men were significant figures in the formative years of modern Turkish literature and nationalist thought. Recaizade Mahmut Ekrem in turn encouraged the nationalist writer and propagandist Mehmet Emin Yurdakul in his work (Akyüz 1964, 548, 550). Ziya Gökalp, often considered the father of Turkish nationalism, was close friends with the Azeri political publicist

4 THE MAKING OF A NATIONAL HERO: A COMPARATIVE EXAMINATION... 71

Ahmet Ağaoğlu, Hüseyinzade Ali (also Azeri), and Yusuf Akçura, a pan-Turkist of Tatar origin. Gökalp worked on the nationalist journal *Türk Yurdu* with Akçura and Ağaoğlu (Georgeon 1986, 373). Gökalp also worked with the nationalist writer Ömer Seyfettin on the journal *Genç Kalemler* (Heyd 1979, 33–34, 36). Within this group of young nationalist leaders, the ideas they had gleaned from the time they spent in Paris were able to take root and develop further, evolving into forms more suitable for the special circumstances in Turkey and Azerbaijan.

In addition to the influence of Romantic-era France, ideas of romantic nationalism in Turkey were further encouraged by exiles from the failed revolutions in Hungary and Poland (Lewis 1982, 135, 345–46). The populist sympathies and the new respect for folk forms that developed at this time (Lewis 1982, 440) provided an ideal context for a poet-hero such as Köroğlu, who championed the cause of the common man, at least in the popular mind.

2.5   Köroğlu's Changing Image in Turkey

One can pinpoint more or less precisely the moment when Köroğlu was reinvented as a national hero in Turkey. This happened at the turn of the twentieth century with the publication of a small volume of poetry by Mehmet Emin Yurdakul, *Türkçe Şiirler*, which was written in the popular idiom and in syllabic meter, and appeared at a time of high nationalist feeling, immediately after the Graeco-Turkish War of 1897. The very first poem in the book[10] can be seen as a deliberate effort to put forth Köroğlu as a new symbol of Turkish national identity. The first stanza asks the reader to ponder Köroğlu's significance: *"Köroğlu ne?"*, or "What is Köroğlu?" It points out that he is everywhere in Anatolia, both outdoors and indoors, from the mountaintops to the very mortar in the walls, offering solace to laborers as his stories are recited in their homes. The second stanza of the poem begins in parallel fashion: *"Fatih ne?"* or "What is the Conqueror?", a reference to Mehmet the Conqueror, whose conquest of Istanbul in 1453 was a transformative moment in Ottoman history. The stanza describes the place Fatih holds in the hearts of the people (Yurdakul 1900, 35–36). It is interesting to note that Köroğlu has been given priority over the renowned Mehmet the Conqueror, most likely because Yurdakul felt that Köroğlu would appeal more directly to his readers.

---

[10] Some personal correspondence precedes the poetry.

72   J. M. WILKS

Mehmet Âkif Ersoy, another nationalist poet most famous for writing the lyrics to Turkey's national anthem, also mentions Köroğlu briefly but sympathetically in his poem *Mahalle Kahvesi*, published in 1911. In this poem, he describes a picture in a coffeehouse depicting Köroğlu carrying off Ayvaz, whom he has just kidnapped, but Ersoy strives to emphasize the kind expression on Köroğlu's face as he rides off with his captive.[11]

Another work from this era that presents a positive image of Köroğlu is worth mentioning. Ömer Seyfettin, a nationalist writer who worked with Mehmet Emin Yurdakul on the journal *Türk Yurdu*, wrote a poem on Köroğlu in syllabic meter, portraying him as a defender of the nation from external enemies; he also expresses sympathy for "social banditry" in his novella *Yalnız Efe* (Sakaoğlu 1987, 82–83). Sakaoğlu has observed that nationalist writers such as Seyfettin and Recaizade Mahmut Ekrem, whose ties to the literary giants İbrahim Şinasi and Namık Kemal have been described above, deliberately romanticized Köroğlu in their pre-Republican works (1987, 81).

However, even in this period, some writers still depicted Köroğlu as violent and crude. Mehmet Kaplan cites a story from a lithograph of 1911–12, in which Köroğlu falls in love with a lovely Turkmen girl. He goes to ask her father for her hand, but the father, not wanting to give his daughter to this ruffian, talks him out of it, pointing out that a woman can be a real headache. He recommends instead that Köroğlu go to Istanbul, where there is a handsome young boy named Ayvaz, the son of a butcher. Köroğlu agrees and follows the Turkmen's advice on how to trick Ayvaz's father to facilitate the kidnapping of the young boy, clearly for sexual purposes here.

Kaplan (1985) acknowledges the role of the intelligentsia and their published writings in shaping Köroğlu's image and also demonstrates how Köroğlu can appeal to those who can identify themselves with him, his crudeness, and immorality. However, he ultimately condemns those who persist in glorifying the past at the expense of the present, believing that such attitudes are based on a reluctance to acknowledge the technological and social changes of modern life. Kaplan bases his judgment on this one version only (101–11), and certainly Turks are not the only people ever to

---

[11] See Saim Sakaoğlu, "Köroğlu Üzerine Yapılan Çalışmalar ve Edebiyatımızdaki Yeri," in *Sultan Baba ve Köroğlu*: 81–82.

4 THE MAKING OF A NATIONAL HERO: A COMPARATIVE EXAMINATION... 73

have idealized a legendary bandit.[12] This retroactive idealization seems to reflect wishful thinking rather than reality.

There are no cases of social banditry that can sustain close historical scrutiny. One can speculate on the psychological factors underlying the idealization of bandits. Common people straining under the yoke of authoritarian oppression may have reasoned that if "The enemy of my enemy is my friend," then bandits who defied the authorities were figures to idealize, even if those bandits did not offer any kindnesses to the common folk. The sheer entertainment value of the bandits' adventures may also have alleviated temporarily the drudgery of peasant life. In any case, Köroğlu and Robin Hood are only two examples of a vast array of such characters in the popular literatures of many parts of the world.

In the early Republican era in Turkey, the idea of Köroğlu campaigning for social justice retained its appeal but was given a far more nationalistic focus. In an attempt to confer on this *destan* the status of greater antiquity, nationalist writer Ziya Gökalp suggested that Köroğlu must have been based on the historical character of Sultan Mahmud of Ghazne, because of the similarity between the names of their favorite companions: Ayāz in the case of Sultan Mahmud, and Ayvaz in the case of Köroğlu, even though in Perso-Arabic script, their names look nothing alike.[13] The Tatar nationalist and pan-Turkist Zeki Velidi Togan suggested that the Köroğlu *destan* must have originated in pre-Islamic times among the western Göktürks, although he never explained his reasons for believing this. Nevertheless, the idea was accepted for a time, even by academician Fuad Köprülü, who himself had ties to Gökalp and other nationalist thinkers (Heyd 1979, 36; Boratav 1955, 911). Another prominent academic figure, Ahmet Kutsi Tecer, collected and studied songs of Köroğlu and even wrote a play about him (Ra'is Niyā 1988, 145). Certainly, the awareness that the Köroğlu

---

[12] Hobsbawm takes Robin Hood as the archetypal social bandit in his book *Bandits*. But even Robin Hood underwent significant romanticizing in the nineteenth century, as Holt points out (see especially Holt 136, 165, 183–86).

[13] In fact, the two names have only one letter in common in Perso-Arabic script, the letter *ya*, while they have only one letter different in Latin script, the letter *v*: Ayvaz = عیوض, while Ayāz = ایاز. Gökalp, having grown up in the Ottoman era, should have known Persian script well enough to know this. Heyd says that Gökalp learned Persian from his uncle when his own education was interrupted by the death of his father (1979, 23). Perhaps Gökalp's Persian had fallen into disuse by the time he made this claim, or perhaps in his eagerness to make the connection, he chose to assume that the names were the same, based on their popular pronunciation.

74   J. M. WILKS

destan was shared by other Turkic groups[14] made it appealing to intellectuals who were committed to the cause of pan-Turkism.

From the 1950s onward, the sympathy of Turkish writers for the problems of rural Anatolia began to take on a more radical hue (Dumont 1978, 87). In 1969, the left-leaning writer Yaşar Kemal wrote his story of the emergence of Köroğlu, *Köroğlu'nun Meydana Çıkışı*, based loosely on the narrative of Aşık Müdami, which had been recorded for the first time in the 1940s by Professor İlhan Başgöz. Kemal's version represents the most extreme softening of Köroğlu's image. In it, Köroğlu is shocked to learn that violence is sometimes a necessity in the life of a bandit. This story also demonstrates the versatility of Köroğlu's image: he can be used either by the political right as a symbol of the nation's defiance in the face of external threats, or by the political left as a protector of the common people from oppressive domestic authorities.

2.6 Ancient Folkloric Motifs and Conflations Relating to Köroğlu's Idealization

Intellectual currents and political developments were not the only factors in Köroğlu's transformation from cruel outlaw to national champion. Some of the motifs embellishing the episodes of the Köroğlu *destan* have a long history in the Caucasus region and eastern Anatolia, and their gradual incorporation into this *destan* probably played a significant role in the transformation of Köroğlu's character. One striking motif is the blinding of the hero's father as the reason for his becoming a bandit. Dumézil found that this motif has a long history in Armenian and Georgian legends (see Boratav 1955, 911–12),[15] and Boratav has acknowledged its pre-existence as crucial in the process of the bandit's idealization into a hero (Başgöz 1978, 318, note 18), providing him with a moral justification for turning to a life of crime.

It has also been suggested that the documented singing talents of another Celali bandit, Deli Hasan (younger brother of the famous Celali, Karayazıcı Mustafa), might have been attributed to the bandit Köroğlu,

---

[14] For example, Mehmet Emin Yurdakul notes in his travel memoirs that his Yomut Turkmen guide near Khiva explained to him that Köroğlu was a famous hero among the Turkmen as well, and the guide recited some verses in *aruz* (classical quantitative meter) in praise of Köroğlu's fighting ability (see Boratav 1931, 93).

[15] Here he cites Dumézil's article, "Les Légendes de 'fils d'aveugle' en Caucase et autour du Caucase," *Revue de l'Histoire des Religions*, Paris, 1938, CXVII, 1: 50–74.

4 THE MAKING OF A NATIONAL HERO: A COMPARATIVE EXAMINATION... 75

whose own musical talents are nowhere documented (Memmedyazov 1982, 37).[16] In many versions, one of Köroğlu's men is named Hasan, and as his men are called *delis*, this yields "Deli Hasan," which may explain the confusion with the historical character. Moreover, it is likely that more than one bandit named Köroğlu and more than one poet named Köroğlu existed, and that some elements of their stories and songs could have been incorporated into the Köroğlu *destan*.

2.7 *Köroğlu's Changing Image in Azerbaijan*

The evolution of Köroğlu in Azerbaijan in many ways resembles and overlaps with the situation in Turkey. As has already been discussed, in many respects Azeri intellectuals were on the same wavelength as their Turkish counterparts, and there was considerable reciprocal influence. As with the Turkish intellectuals, many young Azeris had spent time in Paris, and Romantic notions of nationalism and social banditry played a part in their thinking. Azeri émigrés to Turkey, such as Ahmet Ağaoğlu and Ali Turan Hüseyinzade, were cases in point. Hüseyinzade in particular had a deep influence on Ziya Gökalp. Hüseyinzade's famous slogan, "Türkleştirmek, İslamlaştırmak, Avrupalılaştırmak" ("To Turkify, to Islamize, to Europeanize") was adopted by Gökalp in a slightly modified form: "Türkleşmek, İslamlaşmak, Muasırlaşmak" ("to become Turkish, to become Islamic, to become contemporary"). The variation in the last of the three elements in Gökalp's adaptation of the slogan reflects the different attitudes toward Europe in Turkey as opposed to Azerbaijan. Azerbaijanis were, on the whole, less reluctant to wholeheartedly adopt European civilization as a goal in the modernization process (Hanioğlu 1995, 8; Shissler 2003, 5, 44–45).[17]

---

[16] According to Professor X.G. Köroğlu, Deli Hasan's poetic abilities are mentioned in the history of Iskender Beg Munshi. Evliya Çelebi in his *Seyāhat-nāme* also mentions a poet named Köroğlu twice (V. 283 and I. 638–9) and a bandit named Köroğlu once (V. 18), but he draws no connection between the two. The Armenian historian Arakel (1664) mentions Köroğlu as both a *celali* and a poet, but it is not clear that the bandit from the Bolu region is the subject.

[17] On a related note, also see this volume's Chap. 1, in which Aliakbari discusses Eisenstadt's observation on how "modern" and "European" are not always the same. This quotation from Gökalp shows that, even in these two closely related cases of Turkey and Azerbaijan, the intellectuals involved did not see the matter in exactly the same way. Even here, multiple modernities are evident.

76   J. M. WILKS

In both Turkey and Azerbaijan, the new national identity was shaped by the publications and literary and artistic works of the intellectuals, who were overwhelmingly sympathetic to the cause of modernity. However, there are some important differences in the two cases as well, both in the folkloric background relating to Köroğlu and in the political circumstances in which the publications and artistic productions occurred. Whereas in the case of Turkey, the literary class could proceed with their activities relatively unimpeded by the authorities, in the young nation of Azerbaijan, the heavy hand of Russian authority dictated what books could be published and what artistic works could be produced.

Azerbaijani folklore has additionally conflated Köroğlu with other characters from legend and popular literature. Köroğlu is often associated with the historical figure of Bābak-e Khorrami, a leader in the struggle against the invading Arabs in the ninth century A.D. It has been suggested that, according to legend, Bābak's mother had been blinded, making him "Köroğlu" on his mother's side (Boratav 1955, 912). Whether he is actually identified with Bābak or merely mentioned in the same breath as him, this image of Köroğlu as a defender of Azerbaijan from invaders still persists.[18] Köroğlu's songs and deeds seem to have been conflated with those of other heroes to a certain extent as well: the songs of some prominent figures in the Azeri nationalist movement, such as Kaçak Nabi, Qatır Mehmet, and especially Kaçak Kerem, bear strong resemblances to some of Köroğlu's songs (Ra'is Niya 1988, 178–185; Tahmasıp 1969, 5–7). However, it is in the political circumstances of Azerbaijan that the greatest differences can be seen. In this regard, the story of Köroğlu constitutes a remarkable exception to the generally severe Russian repression of Azeri nationalist sentiments.

Two operas about Köroğlu were written in Azerbaijan, one by Hüseyin Javid, and a later and more important one by Uzeir Hajibeyli (a.k.a. Hajibeyov), who quite deliberately substituted Köroğlu for the traditional Persian hero Kaveh when composing this opera (Ra'is Niyā 1988, 317). As it happened, the earliest performances of the Köroğlu opera by Uzeir Hajibeyov coincided with the so-called Year of Blood (1937–38) in Azerbaijan, when Stalinist authorities conducted a brutal purge of

---

[18] The full quote is given in William Reese, "The Role of the Religious Revival and Nationalism in Transcaucasia," *Radio Liberty Research*, December 5, 1988, quoting from *Pioner Azerbaidzhana*, November 25, 1988: "When the homeland is in distress and its soil encroached upon, the descendants of Babek, Koer-oglu, Dzhevanshir, Nabi, and Khadzhar are ready to fight and perform heroic deeds in the name of the people."

Azerbaijani writers. Many authors were imprisoned or executed on flimsy charges of being insufficiently Realist in their writings, or overly Romantic in their inclinations (Altstadt 2016, 200–01).

However, even amid the ongoing purges, Hajibeyov's Köroğlu opera proved extremely popular within the Stalinist inner circles as well as among the general population. The powerful Stalinist party secretary Mir Jafar Baghirov attended a private showing of the opera for an audience of 200 in Baku in January 1937 and subsequently praised the opera (Altstadt 2016, 188). The opera's public debut, opening to a full house, was in April 1937, just as the persecution of writers was intensifying. One prominent writer, Hüseyin Javid, who had written the earlier Köroğlu opera, attended the opening and was never seen in public again. Köroğlu was widely praised in the press, including such publications as *Yeni Yol* and *Kommunist* (Altstadt 2016, 193). Later, at a showing in Moscow in 1938, Stalin himself was present with many of his cohorts, including Molotov, Voroshilov, Mikoyan, Yezhov, and again Baghirov (Altstadt 2016, 200). Throughout the Year of Blood, the Azeri press continued to praise Köroğlu even as they detailed the trials against the "enemies of the state" at the behest of the Stalinist authorities, who claimed that the modern reading public demanded "sharp political books" (Altstadt 2016, 189). As a result of the success of his opera, Hajibeyov himself was never in danger, even though he never spoke out in strong support of Stalin, and even though his younger brother Jeyhun lived in France and was involved in anti-Stalinist activities there. It is sometimes said that "Köroğlu saved Hajibeyov" (Altstadt 2016, 203).

Therefore, it seems that in Azerbaijan, Köroğlu had a more significant and longer-lasting impact than in Turkey, despite the Russian cultural interference. Apparently, certain features in the Köroğlu *destan* enabled it to resist shifting political winds, so that it was spared much of the harsh treatment meted out in the Soviet era to other Turkic heroic traditions such as Manas, Dede Korkut, and Alpomis.[19] Köroğlu, at least in the versions found west of the Caspian Sea, is a hero of humble origins; his comrades are likewise ordinary men, sons of craftsmen for the most part. It only takes a small stretch of the imagination to conceptualize Köroğlu as a firm believer in internationalism and the brotherhood of peoples, as he welcomes into his band thieves and cut-throats of any ethnic background.

---

[19] For a thorough discussion of the fate of Turkic heroic traditions in Soviet times, see Paksoy (1989). Although I do not agree with Paksoy's assessment of the *destan* genre in general, this work has as its central theme the suppression of popular epics as expressions of national feeling.

78   J. M. WILKS

As in Turkey, in Azerbaijan Köroğlu came to be considered as a champion against oppression of all kinds including economic, even though his principal reason for attacking the rich merchants and pashas was his strong conviction that they were the ones who most deserved to be robbed. Thus, in Azerbaijan during the Soviet era, a fondness for Köroğlu was not perceived as a threat by the authorities, and studies on him and cultural celebrations of him could proceed unimpeded. And yet, perhaps the Soviets should have been concerned about this one national hero who had survived the harsh purges. During the demonstrations of November 1988, the image of Köroğlu was again summoned to inspire courage among the Azeris opposing the Soviet Union. *Pionir Azerbaidzhana* reported, "When the homeland is beset by misfortune, when its land is encroached, the descendants of Babek, Köroğlu … are prepared for battle and deeds in the name of the people" (Altstadt 1992, 209). One very popular chorus from Hajibeyli's Köroğlu opera became a rallying cry for the anti-Soviet protestors during Azerbaijan's independence movement.

Over the years and through many different political developments, academic studies of the Köroğlu *destan* have continued in both Turkey and Azerbaijan. During the Soviet era, the Azeri studies were heavily tinged with Socialist Realism (Altstadt 2016, 187), but even so, it is interesting that a very positive view of the hero's character has persisted in almost all of the studies in both countries, even those studies striving to be historical, despite the lack of hard evidence for any altruistic qualities in the character. To cite one good example of this effusive admiration: "The Köroğlu *destan* is the most precious work of Azerbaijani oral popular creativity. Here the good characteristics peculiar to our people – heroism, love of the fatherland, respect for other peoples, humanism, friendship, brotherhood, hospitality, and other characteristics – have found their rhetorical statement" (Héy'et 1990, 70). Thus, it would seem that the reformers who so deliberately sought to make Köroğlu into a new national hero were successful.

3   CONCLUSIONS

Originally, the oral performances of the popular *destan* centered on a semi-historical figure whose story was, to a degree, conflated with the stories of other legendary heroes of local folklore. From early on, the stories and songs of Köroğlu were collected, recorded, and published in countries of the Caucasus in various alphabets and languages, primarily Azeri Turkish, often with adaptations in the hero's character for different audiences.

The stories were more systematically recorded and published in the nineteenth century, and Chodźko's collection from the 1830s is especially significant. Chodźko's English translation of the collection, in which the hero's image was somewhat softened and gentrified, was published in London in 1842 and found a receptive audience in Romantic-Age Paris. It was further translated and propagated and studied, both in the West and back in the Caucasus. Turkish and Azeri intellectuals in Paris at the time, their own identities in flux, were much affected by French ideas on nationalism and brought these ideas back to their countries and their fellow nationalists. Writers in the nationalist movements in both countries used Köroğlu deliberately in their nationalist works, such as Yurdakul's poem in Turkey and Hacibeyli's opera in Azerbaijan. Ultimately, Köroğlu was celebrated as the embodiment of praiseworthy national qualities, with poems, plays, operas, and statues honoring him.

Certainly, Köroğlu was popular even before being idealized; that is, after all, why his stories were performed so widely and written down so often. The rough bandit of the earlier, mostly oral, versions appealed to popularly and commonly held values. Ordinary people envied his lifestyle. He had what they wanted: power and pleasure, in the form of horses, riches, wine, women, and song. Later, in the published versions, with publishers and collectors such as Chodźko adapting Köroğlu's character for their reading audiences, the roughness of his character decreased. With the influence of Romantic-Age thinking, his character was ripe for idealization into an admirable hero who was capable of saving a nation.

After being romanticized, idealized, and nationalized in publications and works of art, the adaptability of Köroğlu's character helped ensure his survival; both rightist and leftist governments could modify his stories for their own purposes and thus had no reason to suppress them. Hobsbawm (1969) has observed that those bandits whose stories were written down endured the best. They survive in the collective memory as individual personalities, while others merge over time with the collective picture of legendary heroes of the past (111, 114). Thus, the many publications of the Köroğlu story help explain why Köroğlu stands out above the rest: this well-publicized character whose name was always in the air absorbed the positive attributes of other legendary heroes and reflected them onto the nation as a whole, becoming a national icon in the collective mind of the people. This comparative study examines the repurposings and modernizations of the hero in the shaping of modern national identities in Turkey and Azerbaijan, two cases that, despite being similar in some ways, were distinct from one another and were alternatives to the European exemplars.

80   J. M. WILKS

WORKS CITED

Akyüz, Kenan. 1964. La Littérature Moderne de Turquie. In *Philologiae Turcicae Fundamenta*, ed. Jean Deny et al., 469–551. Wiesbaden: Steiner.

Altstadt, Audrey. 1992. *The Azerbaijani Turks: Power and Identity Under Russian Rule*. Stanford: Hoover Institution Press.

———. 2016. *The Politics of Culture in Soviet Azerbaijan, 1920–40*. New York: Routledge/Taylor and Francis.

Başgöz, İlhan. 1978. The Epic Tradition among Turkic Peoples. In *Heroic Epic and Saga*, ed. Felix Oinas, 310–335. Bloomington: Indiana University Press.

Bayat, Fuzuli. 2009. *Köroğlu Destanı: Türk Dünyasının Köroğlu Fenomenolojisi*. Istanbul: Ötüken Neşriyat.

Boratav, Pertev Naili. 1931. *Köroğlu Destanı*. Istanbul: Evkaf Matbaası.

———. 1955. Köroğlu. In *İslâm Ansiklopedisi*, Vol. VI. Istanbul: Maarif Matbaası.

Calmard, Jean. 1983. Chodźko. *Encyclopedia Iranica* V: 502–504.

Canby, Henry Seidel. 1967. *Favorite Poems of Henry Wadsworth Longfellow*. New York: Doubleday.

Chodźko, Alexander. 1971. *Specimens of the Popular Poetry of Persia as Found in the Adventures and Improvisations of Kurroglou, the Bandit-Minstrel of Northern Persia*. New York: Burt Franklin.

Dumont, Paul. 1978. Les Origines de la Littérature Villageoise en Turquie. *Journal Asiatique* CCLXVI: 67–95.

Finnegan, Ruth. 1979. *Oral Poetry: Its Nature, Significance, and Social Context*. Cambridge: Cambridge University Press.

Georgeon, François. 1991. Une Passion Méconnue de George Sand. *Turcica* XXI–XXIII: 259–269.

———. 1986. Les Débuts d'un Intellectuel Azerbaïdjanais: Ahmed Ağaoğlu en France, 1888–1894. In *Passé Turco-Tatar, Présent Soviétique*, ed. Ch. Lemercier-Quelquejay, G. Veinstein, and S.E. Wimbush, 373–387. Paris: Édition Peeters.

Hanioğlu, M. Şükrü. 1995. *The Young Turks in Opposition*. New York: Oxford University Press.

Héy'et, Javad. 1990. *Azarbaijan Şifahi Xalg Edebiyatı*. Baku: Azarbaijan Dövlet Neşriyyatı.

Heyd, Uriel. 1979. *Foundations of Turkish Nationalism: The Life and Teachings of Ziya Gökalp*. Westport: Hyperion Press.

Hobsbawm, Eric. 1969. *Bandits*. London: Weidenfeld and Nicholson.

———. 1992. *Nations and Nationalism Since 1780*. 2nd ed. New York: Cambridge UP.

Holt, J.C. 1982. *Robin Hood*. London: Thames and Hudson.

Kaplan, Mehmet. 1985. *Türk Edebiyatı Üzerinde Çalışmalar*. Istanbul: Dergâh Yayınları.

Kemal, Yaşar. 1969. Köroğlu'nun Meydana Çıkışı. In *Üç Anadolu Efsanesi*. Istanbul: Ant Yayınları.

4 THE MAKING OF A NATIONAL HERO: A COMPARATIVE EXAMINATION...   81

Lewis, Bernard. 1982. *The Emergence of Modern Turkey.* New York: Oxford University Press.

Longfellow, Henry Wadsworth. 1967. The Leap of Roushan Beg. In *Favorite Poems of Henry Wadsworth Longfellow,* ed. Henry Seidel Canby, 109–111. New York: Doubleday.

Memmedyazov, B. 1982. *Göroğli Eposının Döreyişi Xakında.* Ashkabad: Ilim.

Paksoy, H.B. 1989. *Alpamysh: Central Asian Identity Under Russian Rule.* Hartford: Association for the Advancement of Central Asian Research.

Ra'is Niyā, Rahim. 1366/1988. *Kuroğli dar Afsāne va Tārikh.* Tabriz: Enteşārāt-e Nimā.

Reese, William. 1988. The Role of the Religious Revival and Nationalism in Transcaucasia. *Radio Liberty Research,* November 25.

Reichl, Karl. 1992. *Turkic Oral Epic Poetry.* New York: Garland Publishing.

Sadık Beg. *Kurogli-Nāma.* Bibliothèque Nationale Supplément Persan # 994.

Said, Edward. 1979. *Orientalism.* New York: Vintage Books.

Sakaoğlu, Saim. 1987. Köroğlu Üzerine Yapılan Çalışmalar ve Edebiyatımızdaki Yeri. In *Sultan Baba ve Köroğlu,* 79–85. Elazığ: Fırat Üniversitesi.

Shissler, A. Holly. 2003. *Between Two Empires: Ahmet Ağaoğlu and the New Turkey.* New York: I.B. Tauris.

Sümer, Faruk. 1987. Kör Oğlu, Kızır Oğlu Mustafa ve Demirci Oğlu ile İlgili Vesikalar. *Türk Dünyası Araştırmaları* 46. February.

Tahmasıp, M.H. 1969. *Azarbaijan Dastanları.* Vol. IV. Baku: Elm.

Yurdakul, Mehmet Emin. 1317/1900. *Türkçe Şiirler.* Constantinople: Matbaa-yı Ebüzzıya.

CHAPTER 5

Between Poetry and *Reportage*: Raúl González Tuñón, Journalism and Literary Modernization in 1930s Argentina

Geraldine Rogers

1 INTRODUCTION

The chronicle is a privileged sign of the entrance of literature into a transnational media culture. Many important writers have penned chronicles, a somewhat unstructured genre that emerged in the context of journalism and whose practice has brought about literary innovations in other genres, such as poetry and fictional narrative. The most modern form of the chronicle, the *reportage*, or chronicle from "special correspondents," reached its peak with a particular intensity in the first decades of the twentieth century in France, where the contributions of poets and narrators helped to increase the prestige and readership of newspapers. By that time, *reportage*, with its blending of journalism and literature, had become a modernizing genre in Latin America too.

In the 1930s, Raúl González Tuñón, one of Argentina's foremost avant-garde poets, wrote a series of *reportages* about the port of Buenos

G. Rogers (✉)
CONICET, Buenos Aires, Argentina

National University of La Plata, La Plata, Argentina

© The Author(s) 2020   83
R. Aliakbari (ed.), *Comparative Print Culture*, New Directions in
Book History, https://doi.org/10.1007/978-3-030-36891-3_5

84 G. ROGERS

Aires, Patagonia, Paraguay and Spain, which were published in Buenos Aires-based periodicals. These *reportages* confirm the broad circulation and impact in the periphery, during a phase of transnational modernization, of a successful journalistic genre that had emerged in the metropolis of the West. They also reveal other important things, most notably the specifics of the particular use of this genre in light of the technical, aesthetic, social and political local conditions of the unequal modernization process in Argentina. Modernity in Latin America has always been problematic, marked by discrepancies in various spheres including reading and writing practices. As Julio Ramos (2001) states, "the transformation of social communication was quite uneven in Latin America: we would be mistaken to assume the European model, which traces the passage from the liberal era to advanced capitalism, as an explanation for the transformations" from the turn of the century onward. Tuñón's *reportages* and avant-garde poetry also overlap in both themes and techniques, such as the presence of diverse voices within the texts, the hybridization of verses and a textual porosity in relation to contemporary matters. All of this suggests that literary modernization was the result not only of the highbrow European Modernism, but also of exchanges across borders of high/low culture, of genres, and of nations, at a time when the rise of mass culture coincided with the rise of avant-garde art, and particularly in the 1930s, when there were important links between these movements (Benjamin 1934/2005; Huyssen 1986). This chapter discusses the dynamic tension between Tuñón's poetry and *reportage* as these complementary zones converge and diverse. This crossover also demonstrates that Argentine print literary modernity involved particular uses of European templates of journalistic and literary modernization.

2   A Modern Genre

The professionalization of writing and a modern sensitivity inclined toward the contemporary[1] come together with the emergence of the chronicle, a genre that combines literature with information.[2] Between the mid-nineteenth and early twentieth centuries in Europe and America, many

---

[1] Since Baudelaire, the notion of *modernité* has been haunted by the desire to grasp the present (Sheringham 2006; Vaillant 2011).

[2] The *chronique* as a genre emerged in France by the middle of the nineteenth century, although its roots can be traced to the sketches of manners of the previous century in England.

writers and artists entered newspapers and magazines as professional contributors, and this process led to many instances of transference between the fields of art and journalism, which are usually regarded as antagonistic but whose mutual feedback became a source of innovation (Thérenty 2007; Rogers 2010, 2018).

With the development of journalism, Buenos Aires[3] and other urban centers in Latin America began to imagine themselves as part of the growing Western communication network and the expanding international market. From the last decades of the nineteenth century, Argentina's major newspapers began to include collaborations of European authors and Latin American correspondents in London, Paris, New York and Madrid. The most innovative Latin American writers read chronicles in *Le Temps, Journal des Debats* and *Le Mercure de France*, and beginning in the 1890s, these writers produced their own chronicles for local newspapers (González 1993).

The technical advances of the time led to the emergence of a new type of chronicler, the reporter, who was able to go out in search of the news and communicate it promptly and readably. Thus, the chronicle genre began to evolve into its more modern form, the *reportage*, whose distinctive feature consisted of visiting the locations in which events were taking place to gather information in order to produce texts and images that would account for what was seen and heard in situ. Although the *reportage* began in the USA, it experienced a remarkable development in France from 1880 onward,[4] when major newspapers such as *Le Temps* and *Le Figaro* started to send their own reporters to various places in the capital, the deep country and abroad in search of the news. The *reportage* presented contemporary settings and events through subjective narratives and fictional resources, such as the invention of dialogs and the combination of points of view, transporting the reader to the places at which these events occurred via a new form of writing that enhanced the authors' and readers' capacities for observation and empathy. The genre reached its peak in the 1930s, as famous journalists, poets and narrators fulfilled the role of "special correspondents." By that time, authors such as the "flâneur salarié" Henri Béraud, or the *Petit Parisien*'s star journalist Albert Londres, who visited the prisons of L'Île du Diable in French Guiana and

---

[3] The Buenos Aires newspaper *La Nación* began telegraphic service in 1877.

[4] Pierre Giffard's *Le Sieur de Va partout: souvenirs d'un reporter* (Paris: M. Dreyfous, 1880) is a milestone of this process in French journalism.

86   G. ROGERS

documented the world of French gangsters and women trafficking in Buenos Aires, were helping to strengthen and spread this successful genre. In the interwar period, authors such as Blaise Cendrars, Maurice Dekobra, Antoine de Saint-Exupéry, Jean Cocteau and André Malraux, among others, produced *reportages*. According to Boucharenc (2004), this genre, despite being considered minor, was a vector of artistic and political debates of the 1930s.

3   RAÚL GONZÁLEZ TUÑÓN IN THE 1930S ARGENTINA

3.1   The Reporter as a Poet

In the 1920s and 1930s, *Crítica*,[5] the most popular and successful newspaper in Buenos Aires, included in its editorial department a group of writers from the literary avant-garde who were associated with the little magazine *Martín Fierro* (1924–1927).[6] Among them were Jorge Luis Borges, who was hired as the editor of the paper's weekly supplement, and

[5] *Crítica*, founded by Natalio Botana in 1913, developed a reputation as "the people's newspaper" by the 1920s, emphasizing the features that had guaranteed the success of mass journalism since the beginning of the century: a diverse structure, topical photographs, fictionalized news, graphic satire, support from advertising, regular payments to authors and producers, and attractive special issues with unprecedented print-run surges. It used sensationalism to cover crime news and to criticize social problems, and also covered the lives of workers and the world of poverty from a point of view that sought to be in tune with the most vulnerable sectors of the population. Declaring itself "on the people and for the people," the newspaper demonstrated a strong interest in "the popular," which in Argentina was beginning to be correlated with the masses. From 1925 onward, *Crítica* added several writers who had links to the aesthetic *avant-garde* of the *Martín Fierro* magazine to its editorial staff. In 1931, *Crítica* was shut down by the military government, which it had previously supported; its director was imprisoned and then forced into exile. In February 1932, Natalio Botana was able to return to the country and reopen the paper (Saítta 1998).
[6] *Martín Fierro* (1924–27), whose subtitle was "Bimonthly newspaper of art and free criticism," was the main organ of the aesthetic avant-garde of the Florida group, which gathered the most important young innovative writers of the time, such as Jorge Luis Borges, Raúl González Tuñón and Oliverio Girondo. Its program was based on interest in formal innovations, the desecration of art, a simultaneously local and cosmopolitan inflection and anti-Hispanism. Although its concrete acts were less radical than its declarations, its Manifesto rejected academic solemnity in favor of a search for the new and a redefinition of the idea of art. In order to be reaffirmed as modern artists, the writers of the so-called "new sensitivity" rejected the mass culture with which they were actually linked. Their concrete practices, including the newspaper *Crítica*'s hiring of several avant-garde writers to its editorial staff, demonstrated a productive exchange of resources between modern art and mass culture.

the poet Raúl González Tuñón, who wrote several journalistic articles, a number of which were *reportages*.

Tuñón's poetic work meant a modernizing plunge, with some sort of popular surrealism in which the lyrical *I* fused with marginal subjects. His first three books, *El violín del diablo* (*The Devil's Violin*, 1926), *Miércoles de ceniza* (*Ash Wednesday*, 1928) and *La calle del agujero en la media* (*The Street with the Hole in the Sock*, 1930), initiated an avant-garde poetics focused on marginal characters in marginal zones (such as ports, fairs, circuses and suburbs), moving away from Realism and from the pedagogical style that was usual in Argentine left-wing literature. His protagonists are exiles, poor artists (puppeteers, itinerant or circus musicians), sailors of all nations, prostitutes and thieves. The representation of these *others* tends to overlap with the representation of the lyrical *I* ("Escrito sobre una trastienda," in González Tuñón 1928; "El monito del servio," in González Tuñón 1928; "Bajo fondo," in González Tuñón 1926):

> In every port in the world
> There are tramps like me.
>
> I felt that [the gypsies] were my brothers
> And I said at the edge of your laughter:
> –I was born to be a poet
> A Jacobin shirtless poet.
>
> Tonight I shall be with you, brothers (…)
> Open your den and your heart.
> (…) hold my hands
> I am Francois Villon.

The title of the third volume, *The Street with the Hole in the Sock*, suggests traces of surrealism, which are also present in much of the imagery and in verses that are close to nursery rhymes or popular songs, bordering on nonsense. Poetic images detach themselves from rational restrictions, giving way to irrational expansions[7] that create a surrealist atmosphere. The poems are collages of lyrical fragments, lines of dialog, newspaper titles, posters, choruses of children's songs, films and advertising.

---

[7] See "Tres poemas de algún país," "Poemas de la vidriera de una juguetería" (González Tuñón 1930).

88   G. ROGERS

Published on his return from a trip to France, this book creates a cosmopolitan space ("Escrito sobre una mesa de Montparnasse," in González Tuñón 1930):

> I come from Buenos Aires, I tell my unknown friends,
> From Buenos Aires, which is three times bigger than Paris
> And three times smaller.
> And, although my hat and my tie and my riffraff spirit
> Are perfectly european products
> I am sad and cordial as a legitimate Argentine is.

This space of intersections derived from autobiographical experience is superimposed upon the spaces of the newspaper and the cinema, which allow any inhabitant of the transnational media culture to experience imaginary trips. In poems such as "Evelyn Brent," "William Powell" and "George Bancroft," the voices of actors and actresses intertwine with the characters they portray, such as gangsters, women of the underworld or journalists, in a confusion between the fictional and the actual that is typical of media culture ("William Powell," in González Tuñón 1930):

> He always fell under his own terms, facing his fate, as a brave man.
> Out of all the impure men like him, none was pure.
> He justified his triumphs whispering: luck.
> The only fight he lost: against death.

One of the poems included in the same book is signed by an apocryphal author, "Jimmy Herf," the journalist character of *Manhattan Transfer* by John Dos Passos, who is also cited in the epigraph.

Tuñón made particular use of these fragments of modern cosmopolitan culture by stamping the vernacular on them. In his poetical representations of Paris, he used colloquial expressions from the suburbs of Buenos Aires and slang words that were usual in *tango* lyrics, such as "riachuelo," "mataderos," "arrabal," "atorrantes" and "guapo" gangsters, which intentionally give a *porteño*[8] flavor to his French imagery. As Sarlo (1988) and Schwartz (2002) state, such "vernacular cosmopolitism" is a distinctive feature of Latin American avant-garde movements.

The poems are frequently intervened by fragments that resemble the dialogs included in journalistic chronicles. The poet-reporter addresses

---

[8] *Porteño* (slang): from Buenos Aires.

imaginary interlocutors, whether describing Argentine or Parisian scenes ("Escrito sobre una mesa de Montparnasse," in González Tuñón 1930):

Old Bull Mich, the world street
Do you know its gray windows, its fanfares,
A schoolboy's joy when he's free, its girls,
The Daciá Hotel, where my friend Daniel Schweizer lives,
The Luxemburg and the *cabaret des Noctambules*?
[…] The gypsie's curve.
A port decorated with songs from every language
And every voice.
The circus of art, the fair of human culture, on the way to Montparnasse.

Do you know Neuquén?
There, there are cottages made of tree trunks
And grocery stores where saddlebagsand books by Maurice Dekobra are sold.
And Tucumán? In Tucumán, the night can only be sought in the eyes of its women
And guitarrs, so resounding and flowery, seem to be courtyards.

In the same year, Tuñón published *Todos bailan. Los poemas de Juancito Caminador* (*Everybody Dances: The Poems of Johnny Walker*),[9] which features a similar intertwining between poetry and journalism. The book consisted of unbound sheets that allowed the compositions to circulate both together and separately, presenting an alternative to the traditional format of the book. It begins with a few lines referring to the Argentine political context of the time: one of the poems, "Las brigadas de choque" ("Shock Brigades"), could not be included due to censorship, as its previous publication had led to the shutting down of the magazine and to Tuñón's five-day-long imprisonment.[10] The first poem, "Historia de

[9] Here are abundant references in this work to the roaming nature of the poet (walker, stroller) and of his production "on the way". In the same year *Todos bailan* was published, the first issue of the magazine *Caballo verde para la poesía* included "Sobre una poesía sin pureza" ("On Poetry with No Purity") by Pablo Neruda and "Poema caminando" (Poem Walking) by Raúl G. Tuñón.

[10] The poem "Las brigadas de choque" had been published in 1933 in the magazine *Contra. La revista de los francotiradores*. A group of important writers and artists, including Federico García Lorca, Pablo Neruda, León Felipe and Miguel Hernández, among others, signed a declaration against the censorship of Tuñón's poem and against the judicial persecution of the poet (Orgambide 1998).

90   G. ROGERS

veinte años" (Twenty Years History), was a poetic chronicle of the changes that had begun with the collapse of everything since the onset of the Great War in 1914. An international piece of news inspired "Los negros de Scottsboro" ("The Black Men of Scottsboro"), a poem about the black men who had been unfairly sentenced because of racism in Alabama. The execution of the Italian anarchist Severino Di Giovanni in Buenos Aires is referred to in the poem, "Cosas que ocurrieron el 17 de octubre" ("Things that Happened on October 17"), which otherwise seems to be the chronicle of an ordinary day. In these poems, the surrealist imagery provides an experience of the contemporary that is better than the worn-out language of journalism, as crime news clippings, war events and political information intermingle in the poems.[11] These fragments emancipate themselves from a superordinate whole; the enumerations of events are chaotic and avoid expected chronology, opening the way for a random and, because of this, more real heterochronic assemblage of images ("Cosas que ocurrieron el 17 de octubre," in González Tuñón 1935a):

> The automobile jumped into the race with an impressive snore.
> This afternoon, the mayor visited the damp and resentful working-class neighborhoods.
> When we were twenty, we only believed in Art, without life, without Revolution.
> We shall go back to the factories, to the smell of the crowd, to derailments.
> At 5.7 a bomb exploded in front of the Bank of Boston.
> At 5.17, the streetcar fell in the stream […]
>
> ("Fire!, Fire! The house is on fire! The firemen are coming.
> The executed man must already be half rotten in Chacarita cemetery.
> América Scarfó will take some flowers to him, and when we are all dead,
> Dead,
> América Scarfó will take flowers to us.
> Sofa. Bed. Soup. Every insipid turnip. The ball goes on its own").

In this period, Raúl González Tuñón alternated poetry with journalism, and after 1934, combined these with his activity in the Communist Party. He was actively present in Spain, where he traveled many times before and during the civil war, and where he shared his artistic and life experiences

---

[11] See "El general Flor Intrencherado" and "Los seis hermanos rápidos dedos en el gatillo" (González Tuñón 1935a).

with Federico García Lorca, Luis Buñuel, León Felipe, Miguel Hernández and Pablo Neruda, among other artists who shared his antifascist commitment. In 1935, Raúl González Tuñón participated in the First International Congress of Writers for the Defense of Culture, at which many intellectuals, including André Gide, Tristan Tzara, Henri Barbusse and César Vallejo, among others, signed a protest against the censorship and persecution he experienced in Argentina.

In 1936, Tuñón published *La rosa blindada (homenaje a la insurrección de Asturias y otros poemas revolucionarios)* (*The Armored Rose: A Tribute to the Insurrection in Asturias and other Revolutionary Poems*),[12] a milestone of modern political poetry in Spanish.[13] The first edition of this collection of poems, produced by the Graphic Association of Buenos Aires, includes a xylographic cover image by Juan Carlos Castagnino, depicting a woman with her arms held high in a gesture and attitude of struggle (Fig. 5.1). The dedication of the first edition, "Madrid-Buenos Aires, 1935–36," was meant to anchor *La rosa blindada* to contemporary events, on the first anniversary of the Asturian insurrection. Tuñón, a grandson of an Asturian socialist who had emigrated to Argentina, took as his central motive the strike of the miners who declared the Socialist Republic in 1934 and were brutally repressed by the military soon afterwards. As a tribute to this emancipatory struggle, this book privileges the *collective* dimensions in various ways, and each poem is dedicated to an artist who was committed to the antifascist struggle. Here the poet intentionally abandoned the inflections of the Argentine language to adopt the Spanish enunciation of the heroes, which was the same as that of his own ancestors ("no dejéis", "incorporáos"). Without setting aside avant-garde experimentation, he also resumed the poetic forms of Spanish oral folk tradition, such as the "romance," a lyrical structure with octosyllabic verses, refrains, parallelisms and lexical repetitions with a mnemonic function. For him, poetry became a "lyrical testimony," a non-linear chronicle crossed by avant-garde procedures.

---

[12] *La rosa blindada* was published by Horizonte in 1962. The most recent single-volume edition is almost impossible to find today (Tierra Firme 1993). Until fairly recently, it was included in *Poesía Reunida* (Seix Barral 2011); though this collection did include the complete text, it did not include the dedications or the prologues in previous editions.

[13] The poet Juan Gelman, winner of the Cervantes Prize, considered Raúl González Tuñón as one of the main influences in his writing, and called him "the initiator of a path that great Latin American and Spanish poets – Vallejo, Hernández, Neruda, Alberti – would tread later" (1997, 113–114).

Fig. 5.1 The first edition of *La rosa blindada*, with xylography by J.C. Castagnino

In *La rosa blindada*, the collective memory is not only the sum of successive facts in a historical line but a kind of meeting of past and present generations[14] where different struggles for emancipation gather: the Spanish insurrection of 1934, the revolution of October of 1917, the Revolt of the Comuneros in the sixteenth century in Castile,[15] the Paris Commune of 1871[16] and the uprising of the rural laborers executed in Patagonia in 1922[17] ("El cementerio patagónico," in González Tuñón 1936a):

[14] For the crossover of Marxism and Surrealism, see Walter Benjamin's "On the Concept of History" (1940/2003) and "Surrealism and the Everyday" (Sheringham 2006).
[15] See "La historia viva bajo el acueducto inmortal" (González Tuñón 1936a).
[16] See "Cementerio proletario (Jean Allemane)" (González Tuñón 1936a).
[17] See "El cementerio patagónico" (González Tuñón 1936a). In 1922, a violent suppression of a strike of rural workers in the Argentine province of Santa Cruz in Patagonia ended with the mass execution of approximately 1500 workers (Bayer 1972/2016).

In Santa Cruz, between the sea and the mountains,
I have seen the little graveyard of the executed strikers.
Some, badly buried, in the pit they dug themselves,
Stick out the tip of their shoe with dust and lizards.
Others, buried alive perhaps,
A pleading bony hand pecked by crows.
And it is not strange to see the remains of others along the way,
A curious content of the outdoors.
The processions of the dispossessed of the land, the long lines of forced vagrants,
The multitude from every country heading to the south of Earth
In search of bread and death,
The multitude from every country heading to the south of Earth
In search of nostalgia and oblivion,
Stops here, where the oasis of the Patagonian wind, the barren land releases
Its yellow dogs.[18]

"Blues de Río Gallegos," a poem included in *Todos bailan*, was dated "Patagonia, 1932"; similarly, the following poem, "La pequeña brigada," was dated "Chaco Boreal, 1932" ("La pequeña brigada", in González Tuñón 1935a:

The small brigade advances.
Have we heard war, brothers?
Have we seen, brothers?
The small brigade advances.
The head was left hanging
On the wire like a fruit.
We are the small brigade.
We are the sleeplessness, the thirst, the hunger.
Due to the noise of mortars,
The ears will burst
And we will be broken and buried
In arid lands with no crosses.
[...]
We will be brothers, brothers
Someday this has to be.
Have we seen the war?
The small brigade advances.
Have we heard the war?

---

[18] Emphasis is mine.

In the tangled mess of the strike.
Like sharp bodies,
Pale, in twos,
We are walking with no God
With our skulls full of holes.

In several poems from this period, Tuñón reworked documentary materials from his practice as a reporter in the port of Buenos Aires, as well as in Patagonia, Paraguay and Spain. What was *seen* and *heard* re-emerged in these avant-garde verses, with the poetic *I* now a *we* that included the poet's self together with the *others*. In contrast to the poems, Tuñón's reports were written by commission and constrained by the formal, thematic and ideological rules of the publisher.

3.2   The Poet as a Reporter

In March 1932, *Crítica* commissioned Tuñón to go to the port of Buenos Aires to write a series of *reportages* on the situation of unemployed immigrants who had come from Czechoslovakia and Yugoslavia with the hope of finding work in South America. The series was published under the title "Vidas truncas" ("Shattered Lives"), with photographs and drawings that were sometimes displayed as illustrated photograph strips. The *reportage*, embedded in references to authors such as John dos Passos, Sinclair Lewis and Knut Hamsun, was focused on the hidden side of the city of Buenos Aires, seeking to put a stop to the urban hustle and bustle in order to shed light on *the other thing* that was happening while the readers were mostly unaware: "the story of the immigrants with no history". In this manner, he created a space-time that interrupted the alienated consumption of the newspaper ("Una medialuna para el yugoeslavo," in González Tuñón 1932a):

> At this hour, the machines of CRÍTICA are grinding out the 12 o'clock edition; at this hour, an indecisive sun is decorating the English Tower with flashings, [...]; at this hour, the bourgeois men are placing themselves at the tables, with the certainty that what they are going to eat has been earned by the sweat on their brows [...]. And at this hour, quite nearby, the city that [...], **devours the papers' editions** and lives, in short, the comedy and the daily drama, ignoring – in its immense majority – that a man, at the gates of civilization, at the edge of hope, has gone mad with hunger.[19]

[19] Emphasis is mine.

As in his first books of poetry, in which the lyrical I tended to fuse with marginal people, thieves and vagabonds, the setting of the utterance was changing in his *reportage*. Tuñón's use of I as a chronicler who watches from the outside gives way to a *we* in solidarity with the marginalized and unemployed: "But when the night comes falling on us like a police raid, we are already tired of not having done anything, of having completed another irremediable day's travel in the somber route of our fate" ("El inmenso valor de 12 pesos," in González Tuñón 1932a). Thus, he closes the note without the quotation marks or dashes that would single him out as an individual. Even though unemployment was a global issue at the beginning of the 1930s, Tuñón's *reportages* focused on the particular situation of Argentina, "an immense country of wheat" in which local policies imposed by the elites following the coup d'état created hunger and redundancy. This series of chronicles denounces local politics in the moderate terms allowed by *Crítica*, a publication aimed at a broad readership, which had already been shut down by the government. Raúl González Tuñón was better able to express his disapproval of the government in other periodicals.[20]

In April 1932, Tuñón traveled to Patagonia by plane, taking the air route that had been established by the pilots Jean Mermoz and Antoine de Saint-Exupéry, and later bought by the Argentine government from the French company. His ensuing series of three articles, "En el lejano sur" ("In the Far South"), revealed details about this remote territory and questioned the public policies that had left its inhabitants to their own devices. He combined his reasoning and information with brief interviews that brought a plurality of voices to the forefront in the texts, while also including fragments of prose poetry. The reporter's journey was an adventure in itself, both because of the legendary locations he was visiting and because of the experience of flight, which he described as "quite an event," inspired by Saint-Exupéry's account of his experience as a pilot in Patagonia, *Vol de Nuit* (*Night Flight*), published by Gallimard in 1931 and reviewed by *Crítica*.[21] Some of the details that were briefly mentioned in the chronicles reappeared, free of the newspaper's formal and ideological constraints, in the poems "Blues de Rio Gallegos" ("Rio Gallegos's Blues"; footnote: "Patagonia, 1932," in González Tuñón 1935a) and "El cemen-

---

[20] See "Desocupación" (González Tuñón 1935b).
[21] See the unsigned review "Un libro acerca de la Patagonia, por A. S. Exupery," *Crítica*, 26 April 1932.

96   G. ROGERS

terio patagónico" ("The Patagonian Cemetery," in González Tuñón 1935a). Not only did the whaling boats and the wind reappear in these poems, but also the exploitation of rural workers and the memory of anarchist laborers who were executed by the government in 1922 in defense of the interests of English landowners in Argentine territory. What had been seen and heard in situ became a historical memory that could poetically grasp the connections between the past and the present of a period in Argentine history that was characterized by exploitation and struggles for emancipation.

In October of that same year, Tuñón flew one more time as a "special correspondent" to the location of the Bolivian-Paraguayan War in order to write an illustrated series in 14 chapters, "*Crítica* en el infierno del Chaco" ("*Crítica* in the Hell of Chaco"). The notes included fragments of a "song" divided and displayed as an epigraph that three years later would reappear in the poem "La pequeña brigada" ("The Small Brigade"), in the book *Todos bailan* (*Everybody Dances*). The poems, free of the newspaper's ideological framework and connection to the most immediate news, were presented in a more permanent medium, with a constellation of relations that provided the "current thing" with greater historical and literary depth. In notes on this subject that were published in French and Argentine periodicals, Raúl González Tuñón was able to express his own ideas with less reticence.[22]

In 1935, Tuñón, who had already left *Crítica*, traveled to Spain. A year later, the magazine *El Suplemento,* produced in Buenos Aires, began to publish his 12-part series "Redescubrimiento de España" ("Rediscovery of Spain"). The gap in time between his trip and the publication of the chronicles demonstrates the limitations of a magazine that was trying to provide the reader with the sensation of living in the immediate present. This lag is also evident in the previous *reportages* about distant places such as Patagonia and northern Chaco. In these articles, the *special correspondent's* flight is made spectacular as a technical achievement that showcases the level of modernity of a newspaper that seeks to deliver "hot news" to the readers. However, these chronicles were only published after the reporter returned to Buenos Aires, thus representing the disparity between the desire for modernity and the technical resources available. It is precisely this disparity, which was characteristic of a "divergent modernity"

---

[22] See "La Guerre dans le Chaco Boréal" in Henri Barbusse's *Monde* (González Tuñón 1934), and "Sangre en el Chaco" in *Nueva Revista* (González Tuñón 1935c).

(Ramos 2001), that leads to a different use of the genre. In the *Rediscovery of Spain* series, the ephemeral "hot news" *reportage* gives way to deeper and broader coverage of the subject matter, as Tuñón outlines in the second issue ("Sangre en la cuenca minera," in González Tuñón 1932c):

> not only have I found documentation in leaflets, in conversations with fugitives and leaders, but also throughout almost a whole year stay in Spain: in my inquiries, talks, impressions – in the leftist field as well as the rightist field, I have been able to gather the material I shall humbly show to the readers in order to bring them up to date of the sources of the revolution, of its development, its consequences, its possibilities, as something still latent.

The texts and images of this series (Figs. 5.2 and 5.3), published between April and May 1936, served as complements to the poetry of *La rosa blindada,* which was published at the same time.[23]

The poem "Dos historias de niños" ("Two Stories of Children") is a poetic retelling of an event narrated in the third installment of the chronicle, in which Tuñón introduced the "direct" voice of a miner as a testimony.[24] "El tren blindado de Mieres" ("The Armored Train of Mieres") and "La muerte del Roxu" ("Roxu's Death") are also poetic adaptations of events narrated in the same installment. Those poems included in *La rosa blindada* are "lyrical testimonies," as González Tuñón (1962) called them, that use structural devices to dismantle what is predictable about the events in Spain and question the sense of those events, and move away from the realistic to the oneiric in order to access what is truly real.[25]

The mining children that were *reached by the shots of the guards* in the chronicle reappear in the poem "Two Stories of Children," in which the specific time of the chronicle becomes a subjective time that leads the reader to the sensitive core of the event.[26] The poem "El tren blindado de

---

[23] *La Rosa Blindada* was printed in May 1936.

[24] "La primera bomba en el corazón de la cuenca," series "Redescubrimiento de España" in *El Suplemento,* 29 April 1936.

[25] In *Manifesto of Surrealism* (1924/1969), André Breton notes, "I believe in the future resolution of these two states, dream and reality, which are seemingly so contradictory, into a kind of absolute reality, a surreality, if one may so speak. It is a quest of this surreality that I am going, certain not to find it but too unmindful of my death not to calculate to some slight degree the joys of its possession." See also "Lo real y lo fabuloso" and "Más sobre lo real y lo fabuloso" (González Tuñón 1932d, e).

[26] "Towards the middle of October or when the shower of the coal falls on the rails and a red lantern casts a cold ray on the roof that covers the bones of summer. / When all the but-

Fig. 5.2 Series Redescubrimiento de España. (Ibero-Amerikanisches Institut Preussischer Kulturbesitz, Berlin)

Mieres" uses fragments of information, political rallying, elegy and oneiric images that give way to a plurality of meaning in its account of fascist forces' attack on an armored train.

The "Redescubrimiento de España" chronicles and the poetry collection *La rosa blindada* deal with a subject that had enormous repercussions in 1930s Argentina, where many Spanish immigrants and their families were living. Faced with the dangers of fascism, which was very similar to

terflies of small forests and blue mountains have already died. / […] Up, on the truck, he sets off towards the low voice of the desolate kitchens, and the heads of dreamless children roll, under the old coal moons, oh, dead rays […] / I have heard him tell some survivor, and I knew that at the edge of the bloody, burst up, children, at the edge of the mothers with maggots, pigeons and roots, stones and flames, needles and knives, oh mothers of the land of coal and gold, the guards were executing the dead" ("Dos historias de niños," in González Tuñón 1936a).

Fig. 5.3 Series Redescubrimiento de España. (Ibero-Amerikanisches Institut Preussischer Kulturbesitz, Berlin)

the authoritarianism that had existed in Argentina since the 1930 military coup, Tuñón, who had previously been involved with an avant-garde group that rejected Spanish heritage, re-embraces elements of Spanish tradition in order to harmonize himself with the antifascist cause with which he sympathized.

4 CONCLUSION

Tuñón's verses and *reportages* make up a corpus of poetry and journalism that, while different in form, complement each other in their treatments of current events. Journalism converges with the contemporary tendencies of a "poetry with no purity"[27] that ventured into the streets and risked contamination by the heteronomy of the market and politics (Benjamin 1934/2005). At the same time, his poetry avoided the limitations of jour-

---

[27] See the unsigned article "Sobre una poesía sin pureza." *Caballo verde para la poesía* no. 1, October 1935 (Dir: Pablo Neruda).

100   G. ROGERS

nalistic discourse, rescuing the documentary material from merely informative utilitarian logic in order to explore the space between "word and dream, reality and the game of the unconscious" ("Juancito Caminador," in González Tuñón 1935a). The contact between poetry and journalism had lasting consequences in a period of modernization that left traces in both the themes and the forms of the remarkably innovative literature of authors such as Borges and Tuñón. This phenomenon is not foreign to the contacts, on the one hand, between avant-garde art and mass culture, and on the other, between the cosmopolitanism typical of transnational modern cultures and the local culture, a combination that characterized the "peripheral modernity" (Sarlo 1988) of this period. This chapter regards Tuñón's reportage in the 1930s Argentina as a crossover between journalism and avant-garde poetry, and between European and Argentinian modern genres of articulation, and argues that Argentinian literary print modernity, rather than being a replica of its European counterparts, was a distinct repurposing and alternative reconfiguration of European templates of modernization.

WORKS CITED

Baudelaire, Charles. 1863. Le peintre de la vie moderne. *Le Figaro*, Nov. 26, Nov. 29, Dec. 3.

Bayer, Osvaldo. 2016 [1972]. *Rebellion in Patagonia*. Oakland/Edinburgh/Baltimore: AK Press.

Benjamin, Walter. 1934/2005. The Author as Producer. In *Selected Writings, Volume 2: 1931–1934*. Cambridge/London: The Belknap Press of Harvard University.

———. 1940/2003. On the Concept of History. In *Selected Writings, Volume 4: 1938–1949*. Cambridge/London: The Belknap Press of Harvard University.

Boucharenc, Myriam. 2004. *L'écrivain-reporter au coeur des années trente*. Pas-de-Calais: Presses Universitaires de Septentrion.

Boucharenc, Myriam, and Joëlle Deluche, eds. 2001. *Littérature et reportage*. Pulim: Presses Universitaires de Limoges.

Breton, André. 1969. *Manifestoes of Surrealism*. Trans. Richard Seaver and Helen R. Lane. Ann Arbor Paperback/University of Michigan Press.

Buck-Morss, Susan. 1989. *The Dialectics of Seeing: Walter Benjamin and the Arcades Project*. Cambridge, MA: MIT Press.

Bürger, Peter. 1984. *Theory of the Avant-Garde*. Trans. Michael Shaw. Manchester/Minneapolis: Manchester University Press/University of Minnesota Press.

Charle, Christophe. 2004. *Le siècle de la presse (1830–1939)*. Paris: Seuil.

5 BETWEEN POETRY AND *REPORTAGE*: RAÚL GONZÁLEZ TUÑÓN... 101

Durand, Pascal. 2011. Le reportage. In *La civilisation du journal. Histoire culturelle de la presse française au XIXème siècle*, ed. Dominique Kalifa, Philippe Régnier, Marie-Ève Thérenty, and Alain Vaillant. Paris: Nouveau Monde.

Ferenczi, Thomas. 1993. Le grand reportage comme genre littéraire. In *L'Invention du journalisme en France. Naissance de la presse Moderne à la fin du XIXème siècle*. Paris: Plon.

Ferrari, Germán. 2006. *Raúl González Tuñón periodista*. Buenos Aires: Centro Cultural de la Cooperación Floreal Gorini.

Gelman, Juan. 1997. La rosa blindada. In *Recordando a Tuñón. Testimonios, ensayos y poemas*, Selección, prólogo y notas de Pedro Orgambide. Buenos Aires: Ediciones Instituto Movilizador de Fondos Cooperativos.

González Tuñón, Raúl. 1926. *El violín del diablo*. Gleizer: Buenos Aires.

———. 1928. *Miércoles de ceniza*. Gleizer: Buenos Aires.

———. 1930. *La calle del agujero en la media*. Gleizer: Buenos Aires.

———. 1932a. Vidas truncas (Shattered Lives). *Crítica*. Buenos Aires, Mar. 25–Apr. 3.

———. 1932b. En el lejano sur (In the Far South). *Crítica*. Buenos Aires, Apr. 19–24.

———. 1932c. *Crítica* en el infierno del Chaco (*Crítica* in the Hell of Chaco's War). *Crítica*. Buenos Aires, Oct. 16–28.

———. 1932d. Lo real y lo fabuloso (The Real and the Fabulous). *Crítica*. Buenos Aires, Dec.

———. 1932e. Más sobre lo real y lo fabuloso (More About the Real and the Fabulous). *Crítica*. Buenos Aires, Dec.

———. 1934. La Guerre dans le Chaco Boreal. *Monde*. Paris 290, Jan. 6.

———. 1935a. *Todos bailan. Los poemas de Juancito caminador*. Azul: Editorial Don Quijote.

———. 1935b. Desocupación. *Nueva Revista*. Buenos Aires, May 4.

———. 1935c. Sangre en el Chaco. *Nueva Revista*. Buenos Aires, Jan. 3.

———. 1936a. *La rosa blindada. Homenaje a la insurrección de Asturias y otros poemas revolucionarios*. Buenos Aires: Federación Gráfica Bonaerense.

———. 1936b. Redescubrimiento de España (Rediscovery of Spain). Series of Twelve Chronicles. *El Suplemento*. Buenos Aires, Apr. 15–Jul. 7.

———. 1962. The Unforgettable Year 1935. Prologue to the Second Edition. In *La rosa blindada*. Buenos Aires: Ediciones Horizonte.

———. 1993. *La rosa blindada. Homenaje a la insurrección de Asturias y otros poemas revolucionarios*. Buenos Aires: Tierra Firme.

———. 2011. *Poesía Reunida*. Buenos Aires: Seix Barral.

González-Pérez, Aníbal. 1993. *Journalism and the development of Spanish American narrative*. Cambridge: Cambridge University Press.

Huyssen, Andreas. 1986. *After the Great Divide: Modernism, Mass Culture, Postmodernism*. Bloomington: Indiana University Press.

Kalifa, Dominique, Marie-Ève Thérenty, Philippe Regnier, and Alain Vaillant. 2011. *La civilisation du journal. Histoire culturelle de la presse française au XIXème siècle.* Paris: Nouveau Monde.

Laera, Alejandra. 2008. Cronistas, novelistas: la prensa periódica como espacio de profesionalización en la Argentina (1880–1910). In *Historia de los intelectuales en América Latina*, ed. Carlos Altamirano, vol. I. Buenos Aires: Katz.

Orgambide, Pedro. 1998. *El hombre de la rosa blindada.* Buenos Aires: Ameghino Editora.

Rama, Ángel. 1995. *La ciudad letrada.* Montevideo: Arca.

Ramos, Julio. 2001. *Divergent Modernities: Culture and Politics in Nineteenth-Century Latin America.* Trans. John D. Blanco. Durham: Duke University Press.

Rivera, Jorge B. 1998. El camino hacia la profesionalización (1810–1900). In *El escritor y la industria cultural.* Buenos Aires: Atuel.

Rogers, Geraldine. 2010. *Émile Zola en los textos porteños de Rubén Darío: una autoimagen de los escritores modernos en la Argentina finisecular. Anales de Literatura Hispanoamericana* 39. https://revistas.ucm.es/index.php/ALHI/article/viewFile/ALHI1010110173A/21376

———. 2015a. Raúl González Tuñón desencuadernado. Políticas de la literatura, entre el libro y las publicaciones periódicas. *Aletria: Revista de Estudos de Literatura* v. 25. Universidade Federal de Minas Gerais v. 25. http://www.periodicos.letras.ufmg.br/index.php/aletria/article/view/7011

———. 2015b. Poesía sobreviviente: al reencuentro de lo político en *La Rosa Blindada* de Raúl González Tuñón. *Telar* 13–14. http://revistatelar.ct.unt.edu.ar/index.php/revistatelar/article/view/41/0

———. 2018. Jorge Luis Borges in Argentina. *Oxford Research Encyclopedia of Literature.* Oxford/New York: Oxford University Press. http://literature.oxfordre.com/view/10.1093/acrefore/9780190201098.001.0001/acrefore-9780190201098-e-274

Rotker, Susana. 1992. *La invención de la crónica.* Buenos Aires: Ediciones Letra Buena.

Saítta, Sylvia. 1998. *Regueros de tinta. El diario Crítica en la década de 1920.* Buenos Aires: Sudamericana.

Sarlo, Beatriz. 1983. Vanguardia y criollismo. La aventura de Martín Fierro. In *Ensayos argentinos. De Sarmiento a la vanguardia*, ed. Carlos Altamirano and Beatriz Sarlo. Buenos Aires: Centro Editor de América Latina.

———. 1988. *Una modernidad periférica: Buenos Aires, 1920 y 1930.* Buenos Aires: Nueva Visión.

Schwartz, Jorge. 2002. *Las Vanguardias latinoamericanas: textos programáticos y críticos.* México: Fondo de Cultura Económica.

Servelli, M. 2014. De nuestro enviado especial: La crónica periodística de viaje en los diarios Crítica y El Mundo (1920–1930). In *Escrituras a ras de suelo: Crónica latinoamericana del siglo XX*, ed. Marcela Aguilar, Claudia Darrigrandi,

Mariela Méndez, and Antonia Viu. Santiago de Chile: Ediciones Universidad Finis Terrae.

Sheringham, Michael. 2006. *Everyday Life: Theories and Practices from Surrealism to the Present*. New York: Oxford University Press.

Thérenty, Marie-Ève. 2007. *La litterature au quotidien. Poetiques journalistiques au XIXe siecle*. Paris: Editions du Seuil.

———. 2011. "Médiatisation et creation littéraire," "La literature-journal," "Le reel". In *La civilisation du journal. Histoire culturelle de la presse française au XIXème siècle*, ed. Dominique Kalifa, Marie-Ève Thérenty, Philippe Regnier, and Alain Vaillant. Paris: Nouveau Monde.

Thérenty, Marie-Ève, and Alain Vaillant, eds. 2004. *Presses et plumes. Journalisme et littérature au XIX siècle*. Paris: Nouveau Monde.

Vaillant, Alain. 2011. Présentation. In *Baudelaire Journaliste. Articles et chroniques*. Paris: Flammarion.

CHAPTER 6

New Fiction as a Medium of Public Opinion: The Utopian/Dystopian Imagination in Revolutionary Periodicals in Late Qing China

Shuk Man Leung

1 INTRODUCTION

Coined by Liang Qichao 梁啟超 (1873–1929), the term *New Fiction* (*xin xiaoshuo* 新小說) refers to a literary genre with a political function: to rejuvenate the people and the nation through the persuasive power of fictional narrative. Utopian, and in some cases dystopian, visions became a thriving motif in New Fiction after Liang Qichao's political fiction (*zhengzhi xiaoshuo* 政治小說) *Xin Zhongguo weilai ji* 新中國未來記 (*The Future of New China*) was published in the literary journal *New Fiction* in 1902. The word "utopia" originates from Sir Thomas More's (1478–1535) Latin work of the same title, written in 1516. Utopian imagination in New Fiction is different from the Chinese meaning of a perfect world, which usually relates to the virtuousness of ancient China in an inactive, nostal-

S. M. Leung (✉)
The University of Hong Kong, Hong Kong, China
e-mail: leungssm@hku.hk

© The Author(s) 2020   105
R. Aliakbari (ed.), *Comparative Print Culture*, New Directions in Book History, https://doi.org/10.1007/978-3-030-36891-3_6

106   S. M. LEUNG

gic, pessimistic, and unrealistic nature. According to Zhang Huijiuan's (1986, 84–87) interpretation of Thomas More's definition, the nature of utopia is realistic and optimistic in the face of social problems since it advocates a prospective future society, and in this respect, the blueprint of a utopia involves a transformation derived from the decline of social systems and institutions in the real world. Though informed by the West, the utopian imagination in New Fiction is not entirely an imported model of Western knowledge, but a unique blend of traditional Chinese thought, Western knowledge, and most importantly, the then-current political scene. The existing studies merely consider the utopian imagination as a theme in New Fiction,[1] but rarely discuss it from the perspective of modern print culture. My approach here resonates with what Rasoul Aliakbari, recalling Gayatri Chakravorty Sprivak, in the introductory chapter of this collection regards as a method of comparative literature in conjunction with area studies. Through the lens of modern print culture in China, this approach allows us to understand how the comparative literary and cultural nature of utopian imagination in New Fiction was constituted by the literary and political resources of the West and Japan, the political stances of Chinese writers, and the use of New Fiction as an expression of public opinion.

The rise of the modern press played a pivotal role in shaping the emergence of utopian imagination in late Qing novels. After the establishment of the *New Fiction* journal in 1902, similar journals successively emerged, while other types of periodicals began to include a fiction section (Tarumoto 2006, 179–81). A Ying's *WanQing wenyi baokan shulüe* 晚清文藝報刊述略 (A Brief Survey of Literary Journals in the Late Qing) notes that 29 popular literary journals were published during the late Qing (A Ying), comprising about one-tenth of all journals published during the last five decades of the dynasty.[2] The flourishing of the modern press provided not only a solid venue for New Fiction in the processes of production, circulation, and consumption, but also a public platform for developing shared imaginings of a new China. With its utopian view of China, New Fiction established a national narrative about the inevitable transformation

---

[1] Existing studies view late Qing utopian novels thematically, discussing their inheritance from ancient China and translations from the West (Guo 1997, Yan 2008, Zhang 1986). They rarely view it as a print culture discourse developed within the late Qing political and literary setting.

[2] Statistics from the Shanghai Library indicate that at least 257 journals of all types were published in China between 1857 and 1911 (Shanghai tushuguan, 1979).

of China into a nation that would be as progressive as, or even more progressive than, the West. In short, New Fiction was an aspect of Chinese modernization that sought to propagate an ideal image of the new China to the masses through print media.

This article employs the notion of the Chinese public sphere in order to study the way in which late Qing periodicals served as vehicles to popularize this utopian discourse. Rudolf Wagner has applied Jürgen Habermas's concept of the public sphere to the Chinese context, suggesting that, unlike the European public sphere in which a well-educated bourgeoisie comes together for free and open discussion, the Chinese public sphere was stratified, with the Qing court forming the upper tier and newspapers and journals that recruited readers from the educated and low classes forming the lower tier (2001, 1–33). Barbara Mittler has shown that newspapers, especially *Shenbao* (申報) (*Shanghai Daily*), a foreign-owned newspaper, constituted an important part of the public sphere. The Qing Empire issued official gazettes (collectively known as *Jingbao*) as its contribution to public discussion, and *Shenbao* incorporated itself into the Chinese public sphere by reprinting the court gazettes (Mittler 2004 240–42). Where Wagner and Mittler emphasize the role of newspapers in the construction of the Chinese public sphere, I have demonstrated the contribution of fiction journals, which transformed the Qing court's edicts into central issues for public discussion (Leung 2014, 569–81). This article continues my exploration of the role of literature in the Chinese public sphere by examining the fiction sections of revolutionary periodicals in the late Qing period. I argue that utopian novels published in revolutionary periodicals could be considered a medium of public opinion in which writers of fiction contributed to public discourse by responding to the Qing court's political views. The intertextuality between these utopian novels and the editorials that appeared in the same periodicals generated a public voice that resisted the injustices perpetrated by the dynasty.

Focusing on the topic of China's partition (1903–04), this article investigates how three revolutionary periodicals—*Jiangsu* (江蘇) (*Jiangsu Journal*), *Youxue yibian* (遊學譯編) (*Study Abroad and Translation Magazine*), and *Eshi jingwen* (俄事警聞) (*The Alarming News from Russia*)—engaged in discourse in the public sphere to nurture a shared idea of a future China and to overthrow dynastic rule. The first two journals were monthly publications established by Chinese students studying abroad in Japan and were mainly circulated in China, while *The Alarming News from Russia* was published daily in Shanghai and was distributed

108 S. M. LEUNG

both nationally and internationally. An analysis of three novels published in these journals illustrates the significance of the use of fiction as a means of public opinion in revolutionary periodicals.

2   NEW FICTION AS A MEDIUM OF PUBLIC OPINION

The flourishing of the modern press in the late Qing period created a new channel for expressing political views in the public sphere, where they reached the court. Generally speaking, in the past, the Qing court had announced its "edicts and memorials" (*zhaoling zouyi lei* 詔令奏議類) directly to the public, from the top down. The avenue of bottom-to-top speech (*yanlu* 言路), however, was strictly controlled by the Qing court; the usual way for members of the public to express an idea to the court was to submit a proposal (*shangshu* 上書). The emperors fully realized that printing technology could be an influential means of either supporting or subverting imperial power, as Daniel Fried's chapter in this collection has also noted with regard to the Song Dynasty. Similarly, during the Qing dynasty, only official gazettes conveying imperial announcement were allowed to be circulated. The emergence of modern newspapers in China in a strict sense, as Barbara Mittler suggests (2004, 13–23), was in the late nineteenth century, when *Shenbao* was established in Shanghai. In her study of the late Qing public sphere, Joan Judge further states that public opinion (*yulun* 輿論), which was a new mode of representation, appeared in the journals and newspapers of the late Qing, in contrast to the three traditional types outlined by Judge:

> Three such modes of representation can be identified in the traditional period: the imperial mode, with the emperor cast as a reflection of the will of the people and their benevolent protector; the official mode, in which special bureaucratic roles were established to facilitate communication between ruler and ruled; and the elite mode, in which lower and middle-level bureaucrats or literati out of office spoke for those who were excluded from the upper echelons of the dynastic hierarchy. (1994, 66)

Judge suggests that the popularity of print media in the late Qing transformed discourse in the public sphere, as editors, journalists, and columnists drew the attention of the public by addressing social and political issues and arousing a sense of civic responsibility (Judge 66).

New Fiction, as an instrument for expressing political opinions, was an idea that Liang and his contemporaries imported to China from Western and Japanese political fiction. Liang Qichao's "Yiyin zhengzhi xiaoshuo xu" 譯印政治小說序 ("Preface to The Translation and Publication of Political Fiction") argued that fiction (*xiaoshuo*) should express political opinions, and as a result, "the country's public discussion would be changed by every publication" 往往每一書出, 而全國之議論為之一變 (Liang 22). Kang Youwei, Liang's teacher, undertook a review of Chinese bibliography (*mulu xue* 目錄學) in an attempt to introduce the concept of Japanese novels into Chinese intellectual circles. Kang suggested that "the category of fiction" (*xiaoshuo men* 小說門) should be considered an independent category of literature. This proposed category included political fiction by the Japanese writer Suehiro Tetchō 末廣鐵腸 (1849–1896) (Kang 2007, 492–521).

The Japanese concept of political fiction, as Catherine Yeh argues, was heavily influenced by Western ideas. Based on his examination of American and English political fiction, Morris Edmond Speare provided in 1924 the following definition of political fiction, in which

> the main purpose of the writer is party propaganda, public reform, or exposition of the lives of the personages who maintain government, or the forces which constitute government. In this exposition the drawing-room is frequently used as medium for presenting the inside life of politics. (Yeh 1990, 112–13)

Izumi Yanagida's explanation of Japanese political fiction builds on Speare's definition, but he stresses the Japanese context: it was the establishment of a National Diet (*kokkei* 國会) that led to the blossoming of this genre, whose three purposes were reform, propaganda, and exposure (Izumi 39–40). Yanagida further develops Speare's definition and confirms that the purpose of political fiction is to promote one's political beliefs, which essentially means that it functions as propaganda.

Liang Qichao's *The Future of New China* (1902), a powerful work of propaganda, is a political novel that imitates the Japanese style of writing. As Xia Xiaohong points out (2006, 109), Liang was influenced by key works of political fiction from Japan (109). Liang had read Tōkai Sanshi's 東海散士 (Shiba Shirō 柴四郎, 1852–1922) political novel *Kajin no Kigū* (Chance Encounters with Beautiful Women) during his exile in Japan and later translated this work, which was serialized in *Qingyi bao* 清議報 (Pure

Discussion) (Xia 2006, 12). Tōkai Sanshi's *Kajin no Kigū* (Kou, 3) and Liang Qichao's *The Future of New China* share a feature common to works of political fiction: an ambitious political program that criticizes the current political system as it relates to every aspect of communal existence. Liang adopted the genre of the "future record" (*weilai ji* 未來記) to create a utopian tale of a "new China" that allegorically reveals the real-world problems with the sociopolitical system of the Qing dynasty. According to Yamada Keizou (2001, 321–24), the genre of the future record is closely related to other modes of Japanese political fiction. Beginning in the tenth year of the Meiji reign (i.e. 1877), Japanese politicians in particular wrote future records to describe the ideal parliamentary system that they imagined would be established after the fourteenth year of Meiji rule. The titles of these novels usually include a reference to "the twenty-third year," which is seen as being the year of the establishment of a Japanese parliament. Keizou adds that the figure who most influenced Liang was Suehiro Tetchō, who wrote *Nijuu sannen mirai ki* 二十三年未來記 (The Future of the Twenty-three Years). Yamada Keizou (2001, 321–24) suggests that Liang's adoption of the future record shows that Chinese political fiction was strongly influenced by Japanese political novels, which indeed had a great influence on Liang at that time.

Liang Qichao and his contemporaries used fiction to present their political views in the Chinese public sphere. *The Alarming News from Russia* serialized Cai Yuanpei's 蔡元培 (1868–1940) utopian novel "Xinnian meng" 新年夢 (*The Dream of a New Year*) in the editorial section (*sheshuo* 社說) of its 65th issue in 1904. The novel articulates Cai's views on the partition of China and his proposals for a new China, as Cai notes:

> During that period, Western socialists believed that all property should be publicly shared and marriage not allowed. These ideas spread to China and I, Jiemin, [Cai Yuanpei] also believed in them. I wrote *New Year* to express my thoughts on that in *Awakening Bell* [*The Alarming News from Russia*].
> 是時西洋社會主義家廢財產、廢婚姻之說，已流入中國，孑民〔按:蔡元培〕亦深信之，曾於《警鐘》〔按:俄事警聞〕中揭《新年夢》小說以見意。(Huang 1998, 255)

Cai himself confirmed that he was "using novels to express an opinion" 小說以見意. Editors, journalists, and columnists, most of them also politicians, all understood that fiction could be a powerful tool to incite, persuade, and educate the general public.

Of course, literacy was a prerequisite for participating in the Chinese public sphere by reading periodicals. How many readers could New Fiction periodicals reach? The Shanghai international settlement, a core location for publishing and circulating newspapers and journals in the late Qing period, may serve as a representative example. The total population of the Shanghai international settlement was one million, and the literacy rate was about 30 percent, yielding 300,000 potential readers (Chen 2010, 211–12). In reality, however, as Yuan Jin (2001, 20) points out, most periodical readers belonged to the circle of scholar officials (*shidafu* 士大夫). These officials, who were trained in traditional colleges, generally treated fiction as inferior to the Confucian classics; fiction was traditionally regarded as "street gossip" 街談巷語道聽途說 and did not comprise an independent "school of thought" like those recognized in *Hanshu yiwen zhi* 漢書藝文志 (*The Dynastic Bibliography of the Book of Han*) (Ban 1962, 1745). But scholar officials embraced the notion of New Fiction as a political means of Chinese modernization and busily engaged in reading (and writing) novels. Due to their purchasing power, these "traditional" scholars formed a large portion of the market for late Qing literary journals. Wang Shanping (2006, 65–66) shares with Yuan Jin the view that scholar officials were the core readers, but it should be noted that intellectuals studying abroad also read these journals. Moreover, Xu Nianci (1908, 1–10) observed that while "old" and "new" intellectuals made up 90 percent of the readership of late Qing literary periodicals, almost 10 percent of readers were ordinary people.

Most scholars agree that New Fiction was used to expand the reading audience beyond a narrow intellectual circle to include the wider society (Li 2004, 118–25; Yuan 2001, 21–22). Given that fiction was much more readable than the Confucian classics, Liang Qichao has noted that "fiction should therefore seek to teach where the Six Classics have failed to teach, to convey lessons where the official histories have failed to convey [故六經不能教, 當以小說教之; 正史不能入, 當以小說入之]" (1989, 21; English translation by Gek Nai Cheng, Liang 1996, 72). Fiction could serve as a means to enlighten the general public, including "soldiers, merchants, peasants, artisans, cabmen, grooms, women, and young children [下而兵丁、而市儈、而農氓、而工匠、而車夫馬卒、而婦女、而童孺]" (Liang 1989, 22; English translation by Gek Nai Cheng, Liang 1996, 73). Similarly, the three revolutionary periodicals—the *Jiangsu Journal, Study Abroad and Translation Magazine,* and *The Alarming News from Russia*—sought to arouse public awareness of China's partition in the 1900s, particularly the Russian threat to China, as the title *The Alarming News from*

Russia suggests. As Li Jiuhua points out, late Qing periodicals intended to attract the general public as readers. In general, the topics and the style of fiction were chosen to suit the taste of ordinary people. The popularity of the main theme of New Fiction—denouncing the Qing court—and the use of vernacular language served to increase the number of ordinary readers, who were eager to participate in public political discussion (2004, 118–25). Needless to say, although the Western concept of a "civil society" did not develop in the fullest sense at that time (Yuan 2001, 21), it is arguable that New Fiction opened a channel that allowed the general public to engage in discussing the controversies of the moment.

The distribution of New Fiction was another essential factor in cultivating public discussion. As Wagner observed, the Chinese public sphere was a cross-border arena (2001, 1–33), in which periodicals could generally be delivered locally and globally. The four main fiction journals in the late Qing period—*New Fiction Journal* 新小說 *(Xin xiaoshuo)*, *Illustrated Fiction* 繡像小說 *(Xiuxiang xiaoshuo)*, *Fiction Circle* 小說林 *(Xiaoshuo lin)*, and *Monthly Fiction* 月月小說 *(Yueyue xiaoshuo)*—enjoyed various distribution networks. For example, *New Fiction* was available in 75 locations across China, including Shanghai, Beijing, and Hangzhou, and overseas in Tokyo, Yokohama, Nagasaki, and San Francisco (Leung 2014, 562). The general distributors of the three revolutionary journals discussed in this chapter were located in Shanghai: *The Alarming News from Russia* (February 19, 1904, masthead) was distributed by local and international postal services. The *Jiangsu Journal* and the *Study Abroad and Translation Magazine* were founded in Tokyo by, respectively, the Association of Jiangsu Students Studying Abroad in Japan and the Association of Hunan Students Studying Abroad in Japan. These journals were distributed in an area that extended from Japan through Shanghai to the northern and southern regions along the Yangtze River (Xu 2001, 96). The *Jiangsu Journal*'s general distributor in Shanghai served 35 retail outlets across China, including Shanghai, Beijing, Suzhou, Changzhou, Jiangxi, Nanjing, Fuzhou, and Sichuan, and the journal could be purchased overseas in Kobe (*Jiangsu* back cover). *Study Abroad and Translation Magazine*, however, had fewer retail outlets and listed only 11 locations, including Beijing, Fujian, Guangdong, Sichuan, Jiangsu, Hunan, and Hubei (Xu 2001, 93).

3   China's Partition and Revolutionary Periodicals

In 1903 and 1904, various revolutionary periodicals treated China's partition as a serious matter and took a critical stance on two issues. The first was Russia's failure to complete the withdrawal of its troops from Manchuria on

6 NEW FICTION AS A MEDIUM OF PUBLIC OPINION... 113

April 8, 1903; the second was the Qing court's announcement of neutrality in the Russo-Japanese War on February 13, 1904. Public criticism in the *Jiangsu Journal* kept pace with the news of Russian actions in Manchuria. In the late nineteenth century, Russia repeatedly threatened China's sovereignty over Manchuria by constructing a railway in the territory, by securing a base in Port Arthur through the Convention for the Lease of the Liaotung Peninsula (1898), and by using the Boxer Rebellion as a pretext to stage a military occupation of Manchuria in 1900. Russia was eventually forced to withdraw its troops from Manchuria on October 6, 1902, under pressure from Britain and Japan. However, it came as no surprise when Russia reneged on its agreement to complete a second evacuation on April 8, 1903, after pretending to withdraw its troops during the first stage. The Russian government also made seven new demands on China on April 18, 1903, mainly regarding the sovereignty of Manchuria (Fudan daxue 1986, 326; Asakawa 1970, 234). On April 22, the Qing court issued an edict rejecting these demands, stating that "[it is] difficult to promise this loss of sovereignty" 有損主權, 斷難應允 (Wang et al. 1963, 2715). Five days after the court proclamation, the article "Manzhou sabing shijian" 滿州撤兵事件 (The Evacuation of Manchuria) appeared in the first issue of the *Jiangsu Journal,* expressing the view that the Russians were acting immorally because a formal treaty between two countries is like an agreement between two people who are bound by a mutual pledge. The journal condemned the first stage of the withdrawal of Russian troops because it was not a genuine evacuation, and opined that this situation would certainly lead to the partitioning of China. The Qing court's insincerity about implementing reforms and its continuous appeasement of foreign powers exacerbated the threat of partition.

The *Jiangsu Journal*'s perspective of the evacuation of Manchuria was that it would certainly lead to the partitioning of China. Moreover, the *Jiangsu Journal* strongly criticized the Qing court for being insincere about implementing reforms and continuing to fawn over foreign Powers. An important treatise, "Zhina baoquan fenge helun" 支那保全分割合論 ("A Discussion of the Partition and Maintenance of China"), published on September 21, 1903, further charged that the new policy implemented in 1902 by the Qing court was a total illusion:

> Despite the repeated reformative edicts promulgated by the Qing court, let us look at whether the actions taken correspond to their words and deeds. Outsiders find small campaigns, such as sending a few dozen pupils to study abroad and hiring a few military officials for training; and then they hail each other, believing that this is a turning point for the country and call it political reform.

況夫清廷屢下變法維新之詔矣。然審其言行, 有符合者否無也。不察者徒見其小有舉動。如遣數十學生而來游學聘十餘武員以為教習, 便相慶以為清國之轉機在此, 變法在此。 (Yixian 1903, 17)

Sun Yat-sen 孫逸仙 (1866–1925) suggested that the court had failed to carry out the new policy reform that it had announced in 1902 because of the enmity between the Manchu and the Han. The Manchu people thought that the Han would benefit most from the reform, so they refused to accept it (Yixian 1903, 20). This lack of unity was a crucial factor that led to the inexorable partitioning of China.

On October 20, 1903, the *Jiangsu Journal* published a dystopian novel, *Mingri zhi guafen* 明日之瓜分 (*Tomorrow's Partition*) to further illustrate Sun's argument. The author, Guazi 瓜子 (?–?), introduced the story with the words "This is a dream about the partition [of China]" 蓋瓜分之夢 (Guazi 1903, 122). In the novel, the Qing capital has been invaded by the Ten Powers, and the province of Jiangsu has become a British territory, but instead of struggling for survival, the Qing officials (*daqingguan* 大清官) have transferred the sovereignty of the empire to the invaders. The premises of the novel derived from Sun's statements that it would be "better to donate [the empire] to powerful neighbours than hand it to thieves at home" 寧願贈之強鄰, 不願失之家賊, and that "the Manchu people deeply dread the Han people in this way" 滿人忌漢人之深如此矣 (Yixian 20). The author intended to use this dystopian scenario to motivate the Jiangsu people to fight for their survival and ultimately establish an autonomous region.

"Manzhou wenti" 滿州問題 ("The Issue of Manchuria"), an article that was serialized in *Study Abroad and Translation Magazine* beginning on August 7, 1903, discussed the consequences of the failure of Russia's second evacuation from Manchuria, and stated that agreeing to the seven demands made by Russia in April would rob Manchuria of its sovereign rights. Crucially, since China's retention of Manchuria greatly depended on its willingness to adhere to these new demands, the decision should not be left to the court alone, because "China's sovereignty has not been privatized by the Qing court; it is owned by all Chinese citizens" 中國主權非滿政府所私有也, 國民之公主權 ("Manzhou wenti" 1903, 65). "The Issue of Manchuria" argued that the Qing court should follow the will and opinion of the people; otherwise, the people could rightfully overthrow the Qing government. By presenting an anti-utopian vision of a future China, *Study Abroad and Translation Magazine* argued that the only way to rebuild China was to revolt against the Qing dynasty and begin a war with Russia in order to maintain genuine Chinese sovereignty in Manchuria. This argument was continued in a utopian novel, *A World of Yellow Men* (*Huangren shijie* 黃人世界).

Serialized in the same volume as "The Issue of Manchuria," *A World of Yellow Men* predicts the history of China for a period of 20 years, beginning with the 29th year of the reign of Guangxu (i.e. 1904) ("Huangren Shijie" 1903, 99). The defeat of the Russians by Han volunteers is a prelude to the story, which takes place after the Russian invasion of Manchuria, and describes the rape of Manchurian women by Russians. As the situation worsens, Guangxu issues an edict in which he confesses his mistake. Han volunteers step up to help the Qing Empire by restoring the power of the Han people, and by opposing foreign invaders in order to protect the Manchu. Many Han parties call for more volunteers to form an 80,000-strong army whose armor is embossed with a large character, "death" (*si* 死), signifying their willingness to risk death at the hands of the enemy and their determination to regain Manchuria. Sadly, they all perish, and this shocking news leads to the formation of a second army of Han volunteers that consists of four or five hundred thousand people. Every Han shouts "I vow to kill the Russians!" 不殺俄人誓不干休 ("Huangren Shijie" 1903, 100) until all the Russians are finally defeated in battle.

Russia's failure to completely evacuate from Manchuria, combined with its insistence on sharing sovereignty over Korea with Japan, led to the outbreak of the Russo-Japanese War on February 8, 1904. Before that, the Japanese ambassador suggested that the Qing government should remain strictly neutral if Japan and Russia went to war (Asakawa 1970, 363–64). This was because, if China allied with Japan to fight against Russia, Japan would not be able to solely enjoy the benefits of its victory in the war (Zhongguo Shehui Kexue Yuan 1978, 490). The other Powers also advised the court to observe neutrality because of their perceived benefits in the settlement. Thus, the Qing court was forced to announce its neutrality by publishing an edict.

In 1904, *The Alarming News from Russia* published Cai Yuanpei's serialized novel *The Dream of a New Year*, which strongly disagreed with the Qing court's proclamation of neutrality during the war in response to international pressure (Wang et al. 1963, 2849). The first installment of the novel appeared in volume 65 on February 17, five days after China's proclamation of neutrality, and expressed Cai's views on the proclamation:

Unconcerned that our own land is given to someone else as a battlefield! These are members of our family! ("Xinnian meng," February 17, 1904a)

If we do not build a nation now, [I am] afraid that we will have no more chances! For example, Japan and Russia treat Manchuria as their battlefield, and we are outsiders. This is the first time we have been "outsiders"; we have established a precedent but we should not consider it as a reference later, and the announcement of neutrality was not even our decision, but that of a few stupid people who pretended it was. ("Xinnian meng," February 18, 1904b)

> 連自己土地都送給別人做戰場都不管, 這真是家人罷了!
> 但我們現在不切切實實造起一個國來, 怕永遠沒有機會! 譬如日俄兩國, 把滿州做戰場, 我們算是局外。
> 如今第一次的 "局外", 我們先打破了, 以後就無可援例了, 此次局[外]中立的宣告, 何嘗是我們的公意, 不過幾個糊塗東西, 假冒我們的公意做的。

The court claimed that the announcement could secure the security of the State, but Cai believed that no matter which country won the war, the result would lead to the partitioning of China. Therefore, he strongly argued that China should not retain its neutrality, since this would be equivalent to declaring that it was an outsider in the war, and so would automatically lose the right to protect the battlefield after the war. The geographical element was vital to make China into a nation, and the court had no right to deliver the homeland as a gift to foreign powers.

An editorial in Volume 68 of *The Alarming News from Russia* restated the fact that Chinese neutrality would lead to the loss of Chinese sovereignty ("Eshi jingwen," February 20, 1904). The editorial argued that the state's announcement of neutrality was equivalent to the loss of Manchuria, since Manchuria was outside the zone of neutrality referred to in the agreement of February 10 (Zhongguo Shehui Kexue Yuan 1978, 491), and Chinese troops were only allowed to be stationed west of the Liao River. Thus, the "so-called neutrality was essentially the same as relinquishing the land east of the Liao River" 所謂之中立云云, 直無異棄其遼河以東之國土 ("Eshi jingwen", February 20, 1904). This editorial can be seen to continue the argument of *The Dream of a New Year*, as both texts regard the state's neutrality as amounting to the abandonment of Manchuria. In *The Dream of a New Year*, Cai Yuanpei proposed conditions for the establishment of a new China: China should regain control of Manchuria,[3] and foreign countries should surrender all concessions. This

---

[3] China had handed over the Liaodong Peninsula to Russia under the Sino-Russian Secret Treaty of 1896.

would be the first stage of a Chinese utopia ("Xinnian meng," February 19, 1904c). The elimination of concessions was the most important requirement, because the Qing court had been confronted with the crisis of partition since the early twentieth century, and Cai's position was that China should eventually join Japan and fight against Russia. In this case, political fiction and political commentary appeared in the same journal and expressed the same message. The utopian vision advanced in *The Dream of a New Year* reinforced the argument made in the editorial section of *The Alarming News from Russia* by imagining a concrete solution to the political crisis. Cai believed that with Manchuria restored, China would no longer experience international hostility.

4   CONCLUSION: POPULARIZING UTOPIAN VISIONS VIA NEW FICTION

The three novels discussed above, all published in revolutionary periodicals, demonstrate the indigenization in China of the foreign concept of political fiction. These novels inherited both the structure and the themes of Liang Qichao's political fiction, offering blueprints for either a utopian world or a terrifying dystopian nightmare. The utopian imagination in these three novels brings to life the arguments advanced in political commentaries in the same journals by depicting either a prosperous future or a China in shambles. The dystopian vision of *A World of Yellow Men*, for example, dramatizes what would happen if China were to remain weak. These novels adopted the traditional form of chapter-divided novels (*zhanghui xiaoshuo* 章回小說) to accommodate the limited space available in the fiction sections of the revolutionary periodicals, while their timely serialization increased their value as a medium of public opinion.

The intertextuality between the political commentary in the editorials (*zhenglun* 政論) and the novels in these three journals strengthened and foregrounded the political stances advocated in these revolutionary periodicals. The editorials and novels shared a common viewpoint that was expressed in the public sphere in different genres. Political commentary criticized topical issues through examination, observation, and analysis, whereas utopian/dystopian writing imagined the future of China as a strategy for criticizing the court. Because of its psychological and emotional influence, fiction was more capable of molding opinions in the broader society. Liang Qichao and his contemporaries understood how the influence of fiction differed from the influence of newspaper articles and editorials: in particular, narrative fiction invites readers to immerse themselves in an imaginary world. The periodicalists discussed here utilized the foreign concept of political fiction in order to propagate among the Chinese public an alternative political worldview, seeking to convince their readers by shaping their imagination. When used to criticize the Qing court, utopian novels not only presented a political challenge, but also popularized a method of envisioning a future China in order to promote change in the minds of general readers during a turbulent period. At the same time, in contrast to contemporary Japanese and Western models, these writers, by using the traditional format of dividing novels into chapters, and by adopting a utopian/dystopian template, created a distinctive literary modernity that was politically and culturally oriented, one that drew explicitly on the political discourses of the time to imagine alternative futures for a modern China.

WORKS CITED

A Ying 阿英. 1959. *WanQing wenyi baokan shulüe* 晚清文藝報刊述略 [*A Brief Survey of Literary Journals in the Late Qing*]. Beijing: Zhonghua shuju.

Asakawa, Kan'ichi. 1970. *The Russo-Japanese Conflict: Its Causes and Issues.* 1904. Port Washington: Kennikat Press.

Ban Gu 班固. 1962. *Han shu* 漢書 [*The Book of Han*]. Beijing: Zhonghua shuju.

Chen Chun-chi 陳俊啟. 2010. "WanQing baokan zazhi zhong xiaoshuo duzhe qunti gainian de xingsu he xiaojie" 晚清報刊雜誌中小說讀者群體概念的形塑和消解 ["The Formation and Disappearance of the Concept of the Readership in Late Qing Periodicals and Fiction"]. *Hanxue yanjiu* 漢學研究 [*Chinese Studies*] 28 (4): 201–32.

Eshi jingwen 俄事警聞 [*The Alarming News from Russia*]. 1904. February 19, masthead.

"Eshi jingwen zhi kuozhang ci" 俄事警聞之擴張詞 ["Opening Statement of 'The Alarming News from Russia'"]. 1904. *Eshi jingwen* 俄事警聞 [*The Alarming News from Russia*], February 20.

Fudan daxue lishixi 復旦大學歷史系. 1986. *Sha E qinhuashi* 沙俄侵華史 [*A History of the Russian Invasion of China*]. Shanghai: Shanghai renmin.

Guazi 瓜子. 1903. "Mingri zhi guafen" 明日之瓜分 ["Tomorrow's Partition"]. *Jiangsu* 江蘇 [*Jiangsu Journal*] 7: 121–30.

Guo Zhen 郭蓁. 1997. "Lun wanQing Zhengzhi wutuobang xiaoshuo" 論晚清政治烏托邦小說 ["A Study on Political Utopian Novels in the Late Qing Period"]. Master's Thesis, Beijing University.

Huang Shihui 黃世暉. 1998. "Cai Yuanpei koushu zhuanlüe" 蔡元培口述傳略 ["A Brief Oral History of Cai Yuenpei"]. In *Cai Yuanpei jinianji* 蔡元培紀念集 [*The Commemorative Works of Cai Yuanpei*], 249–63. Hangzhou: Zhejiang jiaoyu.

"Huangren shijie" 黃人世界 ["A World of the Yellow Men"]. 1903. *Youxue yibian* 遊學譯編 [*Study Abroad and Translation Magazine*] 11: 95–106.

Jiangsu 江蘇 [*Jiangsu Journal*] 3 (1903): back cover.

Judge, Joan. 1994. Public Opinion and the New Politics of Contestation in the Late Qing, 1904–1911. *Modern China* 20 (1): 64–91.

Kang Youwei 康有為. 2007. "Riben shumu zhi" 日本書目志 ["A Record of a Bibliography of (Books in) Japan"]. In *Kang Youwei quanji di san ce* 康有為全集第三冊 [*The Kang Youwei Collection, vol. 3*], edited by *Guojia Qingshi bianzuan weiyuanhu* 國家清史編纂委員會, 263–524. Zhongguo renmin daxue chubanshe.

Keizou Yamada 山田敬三. 2001. "Weirao xin Zhongguo weilai ji suojian Liang Qichao geming yu biange siwei" 圍繞《新中國未來記》所見梁啟超革命與變革思維 ["Liang Qichao's revolutionary and reformative thought in 'The Future of New China'"]. In *Liang Qichao Mingzhi Riben xifang: Riben jingdu daxue renwen kexue yanjiu suo gongtong yanjiu baogao* 梁啟超‧明治日本‧西方:日本京都大學人文科學研究所共同研究報告 [*Liang Qichao, Meiji and Western: A Research Report of the Humanities and Science Research Center at the University of Kyoto*], edited by Hazama Naoki 狹間直樹, 321–46. Beijing: Shehui kexue wenxian chubanshe.

Leung, Shuk Man. 2014. The Public Sphere and Literary Journals: An Investigation of the Discursive Formation of New Fiction's Utopian Imagination in Late Qing. *Comparative Literature Studies* 51 (4): 557–586.

Li Jiuhua 李九華. 2004. *WanQing baokan yu xiaoshuo chuanbo yanjiu* 晚清報刊與小說傳播研究 [*A Study of the Dissemination of Late Qing Periodicals and Novels*]. Beijing: Zhongguo shehui kexue chubanshe.

Liang Qichao 梁啟超. 1989. "Yiyin zhengzhi xiaoshuo xu" 譯印政治小說序 ["Foreword to the Publication of Political Novels in Translation"]. In *Ershi shiji Zhongguo xiaoshuo lilun ziliao diyi juan: yiba jiuqi yijiu yiliu* 二十世紀中國小說理論資料第一卷: 一八九七——一九一六 [*The Theoretical Materials of Twentieth-Century Chinese Fiction, vol. 1, 1897–1916*], edited by Chen Pingyuan 陳平原, 21–22. Beijing: Beijing daxue chubanshe.

———. 1996. "Foreword to the Publication of Political Novels in Translation," translated by Gek Nai Cheng. In *Modern Chinese Literary Thought: Writings on Literature, 1893–1945*, ed. Kirk A. Denton, 71–73. Stanford: Stanford University Press.

"Manzhou wenti" 滿州問題 ["The Issue of Manchuria"]. 1903. *Youxue yibian* 遊學譯編 [*Study Abroad and Translation Magazine*] 11: 39–71.

Mittler, Barbara. 2004. *A Newspaper for China?: Power, Identity, and Change in Shanghai's News Media, 1872–1912*. Cambridge: Harvard University Asia Center.

Shanghai tushuguan 上海圖書館. 1979. *Zhongguo jindai qikan pianmu huilu* 中國近代期刊篇目彙錄 [*Indexes to Modern Chinese Periodicals*]. Shanghai: Shanghai renmin chubanshe.

Tarumoto Teruo 樽本照雄. 2006. *Qingmo xiaoshuo yanjiu jigao* 清末小說研究集稿 [*Collected Writings on the Study of Late Qing Fiction*]. Jinan: Qilu shushe.

Wagner, Rudolf. 2001. The Early Chinese Newspapers and the Chinese Public Sphere. *European Journal of East Asian Studies* 1: 1–33.

Wang Shanping 王姍萍. 2006. "Xixue dongjian yu wanQing xiaoshuo duzhe de bianhua" 西學東漸與晚清小說讀者的變化 ["The Spread of Western Knowledge to China and the Change in the Readership of Late Qing Fiction"]. *Xian waishi xueyuan xuebao* 西安外事學院學報 [*Journal of Xian International University*] 2 (1): 63–67.

Wang Yanwei 王彥威, Wang Liang 王亮, and Wang Jing 王敬, ed. 1963. *Qingji waijiao shiliao* 清季外交史料 [*Diplomatic History in the Late Qing Period*]. Taibei: Wenhai chubanshe.

Xia Xiaohong 夏曉虹. 2006. *Jueshi yu chuanshi: Liang Qichao de wenxue daolu* 覺世與傳世: 梁啓超的文學道路 [*Enlightenment and Adoption: Liang Qichao's Road to Literature*]. Beijing: Zhonghua shuju.

"Xinnian meng" 新年夢 ["The Dream of a New Year"]. 1904a. *Eshi jingwen* 俄事警聞 [*The Alarming News from Russia*], February 17.

———" 新年夢 ["The Dream of a New Year"]. 1904b. *Eshi jingwen* 俄事警聞 [*The Alarming News from Russia*], February 18.

———" 新年夢 ["The Dream of a New Year"]. 1904c. *Eshi jingwen* 俄事警聞 [*The Alarming News from Russia*], February 19.

Xu Nianci 徐念慈. 1908. "Dingmonian xiaoshuo jie fahang shumu diaocha biao" 丁末年小說界發行書目調查表 ["A Booklist Survey on Fiction in 1907"]. *Xiaoshuo lin* 小說林 [*Fiction Circle*] 9: 1–10.

Xu Xiaoqing 許小青. 2001. "Yijiu lingsan nian liuri xuesheng kanwu de chuanbo wangluo" 1903 年留日學生刊物的傳播網絡 ["The Distribution Network of the Periodicals Founded by the Students Studying in Japan"]. *Zhongzhou xuekan* 中州學刊 [*Academic Journal of Zhongzhou*] 126: 92–96.

———. 2005. "Jinchu shenxiandao xiangxiang wutuobang – lun Lü Sheng Chiren Shuomeng ji de kongjian xiangxiang" 進出神仙島, 想像烏托邦——論旅生《癡人說夢記》的空間想像 ["Go Back to Paradise, Imagine Utopia: Criticism of Lü Sheng's *A Madman's Dream*"]. *Taida wenshizhe xuebao* 台大文史哲學報 [*Humanitas Taiwanica*] 63: 105–38.

Yan Jianfu 顏健富. 2008. "Bianyi/Bianyi: WanQing xin xiaoshuo de wutuobang shiye" 編譯/變異:晚清新小說的「烏托邦」視野 ["Translating/Paraphrasing: Utopia in Late Qing Fiction"]. PhD Dissertation, Taiwan National Chengchi University.

Yanagida Izumi 柳田泉. 1967–68. *Seiji shōsetsu kenkyū* 政治小說研究 [*A Study of Political Fiction*]. Tokyō: Shunjūsha, Shōwa.

Yeh, Catherine. 1990. *Zeng Pu's 'Niehai Hua' as a Political Novel: A World Genre in a Chinese Form*. PhD Dissertation, Harvard University.

Yixian 逸仙 (Sun Yixian 孫逸仙). 1903. "Zhina baoquan fenge helun" 支那保全分割合論 [A Discussion of the Partition and Maintenance of China]. *Jiangsu* 江蘇 [*Jiangsu journal*] 1: 13–21.

Yuan Jin 袁進. 2001. "Shilun wanQing xiaoshuo duzhe de bianhua" 試論晚清小說讀者的變化 [On the Shift of the Readership in Late Qing Fiction]. *Ming Qing xiaoshuo yanjiu* 明清小說研究 [*Ming Qing fiction studies*] 59:18–28.

Zhang Huijuan 張惠娟. 1986. "Leyuan shenhua yu wutuobang – jian lun Zhongguo wutuobang wenxue de rending wenti." 樂園神話與烏托邦——兼論中國烏托邦文學的認定問題 [Chinese Paradise and Western Utopia: Problems in Chinese Utopian Literature]. *Zhongwai wenxue* 中外文學 [*Chung Wai Literary Quarterly*] 15:78–100.

Zhongguo shehui kexue yuan jindai shi yanjiusuo 中國社會科學院近代史研究所. 1978. *Sha E qinhua shi* 沙俄侵華史 [*The History of the Russian Invasion*]. Beijing: Renmin chubanshe.

CHAPTER 7

Nineteenth-Century African American Publications on Food and Housekeeping: Negotiating Alternative Forms of Modernity

Hélène Le Dantec-Lowry

1 Introduction

In Europe and the United States during the nineteenth century, modernity was often associated with major changes in science and the economy, with the concomitant perception of a break with the past and of undeniable progress. I am not suggesting that definitions of "modernity" necessarily entail economic aspects. Rather, I look at modernity as it was widely understood at the time, in order to explore how this definition applied to African Americans. I examine the print-cultural circumstances and the specific thematics of select African American cookbooks and housekeeping guides, demonstrating an alternative Black modern subjectivity grounded in the culture of print and its associated socioeconomic mobility. In situating case studies of African American print culture against the backdrop of White dominance, this chapter does not purport to take into consideration all aspects of "modernity" such as literary, esthetic, and political

---

H. Le Dantec-Lowry (✉)
Université Sorbonne Nouvelle, Paris, France
e-mail: helene.ledantec-lowry@sorbonne-nouvelle.fr

© The Author(s) 2020
R. Aliakbari (ed.), *Comparative Print Culture*, New Directions in
Book History, https://doi.org/10.1007/978-3-030-36891-3_7

123

avant-gardes. I link "modernity" to publishing done by members of a group that was largely excluded from print and whose voices were mostly ignored and in order to do so I will examine publications by African Americans, two guides for servants, Robert Roberts's *The House Servant's Directory, or a Monitor for Private Families* (1827) and Tunis Campbell's *Hotel Keepers, Head Waiters, and Housekeepers' Guide* (1848) and a cookbook, Abbie Fisher's, *What Mrs. Fisher Knows About Old Southern Cooking, Soups, Preserves, Pickles, etc.* (1881).[1] Specifically, I consider how African Americans were able both to appropriate the accepted notion of modernity and to contest it while forging their vision. As such, I aim to contribute to contemporary discussions of "modernity" and "modernization" consistent with contemporary scholarship that interrogates these concepts in terms of their complex and often indirect trajectories, away from seemingly undisputed and universal views of their supposed meaning (Fureix and Jarrige 2015, 42–45; Wittrock 2000).

Part of the transformation of nineteenth-century US society can be attributed to the rise of new techniques that made it possible to publish greater numbers of books, at a lower cost, for the wider readership that developed as literacy rates improved. In the antebellum United States, the vast majority of books were written by white authors and published by white-owned publishing houses—including, at first, a large number of books imported from Britain. African Americans were largely absent from the national discourse, and they had far less access to publishing.

This does not mean that blacks did not write or publish books, but before the Civil War (1861–1865), their success in print was achieved mainly in three ways. First, a few black authors were recognized as writers, such as poet Phyllis Wheatley, whose first collection of poems first appeared in London in 1773.[2] Second, slaves who had run away from plantations in the South told the stories of their lives from birth to their escape into the free North. These slave narratives were either self-published (especially before 1860) or published within abolitionist circles and, regularly, after some revision or editing from white abolitionist friends, they were issued through the northern publishers affiliated to the abolitionist cause, and

---

[1] As indicated in the Introduction to this volume and some of its chapters, modernity has various meanings depending on the approach and the time and place under consideration; see, for example, Gaonkar (2001) and Fureix and Jarrige (2015).

[2] *The Norton Anthology of African American Literature*, edited by Gates and McKay (1997), provides a detailed survey of publications by African Americans since the eighteenth century.

7 NINETEENTH-CENTURY AFRICAN AMERICAN PUBLICATIONS ON FOOD...   125

with the help of organizations such as the American Anti-Slavery Society.[3] Third, as recent scholarship has established, African Americans managed to publish their history, beginning in the 1830s, often to highlight their contributions to American history and produce a counter-narrative that challenged their position in American society. They disseminated their works in various ways, including self-publishing or peddling their books door-to-door, or selling textbooks to black schools. These early publications served as literary and political texts that contributed to the writing of American history, either as testimonials about black heroes or African American participation in the War of Independence, for example, or, later, as texts employing the methods of professional historians even though their authors were very rarely integrated into white schools and universities, including in the free North.[4] These black authors wrote from the margins of US society, which usually failed to recognize their humanity, segregated them, and generally set them apart from the publishing world throughout the rest of the nineteenth century, including the period after the Civil War and the abolition of slavery (1865). It required much effort for a black American to write and to be published.

In this chapter, I will add another small group of nineteenth-century published authors to the current list by looking at commercial books of prescriptive literature which, at first glance, may not appear as specifically African American. Of the 200 known books on food and housekeeping by African Americans, the two guides and cookbook studied in this chapter are the only ones published before 1900 (Tipton-Martin 2015).[5] Examining these books, I argue that it is possible to study the notion of "alternative" modernity and of "multiple modernities" *within* the United States[6] by looking at the dialectical relation between American modernity

---

[3] The first narrative by a former slave, William Grimes, was published in 1825. The number of published narratives increased in the 1830s (Charles Ball, James Williams), and especially in the 1840s (Frederick Douglass, William W. Brown, Henry Bib, among others). For more about the publishing practices of former slaves, see Roy (2017); Zboray and Zboray (2005).

[4] On books in history by African American authors, see Ernest (2004), Hall (2009), Dagbovie (2010), Parfait et al. (2017).

[5] Along with Malinda Russell's short cookbook that is not examined here (see note 19).

[6] As Rasoul Aliakbari notes in the Introduction to this volume, recent research—influenced, for example, by postcolonial approaches and by linguistic and cultural turns—has contested the vision of modernity as essentially Western-European, and as a model that would necessarily expand to the rest of the world, without taking into account the transformation of *both* European colonizing nations and colonized nations during the period of Western Empire-building as well as the various temporal sets of modernity, including value

as defined by the dominant white group on the one hand, and the desire of Blacks to be included in this modernity as part of their quest for justice and progress on the other. I argue that for African Americans in the nineteenth century, the notions of modernity often functioned in tandem with the dominant model, even if blacks could not entirely meet—or did not wish for—the demands and values of this white model, due to their inferior social position. I further propose that Blacks managed to construct their alternative version of modernity. This divergence from the dominant model is apparent in the books that I examine and in the lives of their authors.

2 Housekeeping Guides by Black Authors: Anticipating Efficient Management While Also Seeking Justice

Throughout the nineteenth century, work as a servant was among the most common activities for African Americans, whether as slaves working for their masters in the Big House on the plantations of the South or as free men and women in the Northern states. In the North, in large cities such as Boston and New York, a new class of wealthy financiers employed large household staff as clear signs of their wealth and status. Below them on the economic scale, the growing number of merchants, small manufacturers, and office employees also hired servants, albeit on a smaller scale. In the 1840s and especially the 1850s, newly arrived Irish women competed with black women for jobs as maids, but by and large, African Americans still formed the largest pool of service workers. These men and women were mostly kept at the bottom of a white-dominated social hierarchy and usually given menial positions.

At that time, a sizeable number of black men still worked as domestics in one capacity or another. Service jobs offered them economic opportunities not available to those in many other occupations: work in manufactures and later in factories was not always readily opened to Blacks, especially as rural exodus and growing immigration created a reserve of white workers for America's growing industrial economy, and because

systems and sets of practices different from those of colonizing powers; see, for example, Eisenstadt (2000) and Bhambra (2011). This article demonstrates that it is also important to look at the creation of alternative forms of modernity by different groups within a single nation.

some of those jobs were protected by unions against competition from blacks (Jones 1999). Thus, in the nineteenth century, the service jobs in private homes or public establishments (such as hotels and pensions) were largely held by African Americans, at least until the last decades of the century, when the rising number of immigrants led to more competition for those jobs in a few cases.

Jobs as servants often meant stable employment for blacks, but these were often low-paying and involved long hours and tiring and demanding tasks. For some black men who had supervisory roles, however, these jobs provided a higher social status and even allowed some to enter the growing black middle class. This was the case for Robert Roberts (1780–1860), who published *House Servant's Directory or, A Monitor for Private Families* in Boston in 1827, a text thought to be the first commercially published book by an African American man,[7] and Tunis G. Campbell (1812–1891), author of *Hotel Keepers, Head Waiters, and Housekeepers' Guide*, also published in Boston, in 1848. Both books issued detailed recommendations for, respectively, the organization of service in a private home and the management of hotel staff. The first such guides ever published in the US, these texts tell us much about their authors' will to convey novel ways of approaching work in a society that was beginning to adopt new rules about efficiency and profitability. Therefore, I situate them at the heart of the development of "modernized" capitalism in the US in the first decades of the century, at least concerning service work. At the same time, parts of their text suggest the need to treat workers fairly. Furthermore, the background of Roberts and Campbell as abolitionists and activists for African American rights also indicates their desire to shape modernity in terms that were favorable for their community. I will argue that the apparent contradiction of these goals—including African Americans in a modernizing society on a par with the white Americans while concomitantly defending justice for blacks—shows modernity as a process of constant struggle and reflects two parallel visions of modernity: one white and the other black; one representing the struggle of African Americans to participate in the society that Whites largely controlled, the other delineating the struggle by African Americans to reconcile their vision with that imposed on them by the white-dominated society.

---

[7] This means that his book was published to sell and make a profit for himself and his publisher, outside of the more militant dimension of the slave narratives.

128   H. LE DANTEC-LOWRY

House Servant's Directory,[8] published in Boston in 1827, was written by Robert Roberts, a black man born circa 1780 in Charleston, South Carolina. Although little is known of his early years, the records show that he did housework in Charleston before traveling to Boston with one of his employers, Nathan Appleton, who had stayed in Charleston from 1804 to 1806. Roberts arrived in the North as a free man.[9] Being both literate and experienced in service work helped him secure employment in the northeastern city, where the market revolution created a class of wealthy financiers, whose lavish lifestyle and numerous household employees enhanced their status, as well as a growing class of merchants, small manufacturers, and office employees, who also hired servants (Murrin et al. 2008, chapter 8).

Roberts's *Directory* contains a six-page introduction addressed to the author's "young friends Joseph and David, as they are now entering gentleman's service" (ix), and even though he never mentions their race, it is highly likely that he had African Americans in mind as he calls them his "friends". Moreover, in the 1820s, the vast majority of servants in northern cities were black. The 180-page *Directory* provides a series of detailed entries, interspersed with religious citations, about an array of subjects related to household work (15–153), including "cleaning knives and forks" (18) and making "[e]xcellent paste for the skin" (116), topics intended to make servant work more efficient and superior. "A few observations to cooks" (138) and "A word to heads of families" (154) are added at the end.

What is remarkable about the publication of *The House Servant's Directory* is that it appeared much earlier than other similar guides about housekeeping. To be published at all at the time was very difficult for African Americans; for a black servant, it was all the more challenging. Furthermore, Roberts's guide was published as a book by Munroe and Francis, a well-known publisher established in Boston in the early nineteenth century that printed a variety of books in history and popular literature as well as sermons and biographies. Roberts's guide was concomitantly published by its regular partner C. S. Francis in New York. While the number of copies is difficult to determine, the fact that the *Directory* was pub-

---

[8] Elsewhere, I have examined the resistance to imposed models of race and the new definitions of black manhood in Roberts's *Directory* (Le Dantec-Lowry 2017).

[9] Appleton is found in Boston's archives, and is sometimes referred to as Applegate, depending on the source (Hodges 1998; Harris 2011, 132).

lished again in 1828 and once more in 1837 shows that it was successful. This publication became a standard in the first half of the century (Hodges 1998) when employers bought it either to train their servants or, in wealthy families, for literate butlers to use as a guide for the staff they headed, especially as cities saw a rise in the number of untrained Irish servants and other unskilled staff (Hodges 1998). The increasing number of servants in Boston and the North, in general, in the 1820s and 1830s certainly made this guide a lucrative product for the publishers, who used a novel quarter cloth binding with marbled paper pages to promote sales.

Roberts worked for Christopher Gore, a prominent lawyer and politician with business acumen, between 1825 and 1827, the year Gore died. The "Advertisement of the Publishers" at the beginning of the *Directory* (iii–iv) contains a letter sent by Gore to Munroe and Francis in which Roberts's employer praises the guide, writing: "I have read the work attentively, and think it may be of much use. The directions are plain and perspicuous; and many of the recipes I have experienced to be valuable" (iii). He adds: "Consider me a subscriber for such number of copies as six dollars will pay for, and I think that many more would be subscribed for in Boston" (iii). The positive assessment of Roberts's book by a well-known member of the Boston elite, along with the announced subscription, undoubtedly encouraged the publishers to consider Roberts's *Directory* for publication.

In his guide, Roberts encourages the servant's obedience and subservience to employers. He also insists, however, on the (black) servant's worth and humanity; for instance, he advises employers in his "A word to heads of families" (154–159) to "let [their servants] at least be treated as fellow beings and candidates for a future world" (155).[10] Such dignity was something that African Americans did not often experience in those years, except perhaps from some whites active in the abolitionist movement. Brendan F. R. Edwards argues in his chapter in the present volume, "Print

---

[10] The format of this *Directory* is not very different from well-known household management books published by white women of privilege in the nineteenth century, such as Catharine E. Beecher's *Treatise on Domestic Economy (for The Use of Young Ladies at Home and at School)* published by Harper & Brothers in New York in 1841. Roberts and white women authors were trying to professionalize housework and to inscribe it in modernity, but from different perspectives. White women wrote from the position of employers and focused more on their essential role as teachers to naturally ignorant servants, whereas Roberts's *Directory* explicitly states that servants are indeed capable of doing excellent work with the proper supervision.

130   H. LE DANTEC-LOWRY

Culture and the Reassertion of Indigenous Nationhood in Early-Mid-Twentieth Century Canada", that we should think "not only about the *content* of writing, but the *act* of writing in and of itself". Similarly, when considering publications by African Americans in the nineteenth century, a population that was also exploited and marginalized and generally excluded from the print realm, the *act* of writing and publishing was paramount in asserting their worth. These activities, moreover, allowed African American authors to assume their modernity in the eyes of their communities as well as within the American society as a whole. Publishing provided an alternative vision of blackness, one opposed to the very common negative views and what large segments of the population regarded as their limited aptitudes. Before women writers were considered published experts in housekeeping, Roberts's book demonstrates that African Americans also had specific areas of expertise. His guide offers a narrative of a black agency that contrasts with the dominant discourse of the period.

Roberts's position as a butler in a prominent family with a large staff, and his status as a published author, afforded him a position of privilege in his community. Unlike the growing majority of African American men who were low-paid laborers and seamen, Roberts was a member of a small group of leading blacks who owned businesses, as barbers, hairdressers, and blacksmiths, for example, or held well-paid jobs.[11] The expertise evident in his *Directory* and his success as an author provided him with respectability, not just among blacks, but also more generally. At the same time, black male respectability was not tied simply to one's occupation—most African Americans stood on the lower rungs of the socioeconomic ladder—it was associated with their activism and work towards "racial uplift". Roberts took a stand against slavery, alongside other blacks and white abolitionists protesting, among other things, the capture of free blacks in the North who were subsequently sold into slavery in the South; three of his wife's brothers thus disappeared and were never recovered (Hodges 1998; Le Dantec-Lowry 2017, 79–80). Combined with his activism, his publication contributed to redefining black respectability and fostered alternative modernity specific to the African American experience that included exploitation and racism.

The experience of Tunis G. Campbell leads to comparable conclusions. His *Hotel Keepers* was published in 1848 by another Boston publisher,

[11] For additional information on African Americans in Boston at the time, see Horton and Horton (2000).

7 NINETEENTH-CENTURY AFRICAN AMERICAN PUBLICATIONS ON FOOD... 131

Coolidge, and Wiley. The book's binding, general formatting, and some of the recipes are reminiscent of Roberts's book.[12] Offering precise advice about housekeeping, this guide also explains how to run a private home: "There can be nothing of more importance to a family than the careful attention of faithful servants, in whom confidence can be placed" (5–6). Campbell's book, however, is almost entirely devoted to the management of waiters in a hotel. Although it does not include a table of contents or headings for the various sections, it is clearly structured. The first 97 pages minutely detail the tasks assigned to waiters, signaling where they should be placed in the dining room (as shown in several plates and diagrams) and how they should look and behave. The second part of the book (98–186) contains short recipes for various courses including sauces, roasts, frying, boiling, stewing, soups, and desserts; precise measurements are not specified, in keeping with many cookbooks of the period. This section is followed by a conclusion (187–89) in which Campbell insists on the advantages of his method and argues that proprietors who adopt it can realize significant savings: "The saving in a hotel will thus amount to fifty percent [for a public establishment], and in a private house to twenty-five, upon the usual system" (189). The last three pages (190–92) are reprints of letters addressed to Campbell by customers of the Howard's hotel in New York City, where, in the 1840s, he had first worked as a steward and then succeeded in advancing through the ranks until he became the hotel's principal waiter through 1845.[13]

What is striking about this book, as well as Roberts's, is its attention to detail. Campbell's work could at times be mistaken for a handbook of military rules of conduct. He refers regularly to drills, with phrases such as "drilling the men" (11), a "squad drill" (20), and mentions of "officers" and "a drill serjeant [sic]" (21). These words reinforce the notion of discipline required of the hotel employees and add to the constantly repeated ideas of regularity, order, efficiency at work and the necessary control of the head waiter. Campbell stresses a strong work ethic and high moral qualities, as did Roberts in his guide, in keeping with the labor tenets of capitalism. Precision and exact measurements concerning the placing of

---

[12] Unfortunately, there is little information about the reception of this book. It was published only once; its topic and the timeless information it contains did not necessarily require multiple printings.

[13] Howard's Hotel was a well-known hotel in Lower Manhattan, opened in 1840 by Daniel D. and John P. Howard (Doggett 1846; Lynch 2012, 159–72).

guests, table settings, and the distance of the waiters from the clients' tables are constantly reiterated. In many ways, this type of organization announces the changes that would occur in industrial management in the next few years.[14] Campbell's guide thus participated in defining some of the modern practices that would later grow in the United States. His race-neutral guide does not recognize the work performed by black servants, but the fact that a black man published it includes African Americans in the modernization of work and labor management, once again incorporating them in a system that mostly downplayed their contributions.

On page 190 of *Hotel Keepers*, there is a letter, dated January 23, 1845, by his former employer, Daniel D. Howard, owner of the hotel, who writes the following:

> Tunis Campbell...has been universally esteemed by the patrons of the establishment, as an unusually intelligent, dignified, attentive, and obliging man.
> He is, withal, a man of unblemished moral character, with a disposition to elevate the condition and character of persons of his color. (Howard in Campbell, 190)

This is the only mention of race in the book. Indeed, Campbell writes about hotel employees without ever referring to their age or color, even though he describes tasks distributed by gender. His decision to add this letter, along with those of satisfied guests, was a way for him to establish his credentials as a valid author of a guide on hotel management. It was also perhaps a means to recognize the racial identity of most employees, who were often African American, in an otherwise race-neutral book. The words of Daniel Howard exemplify convincingly the attitude of most whites on race at the time: they perceived blacks as an inferior race that needed to be "elevated". For them, having African Americans as servants was a natural course of action. In spite of the positive adjectives he uses to describe Campbell, Howard does not treat him as an equal. Campbell was also certainly aware that jobs in hotels and restaurants were better paid than positions as domestics in a private home, where various forms of

---

[14] After the War of 1812, the American domestic market was defined by an increase in domestic manufacturing, which was subsequently boosted by improved transportation in a context of mass production and higher demand for consumer goods. In *La modernité désenchantée*, Fureix and Jarrige (2015, Chapter 2) also explain that modernization was tied to new practices of management early in the nineteenth century, before the new forms of production devised by Taylorism.

7 NINETEENTH-CENTURY AFRICAN AMERICAN PUBLICATIONS ON FOOD...   133

exploitation and harassment were common and difficult to avoid (Urban 2018, 245). The attitude of many whites that black men were idle and lazy was also countered by "the black middle class engaged in a 'politics of responsibility' in which servants were encouraged to avoid conflicts with employers" and remain subservient (Urban 2018, 244). This vision is reflected in Campbell's guide. Campbell's involvement in the Reconstruction in the South after the abolition of slavery[15] and his appointment by US Secretary of War Edwin Stanton in 1863, who asked him to supervise the settlement of former slaves in islands in South Carolina, on land that had been confiscated from Confederate whites, demonstrates that he was now fighting to defend the rights of freed men and women. Like Roberts before him, Campbell engaged in the fight for justice for African Americans. Integrating a modernized society also implied political mobilization and a challenge to the prevailing racial and economic order (Hogan 2014; Duncan 2006).

As Eisenstadt argues, "multiple modernities" involve

> a story of continual constitution and reconstitution of a multiplicity of cultural programs. These ongoing reconstructions of multiple institutional and ideological patterns are carried forward by specific social actors in close connection with social, political and intellectual activists, and also by social movements pursuing different programs of modernities, holding very different views on what makes society modern. (2000, 2)

In their books, both Roberts and Campbell attempted to define their work as servants as positions of responsibility. They had the expertise, and this knowledge, as much as their daily routines as servants, allowed them to gain both income and recognition as they helped to foster and improve conditions for prospective employers as well as for other servants. Their books thus stand as proof of how members of the African American community in the nineteenth century gained a distinct, albeit relatively small, voice; a market share; a role in society as print culture expanded as part of

---

[15] The period of Reconstruction is usually understood as covering the years from the end of the Civil War in 1865 to the 1877 departure of the Federal troops that had been stationed in the defeated South to ensure political stability and fair treatment for emancipated slaves. In the next decades, white Southerners would regain control of politics and the economy, segregation would be established and then formalized with the 1896 Supreme Court decision in *Plessy v. Ferguson*, and African Americans would find themselves stripped of their newfound rights (Foner 1988).

new modernity; and the socioeconomic mobility that such expansion produced. They published in years of changing racial relations as abolitionism increased in the North and unrest disrupted slavery in the South.[16] Along with other blacks in the North, these authors struggled for respectability and progress. As James Brewer Stewart argues, leaders in the black community, including in the black church, insisted that progress against discrimination "required unflagging efforts by each to 'uplift' all by living lives of 'respectability' by striving to embrace piety, practice thrift and temperance, comport one's self with well-mannered dignity, and seek all advantage that education offer" (Stewart 1999, 695).

Both the books contributed to the black middle class's vision of respectability as a tool for contested modernity as it subtended the expansion of white middle-class values and prejudices. Dominant values about capitalism were not necessarily challenged; however, another perception of blackness was still asserted. Roberts's involvement in abolitionism and Campbell's participation in the fight for the rights of former slaves during Reconstruction indicate their efforts to take part in American modernity, but on their terms. Stewart convincingly maintains that by pushing for respectability and racial uplift in that period, blacks did not imitate white middle-class values (Stewart 1999, 695); instead, they created their own distinct vision of modernity, one that included the working-class blacks, qualified as "degraded people" by white society.

3 An 1881 African American Cookbook: The West, Gender, and Modernity

Roberts and Campbell were free men when they published in the North, but it was impossible for a black person to publish in the South, not only in the antebellum slave society, but also during Reconstruction, after abolition, when a white-dominated racial and political order was restored. Still, one Southern woman, Abby Fisher, succeeded in publishing her cookbook, *What Mrs. Fisher Knows about Old Southern Cooking, Soups,*

---

[16] For example, abolitionism grew in the 1830s, and some radical abolitionists demanded the immediate abolition of slavery and, for some of them, equal rights for African Americans, as symbolized by William Lloyd Garrison's founding of *The Liberator* in 1831 in Boston. Southern society was shaken by the famous slave rebellion led by Nat Turner in August of the same year.

7 NINETEENTH-CENTURY AFRICAN AMERICAN PUBLICATIONS ON FOOD... 135

Pickles, Preserves, and so on (1881).[17] Fisher was the daughter of a slave mother and a white French father in coastal South Carolina. After years of experience in food-related work, she moved to Alabama, where she married a slave. Later, in 1877, she went west with her family, as Reconstruction ended, and settled in San Francisco, where a wealthy elite grew from the gold rush, profits from the construction of the transcontinental railroad, and increase in the shipping industry (Hess 1995; Haff 2011, 67–73; Brower 2007). She started a successful catering business and later specialized in pickles and preserves. In her "Preface and Apology" she explains that she was encouraged to publish her recipes by her friends and the "patrons in San Francisco and Oakland" and by "ladies of Sacramento during the State Fair in 1879", where she presented her pickles, preserves, and jellies. She was awarded a prize for some of her products, a sign of recognition and proof of good publicity (Wagner 2007, 45–47). Fisher could not write; her book was "written at her dictation". Fisher's publishing experience was quite different from that of Roberts and Campbell. Indeed, *What Mrs. Fisher Knows* was self-published and was printed in San Francisco by the Women's Co-operative Printing Union (WCU)—a printer, not a publisher—at a time when the West Coast city was becoming an important center for printing (see Fig. 7.1). The WCU was founded in 1869 by white women, including Southerners who had moved west and by women associated with the women's rights struggle. Their printing office issued a variety of documents in the 1880s, including legal briefs and corporate reports, a Quaker cookbook and spiritual books. The WCU fought for women's rights in the workforce and pushed for women's employment in the printing business. They obviously encouraged black success as well, as Fisher's book exemplifies. Fisher's business grew and the Fishers owned a mortgage-free house by 1900 (Haff 2011, 71). Her story

[17] For a long time, cookbooks available in the British colonies were imported from England, such as the popular 1821 *Cook's Oracle: Containing Receipts for Plain Cookery on the Most Economical Plan for Private Families*, etc., published by Dr. William Kitchener in Britain, and reissued in the 1820s and 1830s. *American Cookery* by Amelia Simmons is considered the first cookbook published in the US, "for the author" (cover page) in Hartford, Connecticut in 1796 by Hoodson and Goodwin. In 2000, food historian Karen Hess, discovered another cookbook, *Domestic Cookbook Containing a Careful Selection of Useful Receipts for the Kitchen*, published by an African American woman, Malinda Russell in 1866. Little is known about it, however, and I have decided to focus only on Fisher's book, which provides more information in terms of publishing and modernity. Russell's short book was also self-published through a local newspaper, *The True Northerner*, in Paw Paw, Michigan, where she had moved to escape hardships in the South.

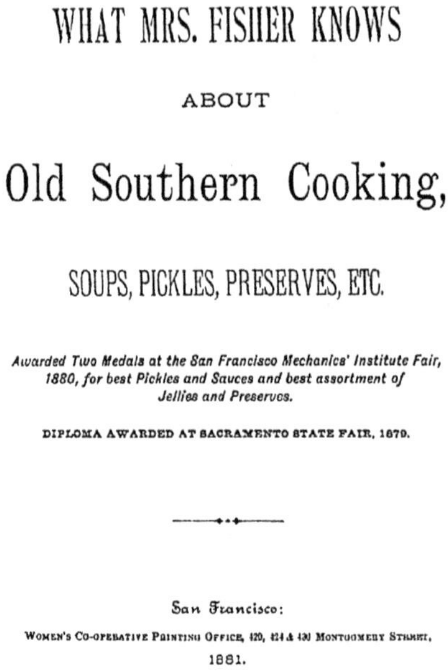

136   H. LE DANTEC-LOWRY

WHAT MRS. FISHER KNOWS

ABOUT

Old Southern Cooking,

SOUPS, PICKLES, PRESERVES, ETC.

*Awarded Two Medals at the San Francisco Mechanics' Institute Fair,
1880, for best Pickles and Sauces and best assortment of
Jellies and Preserves.*

DIPLOMA AWARDED AT SACRAMENTO STATE FAIR, 1879.

———❖———

San Francisco:

WOMEN'S CO-OPERATIVE PRINTING OFFICE, 420, 424 & 426 MONTGOMERY STREET,

1881.

Fig. 7.1 Title page of Abby Fisher, *what Mrs. Fisher knows about old southern cooking, soups, pickles, preserves,* etc. (San Francisco: Women's Co-operative Printing Office, 1881). Primary source edition. Nabu Public Domain reprints, ICG Testing. com. 424741LV00021B/929/P

demonstrates women's solidarity outside racial and class barriers as it helped to constitute new gender-based modernity.

Fisher's 68-page volume includes a table of contents, listing short, precise recipes (160) by genre but in an unusual order, with pies and puddings being placed before soups, for example. Her book contains numerous standard American recipes, proving her skills as a cook. It also exposes her background as a Southerner through various gumbo recipes—part of the African heritage of slave cooks—and corn breads, several "Creole" dishes, including a "Jumberlie" (a misspelling of 'Jambalaya'), and "Sweet

7 NINETEENTH-CENTURY AFRICAN AMERICAN PUBLICATIONS ON FOOD... 137

Watermelon Rind pickle". Adding recipes from a well-recognized cuisine may have helped her compete in the Bay Area food market. The inclusion of such recipes also allowed her to re-appropriate black Southern cuisine at the end of the nineteenth century, an era in which Southern white culture offered a very narrow vision of slavery, often romanticizing former slaves as truthful and happy, and ignoring their contribution to the Southern economy and lifestyle, including its cuisine.[18] Southern cookbooks published in the South in the late nineteenth and early twentieth centuries were all written by white middle-class women who promoted what they described as their critical role in the creation of Southern cuisine. Such assertions elided the labor of the slave cooks and their descendants, as well as African and other influences on the cuisine. The author's preface to *Housekeeping in Old Virginia* (Tyree 1878) acknowledges the contribution of many white women, but not that of black women, to the preparation of her book, even though the title page includes the drawing of a stereotypical smiling black cook at work:

> It will be seen that she [the author] is indebted to near 250 contributors to her book [A list is included]. Among these will be found *many names famous through the land*. Associated with them will be discovered others of less national celebrity, but who have acquired among their neighbors an equally merited distinction for the beautiful order and delightful cuisine of their homes. (viii–ix)

Similarly, the preface of the 1885 *Dixie Cook-book* compilation also states that its recipes were "contributed by well-known ladies of the South" and were "culled, without stint of labor, time or expense, from the treasure-troves of hundreds of the grand old housekeepers of our land who have practically tested what is now given to others". The expression "grand old housekeepers", a reference to Southern white "ladies", obviously eliminates African American cooks (*The Dixie Cook-Book* 1885). Fisher's book placed her in an expanding print culture from which African American women had long been excluded. Her southern recipes provided a counternarrative to that of the white Southern women, and served as an example

---

[18] This romanticized view of the slave past pervaded Southern culture and had spread to other areas of the US by the end of the century through memoirs by former slaveholders, sentimental novels (known as plantation literature), newspaper cartoons, illustrations in advertising, and minstrel shows. They often described the beloved black Mammy, painted as a nanny or a cook. Another view depicted slaves as uncouth and dangerous.

of personal and community "uplift".[19] Fisher's small book was printed by a small printing office and no information is available about the number of copies she sold. It appeared at a time when only a small number of African Americans, and especially African American women, made it into print. This fact in itself suggests different modernity inflected by the concerns, interests, and contributions of black women.

4 Conclusion

The books mentioned in this chapter are extraordinary in many ways. They were written by authors who were born in the South during slavery, at a time when the rates of black illiteracy remained high,[20] and when only a small number of African Americans, and especially African American women, made it into print. If we consider higher literacy rates and an increase in publishing as signs of modernity in the United States, more and more on a par with Europe, then the fact that these African Americans managed to write and publish books is indeed an extraordinary feat.

Proof of their author's achievements, these books also provided their authors with recognizable identities as professionals with specific skills. Regardless of the number of copies sold, these publications challenged common beliefs about the inferiority of blacks. While these authors' status as blacks may have associated them with servants, not only in the South but also in the North and West, the publication of their books elevated

---

[19] Fisher obviously benefitted from her food business, and perhaps also from the sale of her cookbook, especially considering that in San Francisco, low-paid service work was the most common job for black men, and even more so for black women. It is interesting to note, however, that life in San Francisco, albeit less pervasively racist than in the South, was increasingly fraught with problems, including increasing competition with immigrants for jobs, and exclusion of African Americans by white unions (see San Francisco's Digital Archives, http://www.foundsf.org/index.php?title=BLACKS_AND_LABOR, accessed on August 25, 2018). This is perhaps why Fisher, who was identified as "Mulatto" in the 1880 Census, was noted as "white" in the 1900 Census (Haff 2011, 69). Passing as white was a strategy used by light-skinned blacks to avoid lives of segregation and discrimination.

[20] The Census of 1870 was the first to provide national information on literacy rates. It indicated that 81% of African Americans over ten years old were illiterate. Even though the census did not take into consideration regional differences and variation between free blacks and slaves, we know that the majority of them were in the South, where slavery had been abolished only five years prior. In 1850, 36.2% of free blacks aged 20–29 (most of whom lived in the North) were considered illiterate, a figure that further underscores the differences between free and slave, North and South (Collins and Margo 2006).

7 NINETEENTH-CENTURY AFRICAN AMERICAN PUBLICATIONS ON FOOD... 139

them to the rank of experts in their field. By challenging the racial and gender barriers that commonly affected the lives of nineteenth-century African Americans, and also by writing *against* the accepted ideas about their community, these books added agency as a political statement. The growing politicization of the black community and the fight for equal rights, in which Roberts and Campbell were directly involved, meant that their writings acquired added value as an expression of black women's resistance to white hegemony.[21] For this reason, we can say that these texts contributed to the long tradition of protest by blacks against their white detractors, even though the protest was implicit rather than militant. One cannot ignore the labor of black men and women and their participation in the formation and the growth of the US nation, and this phenomenon, too, contributed to the idea of American "modernity". These volumes exemplify the contribution of African Americans, slaves included, who participated in making the United States as a nation in which racial hierarchies and racial erasure would potentially be replaced by alternative *modernity* oriented toward inclusion.

WORKS CITED

PRIMARY SOURCES

Campbell, Tunis G. 1848. *Hotel Keepers, Head Waiters, and Housekeepers' Guide.* Boston: Coolidge and Wiley.

Fisher, Abby. 1881. *What Mrs. Fisher Knows About Old Southern Cooking, Soups, Pickles, Preserves, etc.* San Francisco: Women's Co-operative Printing Office.

Roberts, Robert. 1827. *The House Servant's Directory or, A Monitor for Private Families.* Kansas City: Andrews McMeel Publishing, 2013. Originally Published: Boston: Munroe and Francis.

---

[21] In the second half of the nineteenth century, when Fisher's book was published, the demands for equal treatment and full citizenship by and for blacks—officially granted to them by the Civil War Amendments (abolition of slavery with the 13th Amendment in 1865, civil rights with the 14th in 1868, and the vote for black men with the 15th in 1870)—were progressively less and less respected for various reasons, including the spread of Scientific Racism and Social Darwinism, which provided pseudoscientific reasons for the perception of the black race as inferior, and the popularity of cultural artifacts that popularized the idea that slaves had been well treated by benevolent masters, creating a nostalgia for the Old South in the whole country.

140   H. LE DANTEC-LOWRY

SECONDARY SOURCES

Bhambra, Gurminder K. 2011. AHR Roundtable: Historical Sociology, Modernity, and Postcolonial Critique. *American Historical Review* 116: 653–661.

Brower, Robert. 2007. Solving a Culinary Historic Mystery: Tracing Abby Fisher's Roots to South Carolina. *Repast* XXII (4): 4–7.

Collins, William J., and Robert A. Margo. 2006. Historical Perspectives on Racial Differences in Schooling in the United States. In *Handbook of the Economics of Education*, ed. Eric Hanushek and Finis Welch. Amsterdam: North-Holland.

Dabel, Jane E. 2001. *A Respectable Woman: The Public Roles of African American Women in 19th-Century New York*. New York: New York University Press.

Dagbovie, Pero Gaglo. 2010. *African American History Reconsidered*. Urbana: University of Illinois Press.

Doggett, John, Jr. 1846. *The Great Metropolis, Or Guide to New York for 1846*. New York: Directory Establishment, 156 Broadway.

Duncan, Russell. 2006. *Freedom's Shore: Tunis Campbell and the Georgia Freedmen*. Athens: University of Georgia Press.

Eisenstadt, Shmuel N. 2000. Multiple Modernities. *Daedalus* 129 (1): 1–29.

Ernest, John. 2004. *Liberation Historiography: African American Writers and the Challenge of History (1794–1861)*. Chapel Hill: University of North Carolina Press.

Foner, Eric. 1988. *Reconstruction: America's Unfinished Revolution, 1863–1877*. New York: Harper Collins.

Fureix, Emmanuel, and François Jarrige. 2015. *La modernité enchantée: Relire l'histoire du XIXe siècle français*. Paris: La découverte.

Gaonkar, Dilip Parameshwar. 2001. Introduction to *Alternate Modernities*, ed. Dilip Paramechwar Gaonkar. Durham: Duke University Press.

Gates, Henry Louis, Jr., and Nellie Y. McKay, eds. 1997. *The Norton Anthology of African American Literature*. New York: W. W. Norton & Co.

Haff, Henri. 2011. *The Founders of American Cuisine: Seven Cookbook Authors, with Historical Recipes*. Jefferson: McFarland.

Hall, Stephen G.A. 2009. *Faithful Account of the Race: African American Historical Writing in 19th-Century America*. Chapel Hill: University of North Carolina Press.

Harris, Jessica B. 2011. *High on the Hog: A Culinary Journey from Africa to America*. New York: Bloomsbury.

Hess, Karen. 1995. Introduction to *What Mrs. Fisher Knows About Old Southern Cooking, Soups, Pickles, Preserves, Etc.*, ed. Abby Fisher. Bedford: Applewood Books.

Hodges, Graham Russell. 1998. Introduction to *The House Servant's Directory or, A Monitor for Private Families*, ed. Robert Roberts. New York: M. E. Sharpe.

Hogan, Richard. 2014. Tunis Campbell, Sr. (1812–1891). *Journal of African American Studies* 18: 409–416.

7 NINETEENTH-CENTURY AFRICAN AMERICAN PUBLICATIONS ON FOOD... 141

Horton, James Olivier, and Lois E. Horton. 2000. *Black Bostonians: Family Life and Community Struggle in the Antebellum North*. 1979. New York: Holmes & Meier.

Jones, Jacqueline. 1999. *American Work: Four Centuries of Black and White Labor*. New York: W. W. Norton.

Le Dantec-Lowry, Hélène. 2017. Work, Class, and Respectability in Robert Roberts's *House Servant's Directory or, A Monitor for Private Families* (Boston, 1827). In *Writing History from the Margins: African Americans and the Quest for Freedom*, ed. Claire Parfait, Hélène Le Dantec-Lowry, and Claire Bourhis-Mariotti, 73–87. New York: Routledge.

Lynch, Matthew. 2012. *Before Obama: A Reappraisal of Black Reconstruction Era Politicians*. Santa Barbara: Praeger.

Murrin, John M., et al. 2008. *Liberty, Equality, Power: A History of the American People*. Boston: Cengage Advantage Books, 2012. Originally Published: Boston: Wadsworth.

Parfait, Claire, Hélène Le Dantec-Lowry, and Claire Bourhis-Mariotti. 2017. *Writing History from the Margins: African Americans and the Quest for Freedom*. New York: Routledge.

Roy, Michaël. 2017. *Textes fugitifs. Le récit d'esclave au prisme de l'histoire du livre*. Paris: ENS Éditions.

Stewart, James Brewer. 1999. Modernizing 'Difference': The Political Meanings of Color in the Free States, 1776–1840. *Journal of the Early Republic* 19 (4): 691–712.

The Dixie Cook-Book. 1885. Atlanta: A. Clarkson and Company. https://archive.org/stream/dixiecookbook00wilcgoog/dixiecookbook00wilcgoog_djvu.txt

Tipton-Martin, Toni. 2015. *The Jemima Code: Two Centuries of African American Cookbooks*. Austin: University of Texas Press.

Tyree, Marion Cabell. 1878. Housekeeping in Old Virginia. Louisville. https://www.gutenberg.org/files/42450/42450-h/42450-h.htm

Urban, Andrew. 2018. *Brokering Servitude: Migration and the Politics of Domestic Labor During the Long Nineteenth Century*. New York: New York University Press.

Wagner, Tricia Martineau. 2007. *African American Women of the Old West*. Guilford/Helena: Twodot Books.

Wittrock, Bjorn. 2000. Modernity: One, None, or Many? European Origins and Modernity as a Global Condition. *Daedalus* (Winter): 130–160.

Zboray, Ronald J., and Mary Saracino Zboray. 2005. *Literary Dollars and Social Sense: A People's History of the Mass Market Book*. New York: Routledge.

CHAPTER 8

Progressing with a Vengeance: The Woman Reader/Writer in the African Press

Corinne Sandwith

1 Introduction

According to Stephanie Newell, "debates about gender roles and inter-relationships are inextricable from the rise of print cultures in Africa" (2016, 431); however, scholarship on African print culture traditions to date has shown comparatively little interest in the interventions of African women in these debates.[1] This chapter takes up such an enquiry in the South African context with a letter to the editor by Mrs. Gladys Ramokwena, published in July 1932 in the newspaper *The Bantu World*. As one of the newspaper's "lady readers," Ramokwena notes the absence of articles by women writers and proposes that *The Bantu World* include

---

I would like to acknowledge the support of the Mellon Focus Area research project on Urban Connections in African Popular Imaginaries project (UCAPI).

[1] Notable exceptions include Gadzepko (2005, 2006), Newell (2000, 2013) and Newell and Gadzepko (2004). For scholarship on more contemporary engagements, see Bryce (1997) and Mutongi (2009).

C. Sandwith (✉)
University of Pretoria, Pretoria, South Africa
e-mail: corinne.sandwith@up.ac.za

© The Author(s) 2020
R. Aliakbari (ed.), *Comparative Print Culture*, New Directions in
Book History, https://doi.org/10.1007/978-3-030-36891-3_8

143

a "weekly column devoted to women's affairs" (30 July 1932, 4). In his reply, the editor confirmed that many women did read *Bantu World*, suggesting also that "he would be only too glad to publish articles from women writers, dealing with the life and problems of their sex." True to its word, the newspaper launched a Woman's Page on 1 October 1932, the first of its kind in the history of the African-oriented press in South Africa (For an example of the masthead page, see Fig. 8.1). In an unsurprising irony, the job of editing the women's page, initially titled "Women's Activities," fell to a man: the popular journalist and writer Rolfes Dhlomo, who had recently joined the newspaper as Assistant Editor and who would soon become notorious for his satirical column "R. Roamer Esq."

Ramokwena's correspondence with *Bantu World* raises questions about how African women inserted themselves into the male-dominated world of commercial newspapers in early twentieth-century South Africa and the terms on which this participation took place. By the late 1930s, the white female journalist was an unremarkable, ordinary presence in the world of public print culture, writing articles, contributing letters, and even taking on editorial roles. *The Lady's Pictorial and Home Journal* (1910–1940) and the Communist-aligned *Guardian* newspaper (1937–1962), for instance, were both edited by women; these and other publications, such as *The South African Opinion* (1934–1937), regularly drew on female contributors and column writers (Sandwith 2014; Venter 2014). The same cannot be said for African women, whose interventions in local print arenas tended to be rare and infrequent, most often confined to letters to the editor. Two notable exceptions were Charlotte Manye (Maxeke), who contributed articles in *isiXhosa* on the women question to *Umteteli wa Bantu* in the 1920s (Daymond et al. 2003, April 2012) and Nontisizi Mgqwetho, also writing in *Umteteli*, who defied the conventional distinction between female storytellers and male praise poets by fashioning an unorthodox identity as a Xhosa *imbongi* or praise poet (Opland 2007; Brown 2004, 2008).[2] The launch of the English language women's page in the multi-language *Bantu World* seems to have opened up a different kind of space for women readers. Within a matter of weeks, it had become

---

[2] That women were writing during this period (and that their writing was not always valued) is evident in the fragments that have survived, such as Adelaide Charles Dube's poem "Africa: My Native Land," published in *Ilanga Lase Natal* (13 October 1913) and Florence Jabavu's "Bantu Home Life," an essay published in *Christianity and the Natives of South Africa: A Yearbook of South African Missions* (1928); see Daymond et al. (2003).

8 PROGRESSING WITH A VENGEANCE: THE WOMAN READER/WRITER... 145

Fig. 8.1 Women's Page Supplement (Title Page), *Bantu World* May 1936. (Courtesy of University of Johannesburg Special Collections)

a popular forum in which a small but significant group of educated African women, writing mostly in English, took up the opportunity for public debate through the writing of letters and short articles.

146   C. SANDWITH

This chapter focuses on the details of this heightened, unusual moment of women's entry into the public print culture in 1930s South Africa, looking at how the notion of "woman's sphere," as exemplified in the enduring but generally conservative genre of The Woman's Page, was elaborated in this context; the extent to which it both enabled women's access to print culture and set certain limits on how this could be pursued. The rhetorical strategies and styles that women used to sanction what may have been perceived as an unorthodox publicity, what modes of self-representation, subjectivity, and address were activated, how African women appropriated the form of the newspaper to articulate their concerns, and what kind of female-oriented public sphere was inaugurated, are of special interest here. A central focus in this discussion is the question of gender, a subject of sustained and intense debate during this period. As such, the chapter foregrounds how women used the space of the woman's page to address questions relating to normative gender roles and identities; how "gender trouble" was negotiated in these spaces; what traditional and emergent forms of exemplary femininity were operating, and what was the significance and impact of women's newly established roles as public commentators. Importantly, in highlighting the interventions of the "unofficial gender commentators" of this period (Newell 1997, 1), the chapter explores the extent to which the Western-derived model of modern femininity, on which the women's page was based, was reconfigured and re-oriented by African women letter-writers and contributors. In other words, it considers the extent to which the women's page became host to an alternative or dissenting African modernity in contradistinction to prevailing European norms.

2   DISCUSSIONS

The enquiry into women's entry into print culture traditions has an important bearing on the genesis of African women's written literature more generally. As much western feminist scholarship has revealed, British and North American women's literature traces points of origin to the transitional or preliminary genres of memoir, letter, essay, and pamphlet, all of which provide unorthodox, non-sanctioned, and therefore, less prescriptive spaces for women's writing (Donovan 1990, 47). A similar set of conditions, I suggest, allowed for the emergence of African women's writing in the South African context; thus, the genealogy of black women's literature, comprising autobiography, poetry, political commentary, and fiction, can only be properly traced through an investigation of the history of women's writing in other non-literary forms and forums. By drawing attention to some of the pioneering, albeit trivialized or occluded, journalistic interventions on the part of African women such as Rossie Khabela, Mary Mabel Mpulo, Johannah G. Phahlane, Dora Msomi, and Ellen Pumla Ngozwana, something of the prehistory, or pre-texts, of later black women's writing in South Africa becomes visible. In the exploration of "little known writers and texts," as Newell has argued, "theorisations of African women's creative expression [become] reoriented" (1997, 4).

Ramokwena's engagement with the editor of *Bantu World* is striking for its insistence on the provision of a segregated female space. If the idea of a women's sphere provides a welcome visibility, and perhaps a sanctuary, for women, it also contributes to the Western tradition of gendering space into public/male/important and private/female/trivial concerns. Women have a place on the women's page, but remain outside of the validated social world. Writing about a similar gendering of public debate in the eighteenth-century British periodical, Kathyn Shevelow argues that "the periodicals' characteristic attention to women and 'women's concerns'...served an emerging ideology that, in the act of making claims for women's capabilities and social importance, constructed women as essentially – that is, both biologically and socially – other than men" (1989, 2). Thus, those who "actively solicited women's involvement in the production of the periodical press were also those engaged in containing it" (1).

Despite the explicit gendering of both literacy and human experience that *Bantu World* encouraged, what is also evident is that it acted in very profound ways to legitimate women's lives, aspirations, and achievements. Women readers of the paper regarded the women's page as a sign of their importance and value; in the words of one writer, "Since this paper started, we also feel like human beings'" (10 March 1934, 10). Appreciated for its helpful advice on domestic matters, the paper was granted significance as heroic champion of the women's cause and an important factor in women's emancipation and the redefinition of normative gender (and racial) ideals; as "Daughter of Amanzimtoti" wrote, "We are glad that 'Bantu World' is killing the bad spirit of degrading the character of women of the race in some papers. ... [I]t is only through 'Bantu World' that our efforts can be recognised" (11 March 1933, 10).

148   C. SANDWITH

As Audrey Gadzekpo has argued regarding Ghanaian print cultures, the women's column was "a strong signifier of the presence of women in print culture" (2005, 286). It opened up a space for new writers, enabling the formation of "female reading communities organised around the textual representation of women as readers, writing subjects and as textual figures" (Newell and Gadzekpo 2004, xiii). Numerous letters to the "editress" record the gratitude felt by women readers and their sense of personal vindication. For many contributors, it was as though the existence of the women's page gave licence to female speech. The popularity of the page is evident in its expansion, in November 1935, to a 4-page Women's Supplement, now re-titled "Marching Forward" (*Bantu World* 23 November 1935; for an example from the May 1936 edition, see Fig. 8.1), and in the many occasions when, due to limitations of space, the editress was unable to publish the high volumes of letters and articles she received (*Bantu World* 2 May 1936, 12).

That *Bantu World* would find itself in the vanguard of women's emancipation is linked to the commercialization of African newspapers during this period, with women readers forming a potentially lucrative target audience for advertizers of female-oriented products.[3] As Tim Couzens and others have argued, the 1930s marked the end of a rich tradition of independent African journalism in South Africa, with many newspapers unable to survive the Great Depression. Furthermore, as black disillusionment with segregationist rule intensified, more and more African newspapers were co-opted into a project of ideological containment. The period saw the appearance of a range of new government and industry-friendly newspapers that sought to entrench business interests through advertising (Switzer 1988, 352) and to channel an emerging African radicalism through a repetitive articulation of moderate political views. The weekly Johannesburg-based newspaper *Bantu World*, launched in April 1932 under the editorship of R.V. Selope Thema, was one such newspaper, informed by conservative white political interests, edited by an African man, and targeted at the national African Christian elite. The success of its editorial formula—the promotion of African modernity within a moderate

---

[3] In an illuminating insert, women readers were advised to look very carefully at the adverts on the women's page and to buy the products featured. In this way, readers could lend support to the newspapers but also assist in the "advancement of the race": "It is your duty to your husband, your children and yourself to try these things which are meant to aid the progress and health of the Bantu nation" (5 May 1934, 10).

African nationalism—can be gauged both by its early circulation figures (which were double those of contemporary African papers and which reached a peak of 24,000 per week in 1946) and in its transnational readership extending beyond the borders of South Africa to areas such as Swaziland and Rhodesia (now Zimbabwe) (Couzens 1976, 77; Switzer 1997, 190).

As many scholars have argued, the topic of gender and the related questions of marriage, sexuality, family life, morality, women's education, and the gendered division of labour were the subject of protracted public debate in the colonial period, providing much of the content and even the *raison d'etre* of African print cultural production itself (Thomas 2006, 462; Newell 2013, 127–29). This can be traced in part to the interventionist activities of the colonial mission, which took the intimate arenas of family, the body, gender, and sexual relations as the primary sites of its reformist activities (Burton 2005; Comaroff and Comaroff 2008, 2009; Locher-Scholten 2010). What this entailed was the "subtle imposition" of new modes of being, perception, belief, and habitus (Comaroff and Comaroff 1986, 2; Daymond et al. 2003, 15). As "bearers of culture" to future generations, women were the principal targets of disciplinary regimes centred on the cult of domesticity, separate spheres, and the monogamous nuclear family. As scholars such as Mary Hancock (2001) have suggested, and as this discussion of *Bantu World* confirms, gendered discipline and the female domestic were a constitutive feature of both colonial modernity and emergent forms of anti-colonial nationalism.

Gender debates in this context are also animated by a context of rapidly shifting gender expectations and norms conditioned by increased access to literacy and education (Wilson and Mafeje 1963; Healy-Clancy 2013); they were also influenced by processes of rapid and unregulated urbanization that saw unprecedented numbers of women leaving their family homes, coming to town, and entering the colonial economy as domestic workers, beer-brewers, washerwomen, nurses, and teachers (Gaitskell 1979, 1983; Bonner 1990; Bozzoli and Nkotsoe 1991; Cock 1990). In this context, gender anxieties were fuelled by the increasing prominence in urban centres of single working women who, unencumbered by the regulating ties of family or tradition, seemed to operate outside of accepted female proprieties.

The Bantu World's women's page followed a well-established Western template of admonition and socialization into ideal femininity, a project that was inevitably influenced by a racialized context in which progress was

150 C. SANDWITH

understood as conformity to Western, middle-class ideals. The impact of Christian-colonial values and Victorian gender norms on the page is evident in regular features comprising household tips, recipes, and sewing patterns. Moralizing stories and dramatic sketches (often supplied by the editress) about sexual predators, wifely duties, and the dangers of frivolity reflect a particular preoccupation with women's virtue. The promotion of the qualities of modesty, seriousness, hard work, thrift, diligence, fidelity, tolerance, and forbearance, as well as the more practical talents of household management, etiquette, dress, baby care, and parenting, form the repetitive content of these weekly iterations of exemplary modern femininity.[4] The ubiquity of pious homilies, inspirational poems, and pithy aphorisms confirm the dominance of the sentimental-moralizing mode. In addition, the practice of repetitive citation and "snipping" from papers such as the UK-based *Christian Herald* and the *South African Women's Weekly* underscores the extent to which gendered norms were reinforced through the reproduction and circulation of texts within texts. As Newell has established, the concern with women's morality was also central to African newspapers in colonial West Africa; thus newspapers "played host to a public moral discourse" (2013, 132) in which women's faults and foibles were aired and debated.

The litany of errant women who appear in this space—flirtatious, fickle, slovenly, superficial, treacherous, drunk, avaricious, controlling, promiscuous, outspoken, and ill-mannered—speaks to a particular racial anxiety: in the context of the politics of assimilation and "racial advancement," the aberrant female is tantamount to racial death. According to Lynn Thomas, the handful of male writers who "framed most of the discussion" in *Bantu World* "were concerned to promote an *AmaRespectable* urban femininity that would distinguish their daughters and wives from the disreputable female figures of the prostitute and skokiaan queen" (2006, 468). To this end, and faithful to the Western model, popular modes of address included the device of the white expert in the form of a doctor or nurse, or the formula of a mother-daughter dialogue in which a (white) mother pro-

---

[4] A similar thematic nexus formed the content of magazines directed at white South African women. As Victoria Kuttainen and Jilly Lippmann show in their chapter in this volume, this was also a popular formula of some women's magazines in Australia and Canada.

8 PROGRESSING WITH A VENGEANCE: THE WOMAN READER/WRITER... 151

vides spiritual and emotional guidance to her black daughters.[5] This relationship would have drawn sustenance from those fostered by mission schools, seminaries, and single woman's hostels (Gaitskell 1979).

The equivocal status of the women's page as a tool of emancipation is indicated by the fact that its unveiling in *The Bantu World*, and thus the invitation for women to enter the world of public print culture, was especially designed to coincide with the launch of a beauty competition. This paradoxical combination is based on the understanding that both forms of journalistic "address," the verbal and the visual, present an opportunity to demonstrate civilized respectability, thus emphasizing the political valency of women's public participation in print culture no matter what form it took. Women's entry into the sphere of print is thus understood as a quintessentially modern gesture, something to be celebrated as "progress" and "uplifting" and as the sign of a receding barbarity (Thomas 2006; Weinbaum et al. 2008). The title given to one of the regular full-page sections of the women's page, 'Page of Interest to Women of the Race,' provides further evidence of the links the paper made between gender and racial advancement (see p. 165).

In the tactical alignment of publicity and modernity, the newspaper went out of its way to encourage women's participation in the paper, seeking also to assuage fears of female immodesty: "Be up and doing daughters of Africa! You have nothing to be ashamed of. Take up your pens and write about yourselves... Go into the open and face the world with your men unashamed, undaunted, determined to emulate your white sisters in all that is noble, true and good" (22 October 1932, 9). Despite the declaration of faith, latent misogyny is also apparent in the writer's hope that the competition would also "encourage some of the careless or lazy to give a little more attention to their toilet" (22 October 1932, 9). The newspaper is thus striking for its unusual alignment of beauty and print as equally resonant signs of racial advance. For the "men behind Bantu World," attractive and carefully groomed women were central to the "project of racial uplift that would connect a 'heroic past' to a politically progressive and commercially vibrant future" (Thomas 2006, 472).

The women's page reveals the contradictory pull of the cult of domesticity and the political value of the racial 'proofs' supplied by the record of

---

[5] For a selection of studies of women's pages and women's magazines, see Ferguson (1983), Ballaster et al. (1991), and Hermes (1995, 2005).

women's achievements in education, social activism, and the world of work. In respect of the latter, the paper published dozens of stories of energetic, successful, and self-sufficient women, particularly those, such as Rilda Marta, Frieda Matthews, and Cecilia Lillian Tshabalala, who had been educated abroad, thus asserting the possibility of meaningful action beyond the domestic realm in opposition to the Western missionary ideal.[6] An early women's page feature, for example, engages the political potential of transnational women's solidarities by celebrating the work of women in India who are described as "entering public life as freely as men. They help the men in their struggles for the people. They despised the comforts of home for the battlefields of life" (24 December 1932, 11). While some writers staged their rights to work and freedom in open defiance of patriarchal norms, other working women used the newspaper to negotiate an acceptable compromise, seeking to develop more progressive, public roles for women within patriarchal understandings. In many instances, the terrain of struggle was managed by an extension of their roles of selfless domestic service and wifely duty into service for the community. Through rhetorical appeals to socially accepted values, women were able to pursue their ambitions and desires in ways that offered seeming conformity to socially sanctioned ideas.

Notwithstanding the dominance of the male editress, ordinary women (or at least those writing under female names)[7] were also active participants, something which Thomas' account of the women's page tends to underplay. This involvement is evident in extended debates on the morality of women's work and education, marital relations, *lobola* (bride price), and polygamy. As many eighteenth-century British conduct books attest, early women authors who could not avail themselves of the protection of economic privilege were at pains to justify their unorthodox appearances in print. They did so by adopting the voice of conservative patriarchy, using the space they had claimed to reinforce conventional norms of femininity. They thus justified their own defiance of gender stricture by entrenching those norms for other women (Showalter 1977, 21; Poovey 1984, 42). As I go on to argue, similar patterns of ambiguous conformity

---

[6] For more on Tshabalala and the founding of the organization Daughters of Africa, see Healy-Clancy (2012). See Masola (2018) for a discussion of the "politics of mobility" in relation to *Bantu World*'s coverage of the travels and achievements of prominent African women.

[7] Newell (2013) discusses the problems involving in inferring the gender identity of those who write letters to the press.

are evident in *Bantu World*.[8] Letters and articles by women contributors frequently chimed in with the perspective of the editress, who also launched her own largely didactic column in 1934.

A conservative cultural ethos is evident, for example, in popular writer Johannah G. Phahlane's arguments for the sexual policing of single women and in the numerous complaints about discontented or careless wives, indifferent nursemaids, and powerful skokiaan queens (informal beer-brewers). A particularly spirited example, attributed to Mrs. W. Katie P. Tsolo, gives a sense of what was at stake: "How in the world can we as a race climb the ladder of honour if women of our race keep on giving beer and *segomfana* [hard spirits] to men?... [I]t is a pity because there is no room for me in the Police to help stamping out these pests, pitfalls which befoul our dear and good race. Sisters for the honour and glory of our names, for the honour and betterment of Africa...stop beer making and selling. Am hot and rather serious 'basali'. Our race is blindly going to a cold and lonely grave" (17 February, 10).[9]

While expressing concern for the negative effects of modern mores on women's virtue, many women contributors made a case for women's greater involvement in the public world of men, drawing ideological support from colonial modernity itself and the changing gender roles which it had inspired. In these arguments, echoing the rationalizations of the Christian mission and underscoring a pervasive view of missionaries as rescuers of African women from abusive African men, modern femininity is set against exploitative and degrading indigenous gender practices (Cornwall 2005). In these arguments, colonial modernity is figured as an opening into women's emancipation: "The world in which we live is a different world to that of our grandmothers. The duties of women in those days were to look after her home. A wife was a servant but today she is a helpmate to her husband" (Ramokwena, 30 July 1932, 11). In line with the position of early Western feminists such as Mary Wollstonecraft and Olive Schreiner, the argument for women's emancipation from traditional roles is based on the needs of men and in the interests of the institution of marriage. What is also imagined is a new ideal of companionate marriage based on equality and shared interests.

---

[8] Gadzepko's discussion on women's participation in Ghanaian newspapers (2006) suggests that the argument may also be relevant to the broader African context.

[9] *Basali* is the Sesotho word for women.

154   C. SANDWITH

A further rhetorical strategy in the defence of women's public roles was the alignment of women's work with a national political project of the "advancement of the race." As suggested above, this drew inspiration from the politics of the newspaper more generally; unlike more radical political constituencies at the time, the paper saw assimilation to western norms as a primary route to political and economic rights. In these arguments, women's adoption of non-traditional roles was framed as an attempt to "raise standards." In this way, the political tactic of assimilation and the language of racial progress became important allies in the renegotiation of acceptable female roles and the attempt to re-establish femininity on new grounds. What is also indicated in some of these discussions is a position which bears a close resemblance to what would subsequently be characterized as "womanism," an African-oriented mode of female assertion based on a broader political project and solidarity with African men.

Other examples of the woman's page as a contested negotiated space are evident in how it is almost immediately taken up as a site for the articulation of women's personal stories which, in some respects, pushed the discussion beyond the restrictions of instruction, shaming, and censure. Rossie Khabela, a domestic worker in Johannesburg who wrote in defence of the morality of working women, was a frontrunner in this regard. Khabela describes the financial pressures caused by the death of her father, which, in turn, led to the difficult decision to leave her family home in rural Basotuland to seek work in the city (12 November 1932, 12). Her letter is important for its intimate address, its autobiographical mode, and its strong affective content; it also shifts the conventional voice of authority from the (white or male) expert-professional to the reader herself. As such, Khabela adopts the assertive posture of one who is setting the record straight. In this way, the didactic space of the women's page based on vertical lines of authority and sympathetic patronage is reconfigured on more horizontal lines as a zone of encounter, argument, sharing, support, and solidarity. Arguments in defence of women's work tended to reinforce normative distinctions between "good" women and "bad" ones, a rhetorical formula which, as Antoinette Burton has argued, was also central to the project of colonial modernity (2005, 9). Nevertheless, they made an important adjustment to conservative Western definitions of domestic femininity and exposed the contradictions of the cult of domesticity itself: it was an impossible ideal in a system of racial capitalism that relied on the exploitation of black (female) workers. Interestingly, as a result of this letter, Khabela was installed as a regular contributor to the women's page, thus also suggesting some of the routes through which ordinary women were able to access the world of print (24 December 1932, 10). The same pattern is observed on other occasions, where entertaining letter-writers such as Johannah G. Phahlane (who also wrote under the name "Lady Porcupine"), Dora Msomi, and Mabel Maphumulo were invited to take on more established roles in the paper (Fig. 8.1).

The difficulties in taking up a position in the public sphere, of claiming the authority to write, are evident in the ubiquity of rhetorical gestures of hesitation and apology and the frequent use of pseudonyms. "J.S.D.," for example, concerned that she is "not blessed with the gift of writing," ends her letter with the words, "You see, Mr Editor, I have failed lamentably to convey clearly to your readers what I set out to do. This is my first time to write to a newspaper. So forgive me and rewrite the letter in your own way" (22 April 1933, 11). In other examples, the decision to take up the pen can only be justified on the grounds of powerful feeling: "I am very sorry I cannot write good English or make myself understood but I cannot keep quiet" (3 December 1932, 11). A further noteworthy feature of the protocols of women's address is the frequent deployment of the assertive authorial "I," as in "I am Jessina" or "I am Woman," a device that is also echoed in the trope of speaking and conversation (15 April 1933, 11), mimicking practices of orality. What some of these rhetorical practices suggest is that to write to the paper is not to adopt the position of abstracted social commentator but rather to engage in dialogue with other women; it is, in the words of one correspondent, "to be given a chance to say something to other Bantu girls." What is imagined is an intimate address in which writing is rendered in the oral mode, one that gestures towards female-centred worlds of gossip and sociability. The women's page thus extends the opportunities for female friendship to strangers: "'Bantu World' made us friends without having met in the flesh save in its bright and encouraging columns" (25 March 1933, 12).

Despite interventions of this kind, the mid-1930s saw a more insistent, emotive, and repetitive articulation of conservative Christian norms in the women's page, which led to a pronounced narrowing of the space of debate. The intensifying moral censure, the increased scrutiny of women's behaviour, and the more open expression of misogynist views is perhaps suggestive of a diminution of masculine authority in the world

156   C. SANDWITH

beyond the page. What can be described as femininity under duress, in which the newspaper becomes an important site of social shaming, can also be attributed to the increasing presence of male commentators. At this time, even the usually supportive and affirming editress, who tended to rely on the carrot of the good news story rather than the stick of moral judgement, was moved to take on a more explicitly admonishing role. *Bantu World* journalist Walter Nhlapo, for example, was a particularly outspoken advocate for male moralizing interventions, bolstering a powerful consensus with the cultural capital provided by British writers such as G.K. Chesterton, Robert Herrick, and Edward de Vere. In this context, African women's public interventions had to contend not only with the legacy of the Christian mission and the pressure of "racial advancement," but also with a misogynist Western literary canon. Given the formidable cultural and political resources that were mobilized as checks on unruly women, it is not surprising that many women fell silent or thought it best to ventriloquize the consensual view, thus reinforcing the image of the women's page as a space of conservative articulation. The rarity of contention and questioning in this context makes the existence of such interventions all the more significant. It is to these cracks in the cultural dominant that I turn to in the concluding sections of this chapter.

Several women correspondents take issue with the patriarchal consensus in *Bantu World*, adopting modes of speech that are surprisingly outspoken, angry, dismissive, and direct, in marked distinction from the decorous femininity advocated elsewhere. In her spirited reply to the conservative prescriptions of one male correspondent, Dora Msomi writes: "I say he is talking nonsense; he is one of the location big bugs so should concentrate his attention there ...[His] utterances are not worth more than a grain of sand" (24 February 1934, 10). Another signing herself "A Woman" concurs: "It is getting into our nerves this criticism of us in the papers by men... All they are waiting for is to see some unfortunate woman in error and then they rush to the Press" (10 March 1934, 10). The occasional open confrontation of gendered oppression, "sex prejudice," and male brutality, and the questioning of the cult of domesticity, were also significant. In letters such as these, men rather than women become the focus of hostile and unflattering scrutiny. As "Pietermaritzburg Woman" declared, "[Men] have still got the repressive spirit of driving their women back to servility. They actually think a women's place is in the home" (5 May 1934, 11). Reacting to a particularly heated debate on the behaviour of African nursemaids, Jane Melato draws attention to the racialized context generally occluded in discussions of African women's morality: "It is all right for you to put all the blame on the girls who are employed in European households. But what about the way they are treated? The girl is treated no better than a slave" (30 June 1934, 10). Some readers went as far as to contest the middle-class ideals on which modern femininity in *Bantu World* was based; thus, Mrs. P.T. Teeiso takes "Lady Porcupine" to task for her "stiff," high-flown language, suggesting that the domestic ideal, which she describes in her articles on household management does not match the conditions of most African women: "We have no such amenities madame"; Lady Porcupine should "write on easy subjects which touch on our everyday worries and aims" (11 August 1934, 11).

Two other interventions are worth highlighting, the first from the equivocal Johannah G. Phahlane/"Lady Porcupine" and another particular favourite of the women's page, Ellen Pumla Ngozwana, who submitted articles under the pen-name "Pat." Joining in a growing demand for women's right to work, "Lady Porcupine" dismisses the view that women will be "unsexed" by their entry into male professions, pointing to the many instances of men doing "women's work" with no apparent ill effects. Even so, "every silly clown of a fellow begins to cackle when a cultured and capable woman claims the right to take part in the control of a municipality or state" (30 May 1936, 12). She concludes with a suggestive argument about the distinction between flesh-and-blood women and the constructions of men's fantasy: "If women ever became masculine by becoming logical and ethical, they would no longer be such good material for men's projection" (30 May 1936, 12).

Ngozwana's interventions stand out for the questions she raises about conventional missionary narratives of women's emancipation from African tradition. An article published in 1934 in celebration of the achievements of Frieda Matthews argues that "women are simply progressing with a vengeance" (9 June 1934, 11). Her celebration of what she calls the "triumph of feminism" (9 June 1934, 11) makes an explicitly negative comparison between African women's lives in pre-colonial societies and those facing women in 1930s South Africa: "Some people…believe that the black woman was a slave to her husband, and was treated as such. This is not a true statement as women, even in primitive society, had her own world in which she reigned supreme." While a woman "in primitive society…was given her own sphere in which she moved and was her own mistress," the modern African woman does not have "sufficient scope…to develop" (18 May 1936, 13) (Fig. 8.2).

Fig. 8.2 Women's Page Supplement (Additional Page), *Bantu World* May 1936. (Courtesy of University of Johannesburg Special Collections)

3 Conclusion

My reading of the woman's page in *Bantu World* has emphasized the extent to which it encouraged a hitherto largely silent population of African women readers to enter into the public world of print, thus estab-

8 PROGRESSING WITH A VENGEANCE: THE WOMAN READER/WRITER... 159

lishing its importance as an early or preliminary locale for later traditions of women's literary-cultural expression. This new modern female constituency, navigating complex ideological terrain, both reinforced and questioned dominant norms. In another chapter in this book, Arti Minocha raises questions about the appropriateness of straightforward or unilinear narratives of the arrival and impact of European modernity in colonial contexts, arguing that they cannot do justice to the often muddled, uneven, and contradictory processes and practices that ensued. *The Bantu World* women's page provides further evidence that normative Western print genres and the women's page in particular, were not simply reproduced or mimicked in African spaces but rather became sites of improvisation, refashioning, and indigenization. In *Bantu World*, African women developed an alternative print cultural practice by introducing the modes of orality, autobiography, and affect; they brought subtle alterations in tone, speech styles, performance, and linguistic texture to a space defined by male rationality; and they reconceptualized the rhetoric of women's print not as a site of motherly didacticism and social shaming, but rather as a locus of female friendship, sharing, assertion, and encounter.

In addition, far from being an unequivocal site for the reinforcement of exemplary modern femininity, the women's page offered an ambiguous and often fractious space in which prevailing gender norms could be tested and challenged. Women readers/writers of this period had to contend not only with the constraints of tradition and the latent sex prejudice of an "amarespectable" African nationalist politics, but also with a misogynist western culture that had been yoked to the sign of emancipation. For some women contributors, these contradictions led to a productive questioning and undermining of these normative ideological projects; in this sense, the articulation of African modernity is derived from a "complex process of navigating various identities and places" (Masola 2018, 10).[10] In the face of a potentially debilitating gender consensus in particular, African women readers and writers made judicious selections from both a modern feminist repertoire and a pre-colonial past, thus opening a space for a distinctive African, female-centred culture of print, an alternative modernity, which sought to refashion the cultural dominant to new and more emancipatory ends. In this way, the paper became an important site for the development of distinctive new models of African feminism in solidarity with men and a space in which alternative modes of resistance could be improvised. Along

[10] Arti Minocha, in this volume, makes a similar point about the dialectical tension between existing modes of subjectivity.

160   C. SANDWITH

with the work of Ruth Bush (2017) and Victoria Kuttainen and Jilly Lippmann (in this volume), my reading of *Bantu World* provides further confirmation of the historical importance of women's periodicals and pages in the scripting of an alternative, female-oriented modernity.

WORKS CITED

Ballaster, Ros, Margaret Beetham, Elizabeth Frazer, and Sandra Hebron. 1991. *Women's Worlds: Ideology, Femininity and the Woman's Magazine*. London: Macmillan.

Bonner, Phil. 1990. 'Desirable or Undesirable Basotho Women?' Liquor, Prostitution and the Migration of Basotho Women to the Rand, 1920–1945. In *Women and Gender in Southern Africa to 1945*, ed. Cheryl Walker, 22–50. Cape Town: David Philip.

Bozzoli, Belinda, and Mmantho Nkotsoe. 1991. *Women of Phokeng: Consciousness, Life Strategy, and Migrancy in South Africa, 1900–1983*. London: Heinemann.

Brown, Duncan. 2004. 'My Pen is the Tongue of a Skilful Poet': African-Christian Identity and the Poetry of Nontsizi Mgqwetho. *English in Africa* 31 (1): 23–58.

———. 2008. 'Modern Prophets, Produce a New Bible': Christianity, Africanness and the Poetry of Nontsizi Mgqwetho. *Current Writing: Text and Reception in Southern Africa* 20 (2): 77–91.

Bryce, Jane. 1997. A Life on the Women's Page: Treena Kwenta's Diary. In *Writing African Women: Gender, Popular Culture and Literature in West Africa*, ed. Stephanie Newell, 47–66. London: Zed Books.

Burton, Antoinette. 2005. Introduction: The Unfinished Business of Colonialism. In *Gender, Sexuality and Colonial Modernities*, ed. Antoinette Burton, 1–10. New York/London: Routledge.

Bush, Ruth. 2017. 'Mesdames, il faut lire!' ['Ladies, you must read!']: Material Contexts and Representational Strategies in the First Francophone African Women's Magazine. *Francosphères* 5 (2): 213–236.

Cock, Jacklyn. 1990. Domestic Service and Education for Domesticity: The Incorporation of Xhosa Women into Colonial Society. In *Women and Gender in Southern Africa to 1945*, ed. Cheryl Walker, 76–96. Cape Town: David Philip.

Comaroff, Jean, and John L. Comaroff. 1986. Christianity and Colonialism in South Africa. *American Ethnologist* 13 (1): 1–22.

———. 2008. *Of Revelation and Revolution: Christianity, Colonialism, and Consciousness in South Africa*. Vol. 1. Chicago: University of Chicago Press.

———. 2009. *Of Revelation and Revolution: The Dialectics of Modernity on a South African Frontier*. Vol. 2. Chicago: University of Chicago Press.

Cornwall, Andrea. 2005. Introduction: Perspectives on Gender in Africa. In *Readings in Gender in Africa*, ed. Andrea Cornwall, 1–19. Oxford/Bloomington: James Currey/Indiana University Press.

8 PROGRESSING WITH A VENGEANCE: THE WOMAN READER/WRITER... 161

Couzens, Tim. 1974. The Continuity of Black Literature in South Africa before 1950. *English in Africa* 1 (2): 11–23.

———. 1976. A Short History of 'The World' (and Other Black South African Newspapers). Paper Presented at the African Studies Seminar, University of the Witwatersrand, June 6–26.

Daymond, Margaret J., Dorothy Driver, Sheila Meintjes, Leloba Molema, Cheidza Muszengzi, Margie Orford, and Nobantu Rasebotsa, eds. 2003. *Women Writing Africa: The Southern Region*. Vol. 1. New York: The Feminist Press at CUNY.

Donovan, Josephine. 1990. The Silence is Broken. In *Feminist Critique of Language: A Reader*, ed. Deborah Cameron, 41–55. London/New York: Routledge.

Ferguson, Marjorie. 1983. *Forever Feminine: Women's Magazines and the Cult of Femininity*. London: Heinemann.

Gadzepko, Audrey. 2005. The Hidden History of Women in Ghanaian Print Culture. In *African Gender Studies: A Reader*, ed. Oyèrónkẹ́ Oyěwùmí, 279–296. New York/Basingstoke: Palgrave Macmillan.

———. 2006. Public but Private: A Transformational Reading of the Memoirs and Newspaper Writings of Mercy Foulkes-Crabbe. In *African's Hidden Histories: Everyday Literacy and Making of the Self*, ed. Karen Barber, 314–336. Indiana: Indiana University Press.

Gaitskell, Deborah. 1979. 'Christian Compounds for Girls': Church Hostels for African Women in Johannesburg, 1907–1970. *Journal of Southern African Studies* 6 (1): 44–69.

———. 1983. Housewives, Maids or Mothers: Some Contradictions of Domesticity for Christian women In Johannesburg, 1903–39. *The Journal of African History* 24 (2): 241–256.

Hancock, Mary. 2001. Home Science and the Nationalization of Domesticity in Colonial India. *Modern Asian Studies* 35 (4): 871–903.

Hansen, Karen Tranberg. 1992. *African Encounters with Domesticity*. New Brunswick: Rutgers University Press.

Healy-Clancy, Meghan. 2012. Women and the Problem of Family in Early African Nationalist History and Historiography. *South African Historical Journal* 64 (3): 450–471.

———. 2013. *A World of Their Own: A History of South African Women's Education*. Charlottesville: University of Virginia Press.

Hermes, Joke. 1995. *Reading Women's Magazines: An Analysis of Everyday Media Use*. Cambridge: Polity Press.

———. 2005. *Re-reading Popular Culture*. Malden: Blackwell Publishing.

Jaji, Tsitisi Ella. 2014. *Africa in Stereo: Modernism, Music, and Pan-African Solidarity*. Oxford: Oxford University Press.

Locher-Scholten, Elsbeth. 2010. *Women and the Colonial State: Essays on Gender and Modernity in the Netherlands Indies 1900–1942*. Amsterdam: Amsterdam University Press.

Masola, Athambile. 2018. 'Bantu Women on the Move': Black Women and the Politics of Mobility in *The Bantu World*. *Historia* 63 (1): 93–111.

Mutongi, Kenda. 2009. 'Dear Dolly's' Advice: Representations of Youth, Courtship and Sexualities in Africa, 1960 to 1980. In *Love in Africa*, eds. Jennifer Cole and Lynn M. Thomas, 83–108. Chicago/London: University of Chicago Press.

Newell, Stephanie. 1997. *Writing African Women: Gender, Popular Culture, and Literature in West Africa*. London: Zed Books.

———. 2000. *Ghanaian Popular Fiction: "Thrilling Discoveries in Conjugal Life" and Other Tales*. London: James Currey.

———. 2002. *Literary Culture in Colonial Ghana: "How to Play the Game of Life"*. Manchester: Manchester University Press.

———. 2005. Devotion and Domesticity: The Reconfiguration of Gender in Popular Christian Pamphlets from Ghana and Nigeria. *Journal of Religion in Africa* 35 (3): 296–323.

———. 2013. *The Power to Name: A History of Anonymity in Colonial West Africa*. Athens: Ohio University Press.

———. 2016. Afterword. In *African Print Cultures: Newspapers and Their Publics in the Twentieth Century*, ed. Derek R. Peterson, Emma Hunter, and Stephanie Newell, 425–434. Ann Arbor: University of Michigan Press.

Newell, Stephanie, and Audrey Gadzepko, eds. 2004. *Selected Writings of a Pioneer West African Feminist*. Nottingham: Trent Editions.

Newell, Stephanie, and Okome Onookome, eds. 2013. *Popular Culture in Africa: The Episteme of the Everyday*. London/New York: Routledge.

Opland, Jeff, ed. 2007. *The Nation's Bounty: The Xhosa Poetry of Nontsizi Mgqwetho*. Johannesburg: Witwatersrand University Press.

Peterson, Derek R., Emma Hunter, and Stephanie Newell, eds. 2016. *African Print Cultures: Newspapers and Their Publics in the Twentieth Century*. Ann Arbor: University of Michigan Press.

Poovey, Mary. 1984. *The Proper Lady and the Woman Writer: Ideology as Style in the Works of Mary Wollstonecraft, Mary Shelley and Jane Austen*. Chicago: University of Chicago Press.

Sandwith, Corinne. 2014. *World of Letters: Reading Communities and Cultural Debates in Early Apartheid South Africa*. Pietermaritzburg: University of KwaZulu-Natal Press.

Scanlon, Jennifer. 1995. *Inarticulate Longings: The Ladies' Home Journal, Gender and the Promises of Consumer Culture*. New York: Routledge.

Schreiner, Olive. 1975. *Woman and Labour*. 1911. Edited and Introduced by Adèlemarie van der Spuy and Adriaan S. van der Spuy. Johannesburg: Cosmos Publications.

Shevelow, Kathryn. 1989. *Women and Print Culture: The Construction of Femininity in the Early Periodical*. London/New York: Routledge.

Showalter, Elaine. 1977. *A Literature of Their Own: British Women Novelists from Brontë and Lessing*. Princeton: Princeton University Press.

Switzer, Les. 1988. *Bantu World* and the Origins of a Captive African Commercial Press in South Africa. *Journal of Southern African Studies* 14 (3): 351–370.

———. 1997. *South Africa's Alternative Press: Voices of Protest and Resistance, 1880s–1960*. Cambridge: Cambridge University Press.

Switzer, Les, and Donna Switzer, eds. 1979. *The Black Press in South Africa and Lesotho: A Descriptive Bibliographic Guide to African, Coloured and Indian Newspapers, Newsletters and Magazines, 1836–1976*. Boston: G.K. Hall.

Thomas, Lynn M. 2006. The Modern Girl and Racial Respectability in 1930s South Africa. *The Journal of African History* 47 (3): 461–490.

———. 2009. Love, Sex, and the Modern Girl in 1930s Southern Africa. In *Love in Africa*, eds. Jennifer Cole and Lynn M. Thomas, 31–57. Chicago: University of Chicago Press.

Venter, Isabella. 2014. *The South African Lady's Pictorial and Home Journal* as a Subtle Agent of Change for British South African Women's View of Race Relations in Southern Africa. *Critical Arts: A South-North Journal of Cultural & Media Studies* 28 (5): 828–856.

Weinbaum, Alys Eve, Lynn M. Thomas, Priti Ramamurthy, Uta G. Poiger, Madelaine Y. Dong, and Tami E. Barlow, eds. 2008. *The Modern Girl Around the World: Consumption, Modernity, and Globalization*. Durham/London: Duke University Press.

Wilson, Monica, and Archie Mafeje. 1963. *Langa: A Study of Social Groups in an African Township*. Cape Town: Oxford University Press.

Wollstonecraft, Mary. 1975. *Vindication of the Rights of Woman*. 1792, ed. Miriam Brody Kramnick. Harmondsworth: Penguin.

CHAPTER 9

Fashioning the Self: Women and Transnational Print Networks in Colonial Punjab

Arti Minocha

1 Introduction

This chapter examines print cultures in colonial Punjab in the late nineteenth and early twentieth centuries as gendered spaces that possibly offered new subject positions and modes of articulation to middle-class women. Available print histories of Punjab have adopted closed, spatial frameworks of province or nation and have consequently produced isolated accounts rather than recording the vibrancy of cross-cultural exchange and influence. Print histories have also focussed on literature generated by reform organizations within Punjab and have aligned print with the emergence of communal and national identities. This chapter considers cross-cultural exchanges in the nineteenth-century colonial context as important to the formation of women's identities rather than relegating them only to communal, provincial, and national print histories. It gestures towards influences and networks, facilitated by technology, between women in

---

A. Minocha (✉)
Lady Shri Ram College, Delhi University, New Delhi, India
e-mail: artiminocha@lsr.edu.in

© The Author(s) 2020   165
R. Aliakbari (ed.), *Comparative Print Culture*, New Directions in
Book History, https://doi.org/10.1007/978-3-030-36891-3_9

166   A. MINOCHA

India, outside of their own provincial and national locations, as well as print cultures outside India. It takes into account the mutual influence of travel, commercial publishing, print networks, and "cultural flows" (Appadurai and Breckenridge 1995, 10) between the colonies and the imperial centre on public and print spheres and identity formation.

The cultural terrain of nineteenth-century Punjab, one of the last Indian provinces to be acquired by the British in 1849, was marked by the emergence of multiple publics[1] that successfully used commercial print to negotiate religious identities, solidarities, and civic concerns. The presence of women in these print cultures has been largely overlooked in literary and print historiographies of colonial Punjab, and it has been assumed that women in Punjab were largely framed and recast through colonial and reform discourses while they themselves did not participate as active agents in these print spheres. However, archival evidence indicates that women inhabited and influenced print cultures in multiple ways, as writers, readers, listeners, and consumers of print. This chapter seeks to counter the erasure of women from print histories of Punjab and address the question of their agency through a specific example of one of the first Punjabi (the region, not the language) novels in English by a woman, discussed in the context of the emergence of print publics in Punjab.

Susila Tahl Ram's *Cosmopolitan Hinduani: Depicting Muhammadan and Hindu Life and Thought in Story Form* was published in Lahore in 1902 by the Civil and Military Gazette Press, owned by Dr. Arthur Neve (see *Report*, 1902), sole contractor for printing to the Punjab government. Its publication exemplifies how the nascent print sphere opened up a range of possibilities for women rather than merely containing them.

---

[1] Vivek Bhandari (2007) refers to print publics in Punjab as "multiple publics." See also Neeladri Bhattacharya (2005) who characterizes the publics in Punjab as trying to achieve consensus on the one hand and reaffirming community identities on the other. He refers to them as "fractured" publics (143) and "incommensurable" publics (144). The plural used here suggests that there were various competing and contending groups claiming to represent public interest rather than a singular one. The print space was an important representational space that opened up, especially in the nineteenth-century India, when the medium of print came into the hands of private individuals rather than being monopolized by the colonial state. This space allowed for the generation of public opinion on issues that were perceived as "common good" through debates and discussions in newspapers, periodicals, books and pamphlets. Though ideally accessible to all, the print space consisted of groups and communities with different interests, powers of negotiation and accessibility to the print medium. The communities that constituted these publics are discussed further in this chapter in Sect. 2.

9 FASHIONING THE SELF: WOMEN AND TRANSNATIONAL PRINT... 167

This chapter investigates how Tahl Ram articulates her claim to a modern, cosmopolitan, gendered identity and inserts herself within the emerging print publics. It also discusses the literary and linguistic practices through which the novel's narrator enunciates a self-fashioning that she describes as cosmopolitan.

The formation of publics and print publics and their role in imagining a nation have long been understood according to the influential Eurocentric models of Benedict Anderson and Jurgen Habermas, and more recently through Elizabeth Eisenstein's monumental *The Printing Press as an Agent of Change*. Recent scholarship on print cultures in South Asia has rescripted the story from the narratives of a unilinear flow of European modernity to the colonies, the rupture in indigenous oral and scriptural traditions brought about by print, and even, arguably, the imagining of the nation according to normative European models.[2] The story of the arrival of modernity and formation of publics in colonial Indian contexts is complex and must take into account power relationships inherent in cross-cultural encounters, scriptural practices, literary markets across borders, specificities of location, and transregional and transnational networks. In other words, and as the Introduction to this volume argues, the story of modernity must be "provincialized."

Print cultures acquired trajectories of their own as new technology met with specific cultural, literary, and linguistic practices. Print technologies were not merely indigenized, translated and amalgamated into pre-print intellectual formations and scriptural and oral cultures, but were also actively mobilized to project newer identities into transnational print publics. Therefore, scholars have expressed the need for a revisionary history of South Asian print that needs to be "viewed through critical, postcolonial eyes" (Fraser 2008, 14).

2 THE CONTEXT OF THE NOVEL

This section briefly discusses the cultural and political context of late-nineteenth-century Punjab and the communities that constituted the "multiple publics" referred to above. The latter part of the nineteenth century in Punjab was marked by exigencies of identity politics and religious

---

[2] Scholars who have questioned the normativity of Eurocentric models in the context of South Asian print culture include Robert Fraser, J. Barton Scott, Sandria Freitag, Francesca Orsini, Veena Naregal, Vinay Dharwadkar, Arjun Appadurai, Abhijit Gupta and Swapan Chakravorty.

168   A. MINOCHA

divisions between the Sikhs, Hindus, and Muslims, which were expressed in the print wars enacted by the reformist presses of the Arya Samaj (founded in 1875 by Dayanand Saraswati), the Singh Sabha (founded in 1873) and the Ahmaddiya movement (founded in 1889). These reform groups tried to create seemingly homogeneous religious communities with identifiable cultural markers and social practices, one standardized language for each community, and institutional affiliations for each religion.

The classificatory needs of the colonial state were also instrumental in reorganizing the boundaries of communities in Punjab. The use of particular cultural referents such as language, appearance, devotional practices, marriage practices, and personal laws to identify specific communities made it easy to receive benefits of employment and land that the state gave to particular communities. In the context of Punjab, Neeladri Bhattacharya has argued that "the process of the emergence of the autonomous, reason-bearing individual was cross-cut by an alternative process through which community identities were reworked and reaffirmed" (154). This period of new caste, class and religious formations also saw the consolidation of the burgeoning middle class, which found new opportunities in the fields of education, administration, judiciary, and trade, and used "the associational sphere to postulate its own hegemonic claims" (Stark 2007, 146). Most of these efforts at public good or public spirit centred on access to press, books, education, and the printed word, all of which were important in the creation of modern, middle-class and masculine identities.

Gradually, the "modernizing" middle-class elite wrested the initiative of reform from the colonial state and claimed their right to decide their cultural practices and laws, especially regarding women. Women's bodies, cultural practices, and relationships to the public sphere became discursive arenas in the establishment of class, caste, and religious identities. Print was therefore an important medium through which women entered public discourse and the changing ideas of public space in the nineteenth century. Anxiety over women's conduct and relationships to the public sphere is evident from the titles mentioned in the *Reports on Publications* published by the colonial government and the quarterly catalogues of books registered in Punjab under Act XXV of 1867 and Act X of 1890.[3]

---

[3] Some of these include *Strishiksha* ("The Education of Women"), *Istriyon ka Pahrawa* ("The Attire of Women"), *Fashiondaar Rannaa* ("Fashionable Women"), *Istri Sudhar* ("The Reform of Women"), *Sushikshita Istri* ("The Educated Woman"), *Istri Chikitsa* ("The Medical Treatment of Women"), *Patibrat Dharma* ("The Code of Loyalty to Husband"), and *Istriyon ke Jeevan Charitra* ("Biographies of Women").

2.1 Women and the Print Sphere in Punjab

In order to imagine how women may have inhabited these print spheres, it is important to examine some of their key features. What appears to be inexplicable is that despite low rates of literacy,[4] colonial north India still enjoyed a publishing boom in the 1860s and 1870s. *Reports on Publications* in Punjab from 1867 onwards indicate that the market was inundated with newspapers, periodicals and cheap forms of publication such as pamphlets, tracts, and *qissas* (oral narratives or stories) that ran into thousands of print runs and had an extensive reach. These pamphlets were used by Hindu, Muslim, and Sikh reform organizations to carry out bitter campaigns against each other. Evidence from Punjab proves that literacy was not a precondition for people in general or women in particular to access print cultures. In accounting for the large number of poetry publications in Punjab, the *Report* of 1886 explains how orality co-existed with, and in fact was, a part of the print culture:

> There is inordinate passion for poetry among educated and illiterate people of the Province. In many of the cities and large towns of the Punjab, especially in and about Delhi, poetical societies called musha'arahs, of which the members assemble periodically to recite their ghazals or other poetical compositions. The highest aspiration of these poets is to gain the applause of auditors. In almost all villages groups of inhabitants assemble to hear poetical recitations, which they enjoy and value as a sort of mental treat.

It was, in fact, these habits of oral discourse and forms of literary and social debate that influenced the success of certain print genres, as the *Report* of 1890 indicates even as it shows apprehension about literary tastes of the "masses":

> Though education has helped much to improve the literary capacity of the Province so far as the middle classes are concerned, the masses are still, to a considerable extent, soaked in ignorance which finds consolation in repeating and hearing metrical love tales, elegiac, didactic and devotional love songs. All this gives birth to a host of small poems forming the bulk of productions classified under the head of "Poetry".

---

[4] The statistics for 1902 indicate that the ratio of girls going to school to the total number of school-aged girls was 1:58 (*Report on Public Instruction in the Punjab and its Dependencies for 1901–1902*, Lahore: The Civil and Military Gazette Press, 1903).

Scholars such as Mir and Orsini have argued that forms of orality and performative traditions also continued to be powerful methods of communication and were realigned into the genres of print cultures. Women's periodicals of the time mention tracts and books read in girls' schools, appeals and tracts distributed at Educational Conferences, pamphlets distributed during *melas* (fairs), newspapers read out to groups of people, and women participating in readings and recitals and encouraging each other to read aloud to other women. These are all examples of oral practices being reinforced by print and bringing a large number of "non-reading" people into the fold of the reading public. In these circumstances, reading a book was not only an individualized and isolated activity, but acquired a "public textuality" (Rhodes 2005, 20) as well.

Middle-class women in Punjab gained material access to publishing and print in the second half of the nineteenth century largely through educational institutions, presses set up by reform organizations, and commercial presses set up by middle-class men. Therefore, their entry into the print economy was initiated, mediated, and legitimized by male reformers of specific religious associations.[5] Even so, access to print and education constituted a new literary sphere for women. One of the modes of subjectivity that became possible on grounds of print was a claim to professional authorship and the *intellectual* work that it involved. For middle-class educated women, inclusion in this sphere of writing also meant cultural power and self-affirmation, as is evident in the case of Susila Tahl Ram.

The desire of women to enter the creative domain and chart their own modern literary evolution can also be seen in the women's periodicals of the time. Although little attention has been paid to this genre of women's writing, periodicals give us a rich account of the first stirrings of political and literary subjectivity of women in the "modern" print sphere.[6] It is this sharing of discursive and material space that facilitated a new kind of gendered consciousness among women who have hardly been considered as "political actors" (Nijhawan 2012, 6) in historical literature. Print was thus disseminated via multiple modes of transmission.

---

[5] On this note, see Corinne Sandwith's essay in this collection, which indicates a similar contradiction for women publishing in *Bantu World* where their insertion into the world of commercial publishing was simultaneously marked by the limitations in the issues they could pursue.

[6] Some examples of these periodicals include *Punjabi Bhain*, *Bharat Bhagini*, *Istri Samachar*, *Panchal Pandita*, *Azad Bhain* and *Indian Ladies Magazine*.

2.2 The Author

An example of such a self-conscious claim to authorship is that of Susila Tahl Ram, about whose life very little can be gleaned from available records. Amar Singh, a Rajput nobleman and officer in the Indian army writes in his diary that Susila Tahl Ram was brought up in England and married Tahl Ram, an Arya Samaj follower who was a "rascal" (Rudolph et al. 2002, 382). She did not want to breach Hindu laws; otherwise, she would have divorced him and gone to England to learn creative writing, which would have given her the status of an author. She did not want to take up employment as a governess or teacher in any royal family in India because the status of an independent writer would have been far more respectable than that of a governess. He records that "once she takes service she cannot be independent. She had been presented to Queen Victoria and if she wanted to be presented again after taking employment she could not" (385). Caught in a web of marriage and middle-class respectability, she chose the path of creative work that would give legitimacy to her as a "public intellectual" and perhaps an income as well.

Amar Singh also noted in his diary that he had received three books written by Susila Tahl Ram from her husband. He would give these books to other officers and then hanker after them to collect money from the sale. Susila Tahl Ram also told him that her husband had either spent his money foolishly or given it to the Arya Samaj (384). In the absence of any records of the reception of her writing, Amar Singh's opinion gives us some clues about her reception by middle-class readers (Fig. 9.1):

> She is an Indian lady brought up in England. She writes beautiful Hindi and the book [*Uttam Acharan Shiksha*] too is a good one.... *Cosmopolitan Hinduani* ... is a very nice book indeed. The author is an Indian lady, but her style of writing English is just as good as that of most of the Englishmen. The stories are very good and there is one that is exceptionally real and life-like. This is about a man being married to a young girl and afterwards of their great love and the jealousy of the mother-in-law, that is simply a charming story. (382)

Susila Tahl Ram resurfaced in print again in a few articles in *The Indian Ladies Magazine* and reports written in Hindi for a Jullundar girls' orphanage. In a brief memoir, "First Impressions of Zenana Life," published in *The Indian Ladies Magazine* in 1902, she narrates her experiences on the streets of Benaras when she returns after a seven-year stay in London.

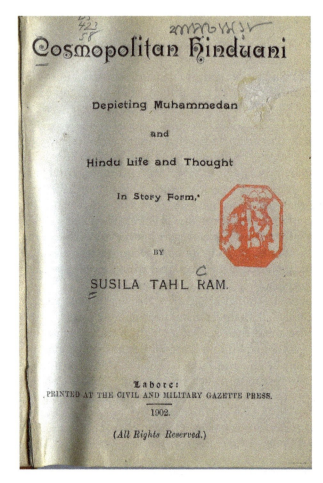

Fig. 9.1 The facsimile of the original cover page of *Cosmopolitan Hinduani*

Zenana women would peep through holes in the walls and scream out to her as she walked through the lanes of Benaras because they wanted contact with the world outside. The listless and confined lives of these bright and intelligent women perhaps inspired a fictional transformation of the vagaries of the present into a readable, finite and hopeful future in the form of this novel.

The Indian Ladies Magazine, published in Madras by Kamala Satthianadhan, was a conscious attempt to build transregional print networks among women. However, the exclusivity and elitism of such print networks is evident in Satthianadhan's comment on her intended audience:

> a considerable number of daughters of India are taking advantage of the opportunities afforded them of a liberal English education, some of them even succeeding in winning University honours. The future of the women of India rests largely with this educated class; and more especially with those belonging to it, who, without losing what is distinctly Indian, have come under the best influences of the West. (Editorial in *The Indian Ladies Magazine*, Vol. 1, July 1901- June 1902)

In the novel *Cosmopolitan Hinduani*, the confidence that this statement expresses becomes a self-conscious anxiety over claiming a representational status that undergirds the articulation of the "New Woman" of the nineteenth century.

2.3   The Plot of the Novel

It is in the context of the reconstitution of religious communities described above that the novel *Cosmopolitan Hinduani* declares its intent to rise above the narrow provincial and communal anxieties and identity politics of that time. It does so by claiming a cosmopolitan outlook, as embodied in its title. The word "Hinduani" in the title of the novel attaches a locally grounded and gendered identity to religion, which was an important marker of identity at that time. The two terms in the title may appear antithetical given the assumption that cosmopolitanism, a concept largely grounded in European political theory, is understood as a desire to establish transnational connections and aspire to world citizenship and is, therefore, inimical to territorial or communitarian boundaries.

How, then, does one reconcile the seemingly local embeddedness of the Hinduani with the expansiveness of the cosmopolitan? How do the ideas of education, home, and marriage that belong to a personal domain connect with the cosmopolitan worldview of a woman in the early twentieth century? The cosmopolitanism that Tahl Ram envisages in the novel is a desire to script a new modernity for Punjabi women of the late nineteenth and early twentieth centuries through education, cultural experience of the West, mobility, renegotiated domesticity and marriage, and a transnational sisterhood.

Consciously employing tropes of the European realist novel such as the omniscient narrator and realistic narrative, Tahl Ram tells the story of Rose Green, an Anglo-Indian woman in late-nineteenth-century Zinatabad in colonial Punjab, and her cousin, Dilawar Jung, with whom she has grown up. Zinatabad is the context for political intrigues, love relationships and associations between the British and the Indians. The novel begins as a love story and is simultaneously placed within the popular literary traditions of the *Bagh-O-Bahar* (tales by Amir Khusro, the title was translated as "Garden and Spring" by Duncan Forbes in 1857) and the *qissa*.

In one of the subplots of the novel, Dilawar's love interest, Rose, is deceived into marrying Yusuf, a cunning upstart with access to the local princely household and the British Residency. At the Residency, Rose is introduced to Amar Devi, daughter of Rai Gyan Chand, who took his daughter to England after the death of his wife and who studied at St. John's, Cambridge while keeping terms at the Inner Temple. Amar Devi's education was also overseen by an Irish professor's wife. The novel presents a differentiated middle class that includes both servile sycophants such as Yusuf, who hanker after power, and well-meaning people such as Rai Gyan Chand and Amar Devi, who have benefited from education and cultural exposure to the West.

The central character, Amar Devi, articulates the idea of a "New Woman" (Tahl Ram 1902, 172). Her amiability and warm hospitality aim at bringing together "the English, the Hindu and the Mohammedan" (58). Her cosmopolitanism is an attempt to transcend the fault lines of religion and caste and establish a liberal and modern subjectivity for women while remaining Hindu. Her cosmopolitanism seems to be set between two seemingly contradictory worldviews: on the one hand, an individual need to better herself, itself a result of her travel and exposure to the West; and on the other, her desire to define a collective politics of Indian womanhood with a transnational reach. The plot follows Rose's torturous marriage and the growing love between Amar Devi and Ugarsen Sarma, whose tender masculinity makes him acceptable to her; they are about to be married as the novel ends. Amar Devi intervenes in circumstances that are oppressive for women and the lower castes, and is instrumental in suggesting ameliorative, rational and progressive measures.

The novel refutes ideas of a woman's progress and liberation claimed by both the colonial administration and the reformist movements. The narrative indicts the reformers in Punjab, both implicitly and explicitly, for having failed to touch the lives of women. Nand Kumar, a pleader "whose voice ominously rolled from the Bar to the platform of the Congress" (191) but is silent when his father compares young girls to dangerous "bundles of snakes" who "must necessarily be united in wedlock before attaining the remarkable age of twelve" (192), provides a trenchant critique of male reformers. His complicit silence continues through his child-wife Hira's torture at the hands of her mother-in-law and her motherhood at the age of 15.

Mr Egerton, a colonial British patriarch, gives an equally unacceptable response when he offers to rescue Rose from a Muslim husband only to be halted by Rose's rebuke: "And you are gracious enough to hold out the hand of salvation" (111). Tahl Ram makes visible this lived, affective but hidden history of women across religions that neither British "saviours" such as Mr. Egerton nor high-minded Indian reformers could ever fathom, their presumptuousness on women's reform notwithstanding. It posits as an alternative an idea of womanhood that transcends religious, caste, and race barriers, and projects a collective future that may well be more progressive.

2.4 Print Networks and Communities of Affect

The print space allows for the narrative representation of affective communities and nurturing relationships between women that were otherwise regarded with suspicion by patriarchal reformers. The Anglo-Indian Rose, her British friend Mrs. Jenkins, Rose's Muslim aunt Gulzar Begum, and the Hindu Amar Devi come together to give Rose "sunshine and the geniality of her deserted friends" (Tahl Ram 1902, 153) and nurture her physically and emotionally as she recovers from a deceitful marriage. This idealized imagined community or sisterhood, however, can only provide a brief alternative to a society that is marked by class and caste anxieties. Everyday beliefs and practices prescribed as appropriate to modernity encode and structure class, caste, and gender relations in the frame of the novel. Lower-class women and servants visiting the pirs "to see the tamasha" (161) are regarded with suspicion. Having claimed legitimacy to tell women's stories authentically, the narrator is conscious of the disconnection between educated middle-class women and women from other classes and castes.

Although Tahl Ram's cosmopolitan imagination establishes the grounds for British women at the Residency and Indian women to meet, these are nevertheless undermined by race and class differences, making them, at best, only tenuous. Tahl Ram debunks the idea that all British women in India were necessarily progressive and able to relate with Indian women on equal terms. The narrator does not idealize cosmopolitanism, which is undercut by the novel's underlying but visible tensions. The fictional conceptualization of this sisterhood, when forged in concrete historical and political practice, is riddled with contradictions.

Tahl Ram's desire to inscribe herself in a domain outside the provincial and the national can also be seen in the context of the increasing trade in printing and publishing at the end of the nineteenth century, and the increased exchanges between British and Indian women. Tahl Ram's cosmopolitan desire for her novel can also be seen in its interpellation into the circulation of ideas between colonies and the metropolitan centre, which was made possible by the rise in the book trade and print transactions at the end of the nineteenth century, and by the increased possibility of travel. The traffic of print between Punjab and other locations worldwide in the colonial period can be gleaned from oral histories and written accounts of travellers from Punjab to the West (sometimes published in England), records of Indian publications or publications about India sold in England, booklists of foreign publishers such as Macmillan with India-specific titles, autobiographical records and communications between foreign publishers and authors in India, records of social and print networks between locations both within and outside of India, missionary records, and records of "inflammatory" material sent by international post intercepted and proscribed by the Punjab government. These sources provide a large array of materials that demonstrate a mutual influence on identity-formation in colonial locations as well as imperial centres. Catalogues of books produced by British publishing companies in India such as Longman, Macmillan, Allen and Unwin, Trubner, Thacker and Spink, as well as those of publications about India in Britain, stand as evidence of the tremendous interest generated in vernacular languages and literatures and their translations by these publication houses.

Special colonial imprints by foreign publishers also made literary works written by women available to readers in India. Bell's Indian and Colonial Library of Standard Literature and Fiction produced works by Mrs. Oliphant, Mrs. Russell Barrington, Mrs. Alexander, Violet Hunt, Mrs. Hungerford, May Edwood, and others (mentioned in *Thacker's Indian Directory*, 1895). Evidence that these works were read by women can be found in the reviews and opinions of these books published in women's periodicals. Early attempts at the "improvement of taste" of people in Punjab were made via translations of Bengali novels such as *Durgesh Nandini, Chandrakanta, Kusumkumari* and *Fatih-i-Bengal*, and Russian novels including the works of Leo Tolstoy, Maxim Gorky and Anton Chekhov (*Report*, 1910). Translations of European novels included Jules Verne's *Journey to the Centre of the Earth* and *Twenty Thousand Leagues under the Sea*, Daniel Defoe's *Robinson Crusoe* and works by Jonathan Swift, Charles Dickens, Thomas Hardy, Francis Bacon, Ralph Waldo Emerson, Johann Wilhelm von Goethe, Miguel Cervantes and Homer, mostly published by the Khalsa Tract Society. *Thacker's Indian Directories* also provide records of works by women authors from Europe that were available through Bell's Indian and Colonial Library of Standard Literature and Fiction. The success of A.H. Wheeler's Indian Railway Library or "one rupee railway library" books, sold at bookstalls at railway stations, is further evidence of the expanding Indian readership of English texts.

The interest in Indian affairs in England was also manifested in organizations such as the Victoria League, which helped women students from India in London, and the National Indian Association, established by Mary Carpenter in Bristol in 1870, which worked to support Indian students in England and women's education in India. The *Journal of the National Indian Association* (published during 1871–1933 in London and renamed the *Indian Magazine* in 1886) and the *Indian Mirror* frequently carried articles by writers located in India and Britain. Catalogues in *Trubner's American, European and Oriental Literary Records*, published in London, record the sales of language-teaching Primers in many Indian languages such as Persian, Hindi, Sanskrit, and Bengali, published in Roman script for Europeans and for Indian students. Indian travellers and writers whose works had been published in England in the latter part of the nineteenth century, such as Toru Dutt, Manmohan Ghose, B.M. Malabari, T.B. Pandian, W.C. Bonnerjee, Dadabhai Naoroji, and Sarojini Naidu entered British literary and print culture through their fiction, poetry, and travel writing. Travel accounts from Punjab that allow us to glimpse the West through Indian eyes include the writings of Hardevi (1888a, b), Raja Jagatjit Singh (1895), the Maharani of Kapurthala (1953), and Jhinda Ram (1893).

Furthermore, references in women's periodicals of the time indicate that reformers feared contact between British and Indian women. Such an inference can also be made from the writings of British women who worked in Punjab, Mission Reports and Journal Reports, and the accounts of Punjabi women themselves. One of the first conscious attempts at organizing a women's collective in Punjab was that of Sarala Debi (1872–1945), the daughter of Swarnakumari Debi, Rabindranath's sister and editor of *Bharati*, a monthly journal, from 1895. She moved to Punjab in 1905 and founded the Bharat Stri Mahamandal (1910), the first women's organization in India, with "the object of bringing together women of all castes and creeds on the basis of their common interest in the moral material progress of women in India" (Chaudhurani 1911, 345, qtd. in Forbes 1996, 70–71). She imagined a collective that was not only pan-Indian in its organization, but sought to bring women from around the world to help each other:

> Bharat Stri Mahamandal... implies a large community encompassing the whole of India beneath its canopy, thus spreading out a mat to encompass all. Bengali, Hindustani, Marwari, Marathi, South Indian and Punjabi women-- all are invited here. Any woman from any nation, such as Europe, America, Iran, Japan or any other country, those who love India and want progress of women in India and are willing to befriend them, are eligible to join the membership of the Assemblage. (Chaudhurani 2010, 313)

Tahl Ram's envisioned women's community can thus be regarded as a precursor to formal women's organizations in Punjab.

2.5 The New Woman and Cosmopolitanism

Tahl Ram sees the "New Woman" as a socially and politically conscious subject who defines her ethics, needs and desires and does not simply replicate a template of Western liberalism. Although her narrative hints at the systemic nature of oppression, the locus of improvement remains the *individual*. Though some historians have critiqued these emerging ideas of liberal middle-class politics in India as derivative and imitative, my examination counters this decontextualized scepticism[7] and views this attempt not as mimicry but as a dialectical tension between available modes of subjectivity. To aspire for liberalism, therefore, is to claim entry for women into the echelons of power and a place in the nascent public sphere, not merely the replication of an imperial Western project. The

---

[7] Tanika Sarkar (2012), for example, points out in her essay "Wicked Widows": "Liberalism, which developed in an imperial West, nonetheless played a revolutionary role in slave insurrections elsewhere" (86).

novel's cosmopolitan subjectivity declares unhindered mobility without the shackles of patriarchal protectionism, challenges the spatial restrictions and morality that defined middle-class Indian women of that time so that they could become part of public space.

Physical and symbolic acts of mobility become important strategies to frame women's agency and rights to cultural experiences. The protagonist, Amar Devi, travels between Zinatabad, London, Munich, the zenanas, the British Residency, gardens, roads, and various other places in India and abroad, and does so alone. Her free and independent movement can be seen as a fulfilment of her desires rather than the nationalist obligations that would come into play a few years later when women would be called upon to join the Swadeshi movement. Another character, Kusum, critiques reformist notions of women's education as a new means of regulating and structuring their lives. In her interpretation, the reformist idea of education "desires us to know enough chemistry to keep the pots boiling, and geography enough to know the different rooms in the house. Yes, to be sure, no better than accomplished cooks and play-things of men" (183). The novel shows that the promise of liberalism and modernity may create an illusion of freedom and thus produce willing subjects, but Kusum's critique is countered by a complex variety of responses from women themselves within the novel.

These fraught responses were echoed by early women's organizations such as the All India Women's Conference (1926), the Women's Indian Association (1917), and the National Council for Women in India, Bharat Stri Mahamandal (1910, Lahore). The cosmopolitan modernity on which such early twentieth-century organizations were modelled often used the language of liberalism to demand women's rights, but this modernity was, nevertheless, shot through with questions of class and caste. In this respect, Tahl Ram's novel anticipates the responses of these institutions to the "women's question".

The novel consciously defines cosmopolitanism from the fringe, reveals a hidden history and experience, and offers a counter-narrative to cosmopolitanism as it was defined in metropolitan Europe. Tahl Ram thus speaks to the critical shift to what has been called "provincialized cosmopolitanism" (Bhambra 2011, 314) that drew attention to the plurality of cosmopolitan practices in non-Western and colonial contexts. *Cosmopolitan Hinduani* was written in the context of literary and political models, mostly male, of cosmopolitan and "progressive" networks. Nauroji's cosmopolitan model in Tahl Ram's contemporary context was more visibly

180 A. MINOCHA

political and was made possible by education, political contacts, and affiliations with organizations and people in the metropolitan centre. His liberal, cosmopolitan subject position was not incompatible with his liberal nationalism (Regan-Lefebvre 2009, 4). Similarly, Annie Besant's use of the discourse of universal human rights to conceptualize the rights of women was compatible with her ideas of Hindu revivalism. Figures such as Dadabhai Nauroji, Josephine Butler, a campaigner for the repeal of Contagious Diseases Act in Britain and India, Annie Besant, and Margaret and James Cousins exemplified cosmopolitan networks that were redefining relations between the ruler and the colonial subjects and in locations not necessarily in India.

2.6 Location in Hinduism

In the context of attempts by religious and reform organizations in Punjab to preserve tradition and vernacularity on the backs of women (Pollock 2002, 53), Tahl Ram's appropriation of cosmopolitan practices can be seen as an attempt to rewrite modernity from women's point of view. Yet this cosmopolitan modernity of Amar Devi must simultaneously hold on to a local Hindu affiliation to mark its identity and cultural difference from the West. At the end of the nineteenth century, when social reform legislation initiated by the colonial state, such as the Age of Consent Act of 1891 and the Rakhmabai case of 1884, aroused protests from revivalists who believed that those legislations interfered with Hindu customs and threatened to anglicize women, Amar Devi's identity within Hinduism would perhaps have given her cosmopolitan desires more respectability. The danger of being ostracized as a deracinated cosmopolitan in a society that was increasingly anxious about defining a "Hindu" identity would have presented itself as a very real possibility to Tahl Ram. The simultaneity of a cosmopolitan consciousness located within the Hindu religion becomes clear towards the end of the novel when another subplot involving low-caste characters is resolved by their inclusion in the fold of a liberal Hinduism. Hinduism thus becomes a benevolent, expansive universalism with a cosmopolitan past rather than a definite set of practices. The "Hinduani" is more a turn towards civic subjecthood than a revivalist claim of authentic religious identity, made current, for example, in Dayanand Saraswati's *Satyarth Prakash* (1875).

2.7 The Choice of Language

The choice of language is always a cultural matter and is instrumental to the expression of identity. Especially in the context of colonial Punjab, language was entangled with issues of modernity and religious identities. Tahl Ram's choice of English as the language for her novel seems to also be a conscious choice of audience that is instrumental to the conception of cosmopolitanism she outlines. *Cosmopolitan Hinduani* seeks to address audiences outside the province and the nation. Local terms are explained to readers who may not be familiar with local practices, for example, "Aftab Jan arrived accompanied by two men, one of whom she addresses as Qazi – a priest who ratifies marriages among Muhammadans" (Tahl Ram 1902, 35). Apart from seeking social networks and audiences, Tahl Ram's use of English for her novel perhaps serves as an entrance into the discursive space of English language and literature, thus consciously inter-pellating it into a field in which networks of the print, the social reach of language and community formation coalesce.

In its first publication, the only one to be recorded in the official "Catalogues of Books" printed in Punjab; a thousand copies were printed at a sale price of three rupees, a considerably high price for books at the time. The price of the book indicates that it was disseminated among mid-dle- and upper-class Western-educated readers, as well as the British in India.

2.8 The Genre of the Novel

The yearly *Reports on Publications* and the quarterly "Catalogues of Books Registered in Punjab," published by the colonial administration and main-tained at the India Office, classify the writing that emerged from Punjab in remarkably precise linguistic, generic, and subject categories such as poetry, novel, biography, drama, history, law, medicine, or religion, shap-ing these categories for Indian vernacular print material in the process and mediating the reception, reading and literary value of English and ver-nacular works. In the *Report* (1903), Lala Hari Das, Registrar of the Punjab Education Department, frames Tahl Ram's "self-conscious story" as a "novel," which implies a clear plot and realism, though this "novel" both follows and disrupts such expectations.

Realism as a narrative mode is suited to "subjective individualism" (Mukherjee 1984, 76) and is thus a reflection of an ideological shift in the way that an individual is conceptualized. The tensions between individual

182   A. MINOCHA

desires and social obligations, especially regarding questions of love, marriage and morality could be effectively framed within the linear and prosaic narrative form of the novel rather than a more stylized one. The literary aesthetic of rational dialogue is more suited to the new mode of conjugal relations, although the narrative sometimes hearkens back to the forbidden love and mystical experience of the Laila-Majnu tradition as a lyrical aesthetic ideal. Javed Majeed (2012) has pointed out "how the self-conscious sense of being modern was used by South Asian writers as an ideology of aesthetics in order to distinguish themselves from their traditional predecessors" (264) and is a hallmark of modern South Asian literature.

3   CONCLUSION

The novel *Cosmopolitan Hinduani* marks an effort to enter and counter a space that was already mediated and encoded for women, and to negotiate a new matrix of power relations in print space. I have examined and historicized the novel in the context of the processes that made it possible for a particular kind of enunciation by a woman to enter the print economy and culture of its time. Susila Tahl Ram's participation in the thriving print culture of Punjab suggests the constitution of an alternative, women-oriented, cosmopolitan literary modernity that was distinct from the Western, British, and Indian models. This enunciation of a modern subjectivity reminds us, in particular, that modernity and cosmopolitanism must be examined through cross-cultural frames, that modes of subjectivity in the colonial period were not necessarily tied to religion and nationalist frameworks, and that women were able to imagine networks that challenged conventional geographies of empire and metropolis.

WORKS CITED

Anderson, Benedict. 1983/2006. *Imagined Communities: Reflections on the Origin and Spread of Nationalism.* London: Verso.

Appadurai, Arjun, and Carol Breckenridge. 1995. Public Modernity in India. In *Consuming Modernity: Public Culture in a South Asian World*, ed. Carol Breckenridge, 1–20. New Delhi: Oxford UP.

Bhambra, Gurminder K. 2011. Cosmopolitanism and Postcolonial Critique. In *The Ashgate Research Companion to Cosmopolitanism*, ed. Maria Rovisco and Magdalena Nowicka, 313–328. Farmham: Ashgate.

Bhandari, Vivek. 2007. Print and the Emergence of Multiple Publics in Nineteenth Century Punjab. In *Agents of Change: Print Culture Studies after Elizabeth L. Eisenstein*, ed. Sabrina Alcorn Baron et al., 268–286. Amherst: University of Massachusetts Press.

Bhattacharya, Neeladri. 2005. Notes Towards a Conception of the Colonial Public. In *Civil Society, Public Sphere and Citizenship: Dialogues and Perceptions*, ed. Rajeev Bhargava and Helmut Reifeld, 130–156. New Delhi: Sage Publications.

Brinda, Maharani of Kapurthala. 1953. *Maharani: The Story of an Indian Princess*. New York: Henry Holt.

Catalogues of Books Registered in Punjab Under Act XXV of 1867 and Act X of 1890, 1867–1921, India Office Records, British Library.

Chaudhurani, Sarala Debi. 1911. A Women's Movement. *Modern Review* 10: 344–350.

———. 2010. *The Many Worlds of Sarala Devi: A Diary*. Trans. Sukhendu Ray. New Delhi: Social Science Press.

Dharwadkar, Vinay. 1997. Print Culture and Literary Markets in Colonial India. In *Language Machines and Technologies of Literary and Cultural Production*, ed. Jeffrey Masten et al., 109–136. London: Routledge.

Eisenstein, Elizabeth. 1979. *The Printing Press as an Agent of Change: Communications and Cultural Transformations in Early-Modern Europe*. 2 Volumes. Cambridge: Cambridge University Press.

Forbes, Geraldine. 1996. *The New Cambridge History of India, IV. 2: Women in Modern India*. Cambridge: Cambridge University Press.

Fraser, Robert. 2008. *Book History Through Postcolonial Eyes: Rewriting the Script*. London/New York: Routledge.

Frietag, Sandria. 1991. Introduction. *South Asia: Journal of South Asian Studies* 14 (1): 1–13.

Gupta, Abhijit, and Swapan Chakravorty, eds. 2016. *Founts of Knowledge*. New Delhi: Orient Blackswan.

Habermas, Jurgen. 1989. *The Structural Transformation of the Public Sphere: An Inquiry into a Category of Bourgeois Society*. Trans. Thomas Burger. Cambridge, MA: MIT Press.

Hardevi. 1888a. *London Yatra*. Lahore: Oriental Press.

———. 1888b. *London Jubilee*. Lahore: New Imperial Press.

Majeed, Javed. 2012. Literary Modernity in South Asia. In *India and the British Empire*, ed. Douglas M. Peers and Nandini Gooptu. Oxford: Oxford University Press.

Malhotra, Anshu. 2002. *Gender, Caste, and Religious Identities: Restructuring Class in Colonial Punjab*. Delhi: Oxford University Press.

Mir, Farina. 2010. *The Social Space of Language: Vernacular Culture in British Colonial Punjab*. New Delhi: Permanent Black.

184   A. MINOCHA

Mukherjee, Meenakshi. 1984. Reality and Realism: Indian Women as Protagonists in Four Nineteenth Century Novels. *Economic and Political Weekly* 19 (2): 76–85.

Naregal, Veena. 2001. *Language, Politics, Elites and the Public Sphere: Western India Under Colonialism.* New Delhi: Permanent Black.

Nijhawan, Shobna. 2012. *Women and Girls in the Hindi Public Sphere: Periodical Literature in Colonial North India.* New Delhi: Oxford University Press.

Orsini, Francesca, ed. 2012. *The History of the Book in South Asia.* Surrey: Ashgate.

Pollock, Sheldon. 2002. Cosmopolitan and Vernacular in History. In *Cosmopolitanism,* ed. Carol A. Breckenridge et al. Durham/London: Duke University Press.

Ram, Jhinda. 1893. *My Trip to Europe.* Lahore: Mufid-I-Am Press.

Regan-Lefebvre, Jennifer. 2009. *Cosmopolitan Nationalism in the Victorian Empire: Ireland, India and the Politics of Alfred Webb.* Basingstoke: Palgrave Macmillan.

Report on Publications Issued and Registered in the Several Provinces of British India During the Year 1902. Calcutta: Office of the Superintendent of Government Printing, 1903. India Office Records, British Library.

Rhodes, Jacqueline. 2005. *Radical Feminism, Writing, and Critical Agency: From Manifesto to Modern.* Albany: State University of New York Press.

Rudolph, Susan Hoeber, Lioyd I. Rudolph, and Mohan Singh Kanota, eds. 2002. *Reversing the Gaze: Amar Singh's Diary: A Colonial Subject's Narrative of Imperial India.* Boulder: Westview Press.

Saraswati, Dayanand. 1908. *Satyarth Prakash.* Trans. Durga Prasad. Lahore: Virjanand Press.

Sarkar, Tanika. 2012. Wicked Widows: Law and Faith in Nineteenth-Century Public Sphere Debates. In *Gendering Colonial India: Reforms, Print, Caste and Communalism,* ed. Charu Gupta, 82–108. Hyderabad: Orient Blackswan.

Scott, J. Barton, and Brannon D. Ingram. 2015. What Is a Public? Notes from South Asia. *South Asia: Journal of South Asian Studies* 38 (3): 357–370.

Singh, Raja Jagatjit of Kapurthala. 1895. *My Travels in Europe and America 1893.* London: Routledge.

Stark, Ulrike. 2007. *An Empire of Books: The Naval Kishore Press and the Diffusion of the Printed Word in Colonial India.* Ranikhet: Permanent Black.

Tahl Ram, Susila. 1902, February. Spring at the Kutub. *The Indian Ladies Magazine* 1 (8): 355–358.

———. 1902. *Cosmopolitan Hinduani: Depicting Muhammadan and Hindu Life and Thought in Story Form.* Lahore: The Civil and Military Gazette Press.

Trubner's American, European and Oriental Literary Record, Vol. 2, January–December 1882. India Office Records, British Library.

CHAPTER 10

Crafting the Modern Word: Writing, Publishing, and Modernity in the Print Culture of Prewar Japan

Andrew T. Kamei-Dyche

1 INTRODUCTION[1]

In late nineteenth-century Japan, the state attempted to formulate a distinct modernity that would mark the country as an equal to the Western powers while at the same time according it a unique status through the careful reconfiguration of "tradition." However, the categories of "modern" and "tradition" constituted fiercely contested spaces of meaning, and the expanding print culture of the early twentieth century was replete with intellectuals and writers attempting to formulate alternative modernities that conformed neither to the configuration represented by the state nor to those of the Western powers. This chapter seeks to shed light on this phenomenon by examining the vibrant print culture of prewar Japan, and the roles of various writers and publishers in fashioning the contours of that culture.

[1] All Japanese names are given in Japanese order, with family name first, except for individuals publishing in English.

A. T. Kamei-Dyche (✉)
Aoyama Gakuin University, Sagamihara, Japan

© The Author(s) 2020
R. Aliakbari (ed.), *Comparative Print Culture*, New Directions in Book History, https://doi.org/10.1007/978-3-030-36891-3_10

185

2   Prewar Print Culture

Printing in Japan dates back to the Nara period (710–794), but the potential of the technology went unrecognized and during the Middle Ages was mainly limited to temples.[2] Moveable-type printing technology arrived from both Europe and Korea during the sixteenth century, but failed to supplant woodblock printing. An active print culture (出版文化, *shuppan bunka*) flourished during the early modern era (1600–1867), when a revolution in woodblock printing led to a cornucopia of books and the colorful *ukiyoe* (浮世絵) art prints that later inspired generations of Western artists. The world of print experienced a second revolution when Japanese society embarked on a rapid program of state-sponsored modernization in the first half of the Meiji period (1868–1912). This was a time when the technologies, institutions, and ideologies of the modern West flowed into Japan in a great torrent. New buildings, transportation grids, and communication networks changed the cityscape, while new models of the family and gender roles, heavily influenced by patriarchal notions of the "familial state," changed the social geography. The dawn of print modernity at the end of the nineteenth century was the result of two developments: technological innovations such as mechanical steam-powered presses dramatically increased printing capacity while making printing cheaper and more efficient, and the growth of an educated readership due to the public education system fueled demand for printed works. The early twentieth century was an era of expanding media, with mass-market advertising, recorded music, plays, film, and an enormous boom in print culture.[3] Newspapers and magazines flourished, and bookstores and libraries proliferated, making it easier for writers to get their ideas into print and readers to access those ideas (see Mack 2010; Satō 2002). The expansion of the middle class also meant that more families had disposable income available to purchase books and periodicals.

The rapid changes in Japanese society opened a series of spaces—political, social, and cultural—in which Japanese could seek to formulate a distinct modernity as an alternative to the Western designation being imposed

---

[2] The marginalization of print in Japan during the medieval era marks an interesting point of contrast with China, where, as Daniel Fried illustrates elsewhere in this volume, a significant print culture was already flourishing.

[3] Silverberg (2009) has demonstrated how mass culture had the potential to challenge state ideology, often with a self-aware ironic sensibility. On the transformative effects of technology on literature, see Gardner (2006) and Jacobowitz (2015).

10 CRAFTING THE MODERN WORD: WRITING, PUBLISHING... 187

from abroad. However, the state sought to pre-empt this development by rapidly disseminating its own official discourse on modernity. To fend off the risk of colonization, the ex-samurai elites who made up the government endeavored to forge a society that could meet all of the Western criteria of a "modern" nation-state, while at the same time asserting a unique Japanese character or spirit that could transcend this ostensible Westernization process. This was deemed necessary to calm the domestic population during the tumultuous social transformation, while simultaneously demonstrating to Westerners that Japan was both a fully modern society akin to the Western powers and a distinct nation with a traditional heritage marking it as unique. The result was Japanese modernity being marketed to domestic and foreign audiences alike as a peculiar combination of what the ruling elite understood as "modern" (Western, and by extension universal) elements and "traditional" (Japanese, and therefore unique) elements.[4] By the turn of the century, the basic tenets of this ideological system held firm despite their increasingly obvious contradictions, particularly after Japan's victories over China (1895) and Russia (1905) prompted writers both to approach the West more skeptically and to take a renewed look at Japan's cultural heritage.

Print culture represented a significant arena in which to contest the state-sanctioned discourse on modernity and craft alternative configurations.[5] Naturally, the state recognized this, and sought to control the media to limit its subversive potential and use it for its own ends (see Kasza 1988; Rubin 1984; Treat 2018). Therefore, there was a constant struggle among writers and the state over the meaning of being modern, as these competing forces echoed each other's discursive practices in an attempt to win the minds of the masses.

What resulted was a series of articulations of modernity in print culture that frequently responded to the official discourse and to Western designations of modernity, through subtle or satirical means. It must be said that these articulations did not comprise one single distinct vision of the mod-

---

[4] The attempt to articulate an official discourse on modernity, and the complex role therein of a Japanese "tradition," encompassed a broad range of political, social, and ideological components. These included a new calendar based on the Gregorian one but with seasonal events adapted from the lunar calendar, a standard language, a new nobility combining European and Chinese conventions, and new "national" customs. For more on various "invented traditions," see Vlastos (1998).

[5] Several scholars have noted the democratic potential of print culture at the time, such as Nagamine (2004) and Miyashita (2008).

ern erected as an alternative to the hegemonic official discourse; indeed, it was the monolithic, all-encompassing nature of the official enterprise that prompted anxiety in so many writers and publishers to begin with. It is not surprising that their alternatives therefore constituted a range of formulations rather than a single cohesive force. Nevertheless, there were several key characteristics that encompassed the bulk of these articulations of modernity. First, they often drew on configurations of tradition that complicated, transcended, or entirely undermined the configuration comprising the official discourse. Drawing attention to the variety of experience in traditional thought and social structures, or competing conceptions therein, problematized the official line of a cohesive traditional Japan. Second, there was a great amount of synthetic meshing of indigenous literary genres, motifs, and book design elements with imported Western ones to produce new innovations in both the content and structural form of published works. Third, there was a playful approach to categories, both literary and social, including of course "tradition" and "modern," "Japanese" and "Western." Playfulness also characterized the final major characteristic, a pushing back and forth regarding social norms and mainstream political and cultural values, including prescribed class and gender roles. At times this only reinforced official discourse, but more frequently it problematized or undermined this discourse's totalizing assumptions. In other words, modernity as configured in prewar Japanese print culture was not so much anti-state as it was intrinsically skeptical about the state's articulation of modernity and the hegemonic pretensions thereof.

These characteristics can be seen throughout the print world of early twentieth-century Japan, from manga and mass-market magazines to print advertising, but the rest of this chapter focuses primarily on examples from middlebrow and highbrow publishing; in other words, works that were aimed at a higher-educated, primarily urban middle-class readership. My intention is not to exhaustively survey print culture—indeed, space prevents much beyond scratching the surface—but to simply offer some clues about how the print culture of the era gave rise to alternative configurations of modernity.

3   Writing

The early twentieth century witnessed a range of voices struggling to assert their own articulations of modernity through print culture. Significant increases in education reduced illiteracy rates, while the growing social awareness of the readership encouraged writers to explore socio-economic issues, including the heightened anxiety that had come to afflict much of the urban population.[6] At the same time, the state frequently sought to co-opt writers to shore up the intellectual and cultural capital supporting the official line, often by trying to locate the origins of modern policy in the traditional past.[7] Some Japanese intellectuals were enthusiastic proponents of the official articulation of modernity. For example, Inoue Tetsujirō (井上哲次郎, 1855–1944), an influential philosopher and educator at Tokyo Imperial University, strongly supported state ideology.[8] He eagerly lectured on *bushidō* (武士道), an ideological product of the late years of the early modern era—when the samurai were civil servants who spent little, if any, time fighting—that had been reinterpreted as an ancient code informing the morality of all (loyal) Japanese and which the Imperial Japanese Army considered particularly useful (see Benesch 2016).

Others dissented, directly or indirectly challenging the state's officially-sanctioned modernity and offering up their own alternatives, often incorporating articulations of the modern and traditional that undermined the official model. Prewar print culture was thus a contested terrain of meaning in which various configurations of modernity competed for influence. One of the ways this occurred was in works of fiction that depicted particular aspects of struggle or negotiation among elements framed by authors as traditional or modern. For example, in Mori Ōgai's (森鷗外, 1862–1922) 1910 short story "Fushinchū" (普請中, Under Reconstruction), Japan, depicted with the metaphor of a hotel under renovation, is portrayed not as a splendid modern nation with a traditional spirit, but as a confused institution attempting to be two things at once while never truly succeeding at either.[9]

Natsume Sōseki (夏目漱石, 1867–1916), perhaps Japan's greatest early-twentieth-century author, depicted individuals struggling to achieve,

---

[6] Elementary schools were first implemented in 1872, and at first less than one-third of applicable children enrolled. By the turn of the century this had risen to more than 81%, and to 98% by 1910 (Monbushō 1967, 132). On state ideology and education, see Horio (1988); on readership, see Maeda (1973); on illiteracy, see Rubinger (2000).

[7] This approach was also employed by officially-sanctioned works marketed at Western audiences, such as Ōkuma (1909).

[8] While there is no complete set of Inoue's works, there are partial compilations, notably *Inoue Tetsujirō-shū* (2003).

[9] "Fushinchū" was published in *Mita Bungaku* (三田文學), a literary journal founded at Keio University that same year. For the collected works of Ōgai, see *Ōgai Zenshū* (1971–75).

190 A. T. KAMEI-DYCHE

or even comprehend, some sort of identity to which they could cling in a world of confusion and turmoil in which they possess little if any true agency, in works such as *Sanshirō* (三四郎, 1908) and *Kokoro* (こゝろ, 1914).[10] Sōseki's novels frequently engaged with issues of continuities and ruptures in Japanese tradition as well as with cultural differences with Western societies, but provided no answers, and his characters found little resolution to the conflicts that shaped their experience of the modern. Sōseki appeared to be saying that, contra the state, only through individual self-reflection could moderns find any meaningful identity and value in their lives—notions he made explicit in a 1914 speech to students at Gakushūin, in which he clearly put individualism before nationalism.[11] Even though Sōseki's sentiments may have been anathema to them, the establishment sought to co-opt him anyway, with the prime minister inviting him to a prestigious writers' gathering and the Ministry of Education offering him an honorary doctorate, both of which he publicly turned down.[12] Ōgai was more open to official recognition, but still balked at government attempts to limit free expression, and neither writer offered anything resembling the triumphalist nationalistic novel for which the authorities yearned.[13]

Sōseki was one of a number of writers who experienced success by combining the modern Western novel format with sensibilities and aesthetics from the Japanese literary tradition. While today these novels are studied as single-volume finished products, at the time most novels were published in magazines or newspapers in serial format. Unlike premodern classics, including military tales such as *Taiheiki* (太平記) or *Heike Monogatari* (平家物語), which were guaranteed sellers, many modern works were only republished in book format after the conclusion of a successful run assured publishers of a worthwhile investment.[14] Short fiction and essays in the late nineteenth and early twentieth centuries most frequently appeared in

---

[10] For Sōseki's collected works, see *Sōseki Zenshū* (1993–99).

[11] Gakushūin was the Peers' School, for children of the nobility. For Sōseki's speech on 25 Nov. 1914, see Rubin (1979).

[12] The gathering, called the Useikai (雨声会), met at Prime Minister Saionji Kinmochi's residence in June 1907. The honorary doctorate was arranged in 1911, and Sōseki weathered considerable criticism in rejecting it.

[13] On Ōgai and the state, see Hopper (1974), and on writers and state-building see Starrs (1998).

[14] Particularly successful serial novels could become publishing sensations upon being republished as single-volume works, even running through hundreds of printings.

coterie journals, usually centered on a particular educational institution, limited in reach to their city of publication, and produced in tiny print runs, many less than a thousand copies. These journals, many of which were published monthly, counted on the efforts of their members and the tenuous distribution networks of publishers and bookstore owners to reach their largely highbrow readership. Sōseki, in contrast, enjoyed a nationwide reach through the *Asahi Shinbun* (朝日新聞) newspaper, one of the major national dailies available at numerous shops. His work was therefore readily accessible to a middlebrow readership.[15]

A large body of scholarship has examined the dominant trend in novels at the time, known as *watakushi shōsetsu* (私小説), also read as *shisōsetsu,* or "I-novels," which ostensibly conveyed the author's authentic voice. As Tomi Suzuki (1996) has argued, the I-novel discourse was predicated on a contrast with Western novels, with the latter being seen as fictional constructs while the former were supposed to reflect a "direct expression of the author's lived experience" (3). The direct articulation of the modern experience thus represented a contrast with modern Western literature, in that the latter privileged the mediation of experience through fiction. At the same time, the I-novel discourse functioned as a rhetorical device with which authors created literary manifestations of themselves that asserted the primacy of their experience while simultaneously existing in a space distinct from the "real" historical author.

Other prewar writers turned Sōseki's approach on its head by combining established Japanese genres and literary forms with an explicitly modern topic or ethos, as Yosano Akiko (与謝野晶子, 1878–1942) did by using classical poetic forms to depict the scenes and sentiments of modern life.[16] Akutagawa Ryūnosuke (芥川龍之介, 1892–1927) drew on *Konjaku Monogatari* (今昔物語) tales to craft short stories that

---

[15] Sōseki's column contributed to changing popular (generally negative) perceptions about journalism and fostered an environment in which influential writers were increasingly recruited by newspapers to write on not only literary but also social issues. Newspapers would also send writers on trips to produce exotic travel accounts, resembling the situation in other early twentieth-century contexts such as that of Argentina covered in Geraldine Rogers' chapter in the current volume.

[16] Yosano's poetic style caused consternation among the literary establishment, while at times her themes incurred nationalist wrath, as was the case with her 1904 "Kimi Shinitamaukoto Nakare" (君死にたまふことなかれ, You Must Not Die), pleading with her younger brother to return from the Russo-Japanese War alive, which was interpreted as expressing an antiwar sentiment. For her collected works, see *Teihon Yosano Akiko Zenshū* (1979–81).

192   A. T. KAMEI-DYCHE

appeared akin to folk tales on the surface but incorporated psychological complexity and reflected current concerns over ethics and the limits of human perception.[17] Meanwhile, the work of Tanizaki Jun'ichirō (谷崎 潤一郎, 1886–1965) was informed by his own theory of aesthetics that articulated the acceptance and welcoming of literal and figurative shadows in contrast to a Western desire to dispel these same forces.[18] While Tanizaki's works posited the existence of a distinct Japanese sensibility, as the official discourse had done, Tanizaki's articulation was decidedly unstable and embraced themes such as crippling neuroses and subversive sexuality.[19] Similarly, the state's ideology of the family, intended to be a solid bedrock of social control, was undermined by fictional portrayals of alternative family models, as Ken Ito (2008) has ably demonstrated. Prewar print culture also featured translations from Western languages, which continued at a tremendous pace. Translators, many of whom were authors in their own right, chose to translate works that spoke to current debates and reflected their sentiments on the official discourse.[20]

The print culture of the era also offered the potential for more inclusive or progressive articulations of modernity among marginalized segments of the population, particularly women. The official discourse claimed to be forward-thinking in that it addressed women and presented the state as having liberated them from a repressive feudal existence. However, the state's conception of the modern woman was both illusionary and self-serving. It was illusionary because in many ways, the modern state was a more overtly patriarchal and repressive force than its early modern predecessor. Women still lacked most of the rights accorded to men, but now this inequality was entrenched through legal inscription; conversely, Western ideas of "ladylike" behavioral norms, often encouraged by well-

---

[17] For Akutagawa's collected works, see *Akutagawa Ryūnosuke Zenshū* (1995–98).

[18] Tanizaki set forth his ideas in *In'ei Raisan* (陰翳礼讃, In Praise of Shadows), serialized in 1933. For Tanizaki's collected works, see *Tanizaki Jun'ichirō Zenshū* (1981–83).

[19] Tanizaki's blend of classical tropes with modern sexual mores never sat right with the authorities, although he was able to get a lot past the censors. See Rubin (1984), 137–41 and 235–245.

[20] Since the 1870s, when translations of Western texts rapidly increased, the works chosen reflected the aspirations and concerns of intellectuals, ranging from Jules Verne's *Around the World in Eighty Days* (translated in 1878), popular for its world adventure theme and emphasizing the power of technology to elevate some nations over others, to Samuel Smiles' *Self-Help* (translated in 1871), which was read in a quasi-Confucian vein as a call to elevate the nation through individual effort. On the methods by which translators adapted Western works to the Japanese cultural context, see Miller (2001).

meaning Westerners, deprived Japanese women of some of their alternative sources of agency. For example, whereas women formerly of the samurai caste would have been expected to acquire a degree of martial arts proficiency, this was discouraged as inappropriate for modern women who were expected to be demure. At the same time, the official discourse was self-serving because it celebrated women as "good wives, wise mothers" (良妻賢母 *ryōsai kenbo*) who would serve the state by looking after their husbands and raising sons. The state portrayed this as naturally following from Japanese tradition, while discarding genuine ancient sources of female agency: it celebrated the sun goddess Amaterasu as the founder of Japan's royal house, and by extension the nation, while neglecting the spiritual power associated with the feminine principle in antiquity, and paraded the royal women while stripping them of any right to inherit the throne.[21] Many otherwise progressive male intellectuals acquiesced to this ideology, fearful of the consequences of unbridled female agency.

Women writers responded by carving out their own space, using the arena of print culture to undermine the official articulation of modernity and substitute their own (see Mackie 1995).[22] Some women writers revealed the contradictions in prescribed social roles by shedding light on the struggles facing women and their communities; for instance, Higuchi Ichiyō (樋口一葉, 1872–96) drew on her lived experience to portray the everyday lives of the poor and marginal.[23] Generally, however, women writers were lauded by the male-dominated literary establishment only if they avoided social issues and instead crafted elegant and idealized voices, sharply distinct from the "authentic" voices desired from male writers (see Lukminaite 2016). Women also exercised agency as readers, gradually becoming conceptualized as a distinct readership. Magazines specifically aimed at women began in the 1880s and experienced a boom in the 1910s and 1920s (see Frederick 2006; Patessio 2010, 191–213). Many magazines in the 1910s had monthly circulations in the tens of thousands; by the late 1920s some, such as *Fujin Kōron* (婦人公論, Ladies' Review) had circulations of over 100,000, while *Shufu no Tomo* (主婦の友, Housewife's Friend), perhaps the most popular, hit well over 200,000 (Frederick 2006, 6). Such magazines were general-interest

---

[21] Japan has had eight historic women sovereigns, the last of which was Go-Sakuramachi (1740–1813, r. 1762–71), but even though male rulers had been preferred, there had never before been a legal apparatus in place to prevent women from ascending the throne.

[22] On women writers in modern Japan, see Copeland (2000), Copeland and Ortabasi (2006), Suzuki (2010) and Tanaka (2000).

[23] For the collected works of Higuchi, see *Higuchi Ichiyō Zenshū* (1974–81, 1994).

194   A. T. KAMEI-DYCHE

publications marketed to housewives and students alike. They enjoyed a broad reach thanks to subscriptions and mail, and groups of friends or students would often contribute to a single subscription for multiple periodicals and circulate them. Despite being targeted at women, however, these magazines were overwhelmingly helmed by male editors and frequently dominated by male writers. Women contributors were usually dissuaded from commenting on women's rights and related issues.

Hiratsuka Raichō (平塚らいてう, 1886–1971) found the situation intolerable, and was involved in starting the journal *Seitō* (青鞜, Bluestocking) in 1911 to give women writers an outlet and advance feminism.[24] She wrote, "In the beginning, woman was truly the sun. An authentic person. Now she is the moon, a wan and sickly moon, dependent on another, reflecting another's brilliance" (Hiratsuka 2006, 157).[25] This reference to the sun goddess Amaterasu represented a brilliant coup on Raichō's part: by invoking this myth, she not only sounded a clarion call for women to stand up and assert their agency in fashioning a modern society, but she did so by skillfully using ancient Japanese tradition to counteract the government's "good wife, wise mother" efforts.[26] It was even more effective because of the Japanese state's own use of the Amaterasu myth in the new state religion, so that Raichō was effectively turning official propaganda back on itself. Whereas the official discourse urged modern women to embrace tradition and serve the state, Raichō urged them to embrace tradition to empower themselves. Both articulations of modernity framed a role for women in terms of reconfigured tradition, but one pointed toward subservience and the other toward liberation.

Raichō received 100 yen from her mother to cover the first issue's printing (Hiratsuka 142–43). With a print run of only 1000 copies (priced at 25 sen [0.25 yen] each), her beginning had more in common with coterie

---

[24] In seeking to craft a literary space for women Raichō reflected a similar concern to that of writers and readers in other nations. One such example was Gladys Ramokwena, the 1930s Johannesburg reader who, as Corinne Sandwith explains in her chapter in this collection, desired a space for women writers in her newspaper. In Japan at the time, however, women journalists were exceedingly rare and, rather than pushing the male-dominated newspapers to provide a female literary space, Raichō and her colleagues deemed it more practical to establish one themselves through their own journal.

[25] For a partial collection of her works, see *Hiratsuka Raichō Chosakushū* (1983–84).

[26] Raichō herself suggested the sun and moon imagery just spontaneously occurred to her rather than being based on careful reasoning (Hiratsuka 2006, 160), but such false humility was common in her personal writings. She poured tremendous effort into her work but was always quick to downplay it.

journals than the mass-market magazines, but Hiratsuka and her group were well organized: they solicited advertisements, paid for announcements in the newspapers, and sent postcards to notable women to recruit subscribers (Hiratsuka 2006, 150–56). The journal was a resounding success, but as its writers more assertively argued about women's issues, the literary establishment and mainstream media spread rumors about the creators, prompting fierce rebuttals from Raichō. Abandoning subtlety, she directly attacked the "good wife, wise mother" ideology and incurred the wrath of the state, which intensified its censorship of women's writings and magazines. By the time *Seitō* ceased publication in 1915, however, it had already affected the literary landscape, by demonstrating how innovative women could use the power of print to assert their own articulation of modernity in defiance of that imposed upon them by the state.

4 PUBLISHING

Publishers also played a key role in the struggle over meaning and the shaping of the "traditional" and the "modern" that informed the various articulations of modernity in prewar print culture. The late nineteenth century witnessed the concentration of the Japanese publishing industry in Tokyo, a development that was reinforced rather than undermined in the wake of the devastation of the Great Kantō Earthquake in 1923. The industry had also become greater in its reach and more specialized, with both mass-market companies and smaller-scale highbrow operations flourishing. Decreased printing costs, improved distribution networks, and effective marketing tools all made it easier to enter the book trade. From the late 1920s, the *enpon* (円本, 1-yen book) movement, initiated by the publisher Kaizōsha (改造社), resulted in a wider range of books being made affordably accessible to more readers than before, albeit with a dramatic cut to many publishers' profit margins.

At times, the shifting social context offered opportunities for astute publishers to assert their power in the marketplace of ideas. For example, when the 1920s-era *kyōyōshugi* (教養主義) self-cultivation movement enhanced the public education system's emphasis on reading as essential for the development of moral character and of the nation, Iwanami Shigeo (岩波茂雄, 1881–1946), founder of the highbrow publisher Iwanami Shoten (岩波書店), seized the opportunity to promote a conception of Japanese modernity based on the importance of rationality and moral philosophy. Being a modern Japanese, in Iwanami's view, required a thorough knowledge of the Japanese philosophical tradition coupled with the logic of modern Western philosophy, particularly German idealism. Naturally, this necessitated purchasing a large body of Iwanami publications by contemporary Japanese scholars and intellectuals discussing these schools of thought.[27] Iwanami's articulation of Japanese modernity as springing from citizens' mastery of philosophical tradition clearly contrasted with the state's emphasis on decorum and social control. However, no small number of other publishers found a way to make their efforts dovetail with those of the state while still taking advantage of intellectual trends, such as identifying rationality as the key to competing with the West and using this angle to sell philosophy textbooks.

Publishers also used design and marketing to influence the contemporary discourse. Books were carefully designed to convey their place in the contests over meaning by appealing to, or conversely subverting, expectations of how a modern book should look. Publishers would forge links with artists to develop their products and promote them on a scale heretofore unseen. Some authors were excited by the possibilities that modern art afforded and the capacity of technology to realize those visions. For example, Sōseki was inspired by Art Nouveau during a sojourn in the United Kingdom from 1900 to 1902, and arranged for the illustrations in the book version of his immensely popular 1905 novel *Wagahai wa Neko de aru* (吾輩は猫である, I Am a Cat) to be done in that style. The pretentions of the novel's narrator, a housecat satirically observing human society, are reflected both by Western artistic conventions such as using "Egyptomania" imagery to show the cat as godlike, and the traditional Japanese language such as honorific terms, like "*wagahai,*" that were appropriate to a high-status speaker. In this way Sōseki combined image and text, European art and traditional Japanese language, to playfully mock the cat's delusions of grandeur. In so doing, he also poked fun at his contemporaries and their confused, but often pretentious, navigations among the categories of tradition and modernity. Starting with *Kokoro*, Sōseki published all of his remaining book editions with his disciple, the aforementioned Iwanami Shigeo. He did this not only to help Shigeo's business by lending his immense cultural capital, but also to be able to completely orchestrate the design of his books. He was free to recruit his favorite artists, experiment with the bindings, and even incorporate his

---

[27] On publishers in the intellectual climate of the 1920s, see Takeuchi (2003) and Mack (2010).

own work, such as a cover design based on a rubbing made of a stele in China.[28] The design of *Kokoro* combined traditional Chinese-inspired landscapes with dreamy Art Nouveau stylistics, and represented a transformative moment in prewar print culture when books truly came to be seen as works of art in their own right (Figs. 10.1 and 10.2).

Authors also promoted their own work. Sōseki, for instance, helped design advertising posters and used his famous calligraphy both for advertising and for Iwanami's shop sign. This was no minor feat, because publishing had been previously regarded as a dirty and unsophisticated trade, and the direct involvement of writers with the business aspects of the literary world was shocking. It shaped the entire modern experience of literature and contributed to the rise of celebrity authors, one of the first major examples of whom was undeniably Sōseki himself. The image of the *modern* author as an authentic self-made person, crafting his/her own work

Fig. 10.1 Dust jacket illustration from volume one of *Wagahai wa Neko de aru*, depicting the cat as an anthropomorphic Egyptian deity toying with humanity. (Source: Nihon Kindai Bungakukan/Holp Shuppan 1976 replica)

[28] On Sōseki's favorite artists and their influence, see Yamada (2000).

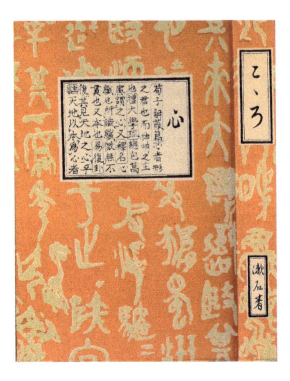

Fig. 10.2 Cover of the Iwanami Shoten one-volume edition of *Kokoro* (1914). (Source: Nihon Kindai Bungakukan/Holp Shuppan 1972 replica)

like a professional producing a work of art, was an ideal he had fostered that endured long after him.

Publishers wielded significant authority because the various conceptions of "tradition" and "modern" that accompanied the competing articulations of modernity had also fueled a debate over literature itself. "Literature" as a category, and the notion of a national literary inheritance, were amorphous conceptions that received increasing attention in the prewar era. This led to the necessity of establishing a canon, and consequently various publishers sought to package their own visions of the "classics" (see Shirane and Suzuki 2000). Here, too, the state was ahead of the game: beginning in the 1870s, authorities had commissioned studies that would construct a canon to present to the world, lest the Western powers regard Japan as a state without a national literature. The state drew on literary history to argue for an essential Japanese national unity since ancient times, using the weight of tradition to lend credence to the idea of a people and state unified under the sovereign. This was part of a broader initiative that also funded historical studies and archeology in order to play up a mythic narrative of the royal family and construct a historical legitimation for the state (see Low 2012; Mehl 2017). The official canon became part of the public education system.

Publishers, however, were intent on formulating their own canons instead of merely parroting the official line. Premodern literature offered flexibility, for historically there had been a variety of literary and philosophical canons. Moreover, publishers were aware of the demand for contemporary "classics" and for the best of Western literature. This led to yet another series of conflicts as publishers struggled to navigate the landscape of meaning to formulate their own canons of classics, traditional and modern, Japanese and foreign. This resulted in the creation and marketing of a range of multi-volume collections that purported to contain the essential texts of one or more of these great categories. In the case of Japanese literature in particular, the 1890s witnessed several such collections, and by the mid-1920s, these were numerous. These collections ranged from series with less than ten volumes to gargantuan enterprises spanning hundreds of volumes, such as the 266-volume *Nihon Koten Zenshū* (日本古典全集, Complete Works of Japanese Classics) which began in 1925 and whose editors included Yosano Akiko. Some of these collections were carefully constructed products with a set number of volumes, published in the same format, and designed to be displayed as a symbolic form of cultural capital, as was the case with the influential 63-volume *Gendai Nihon Bungaku Zenshū* (現代日本文学全集, Complete Works of Contemporary Japanese Literature) begun in 1926 (see Mack 2010, 91–138).[29] Each volume in series like these usually cost only 50 sen (0.5 yen) to 1 yen, and they were usually purchased via subscribing at a bookstore or in response to advertisements.

Other canons were designed as ongoing imprints, such as Iwanami Shoten's *Iwanami Bunko* (岩波文庫) pocketbook series, inspired by the German Reclams Bibliotek and intended to deliver a wide variety of classics into the hands of the masses cheaply and easily. Seizing on the contemporary self-cultivation rhetoric to advance his own notions of the importance of scholastic and philosophical knowledge, Iwanami Shigeo wrote, in a short piece included in every Iwanami Bunko volume, that "people have an urgent demand that knowledge and beauty be recaptured from the monopoly of the elites. *Iwanami Bunko* was born to meet that

---

[29] 340,000 people enrolled in the series when it began (Mack 2010, 120).

demand" (1998, 94–95). He was so successful in this endeavor that the series ultimately established the *bunkobon* (文庫本) publishing format that remains one of the standards of the industry in Japan today. Iwanami also popularized the concept of publishing authoritative sets of the collected works of a given modern author, as well as producing sets of historical lectures and academic studies. His company ultimately not only produced several enduring literary canons, but also established itself as the premier intellectual publisher, shaping the world of education and research for decades to come.

5   Conclusion

In the early twentieth century, Japanese print culture gave rise to a variety of articulations of modernity that contested the official conception, an ideological structure that the state had cobbled together in the late nineteenth century in an attempt to unite the domestic population behind its policies while ensuring that Japan would appear comparable to then-current Western articulations. This chapter has discussed some of these alternative articulations, and showed how they drew on the power of print to reach new readers, problematize or satirize social trends, or use new design models incorporating both Japanese and Western elements. Like the state, they frequently drew upon configurations of "traditional" and "modern" categories, but in vastly different ways than the official discourse had done.

The expansion of an educated readership at the same time that innovations in publishing increased the means of reaching more of that readership opened a new space for debate over meaning. Prewar print culture thus represented a medium in which numerous forces could proffer articulations of modernity that differed from, or even directly challenged, the state's own official configuration. These forces included both writers and publishers, even in tandem, presenting their own conceptions of the "traditional" and the "modern," which left readers with not just a single "Western" or "official" model, but a myriad of articulations of Japanese modernity with which to engage, which continued to develop or be reframed as the prewar era wore on. Ultimately, the state was able to assert the primacy of its own articulation over the others by intensifying censorship and significantly crippling the potential of print culture in the 1930s. However, this did not long endure, for when the restrictions on the media were lifted after the Second World War, the debates resumed, often along the lines that had been established in the prewar era.

Works Cited

芥川龍之介 Akutagawa, Ryūnosuke. 1995–98. 『芥川龍之介全集』 *Akutagawa Ryūnosuke Zenshū*. 24 vols. Tokyo: Iwanami Shoten.

Benesch, Oleg. 2016. *Inventing the Way of the Samurai: Nationalism, Internationalism, and Bushido in Modern Japan*. Oxford: Oxford University Press.

Copeland, Rebecca. 2000. *Lost Leaves: Women Writers of Meiji Japan*. Honolulu: University of Hawai'i Press.

Copeland, Rebecca, and Melek Ortabasi, eds. 2006. *The Modern Murasaki: Writing by Women of Meiji Japan*. New York: Columbia University Press.

Frederick, Sarah. 2006. *Turning Pages: Reading and Writing Women's Magazines in Interwar Japan*. Honolulu: University of Hawai'i Press.

Gardner, William O. 2006. *Advertising Tower: Japanese Modernism and Modernity in the 1920s*. Cambridge, MA: Harvard University Asia Center.

『現代日本文学全集』 *Gendai Nihon Bungaku Zenshū*. 63 vols. Tokyo: Kaizōsha, 1926–1931.

樋口一葉 Higuchi, Ichiyō. 1974–81, 1994. 『樋口一葉全集』 *Higuchi Ichiyō Zenshū*. 6 vols. Tokyo: Chikuma Shobō.

平塚らいてう Hiratsuka, Raichō. 1983–84. 『平塚らいてう著作集』 *Hiratsuka Raichō Chosakushū*. 7 vols. Tokyo: Ōtsuki Shoten.

———. 2006. *In the Beginning Woman Was the Sun: The Autobiography of a Japanese Feminist*. Trans. Teruko Craig. New York: Columbia University Press.

Hopper, Helen M. 1974. Mori Ōgai's Response to Suppression of Intellectual Freedom, 1909–12. *Monumenta Nipponica* 29 (4 Winter): 381–413.

Horio, Teruhisa. 1988. *Educational Thought and Ideology in Modern Japan: State Authority and Intellectual Freedom*. Trans. Steven Platzer. Tokyo: University of Tokyo Press.

井上哲次郎 Inoue, Tetsujirō. 2003. 『井上哲次郎集』 *Inoue Tetsujirō-shū*. Nihon no Shūkyōgaku Series, 9 Vols. Ed. Shimazono Susumu and Isomae Jun'ichi. Tokyo: Kuresu Shuppan.

Ito, Ken K. 2008. *An Age of Melodrama: Family, Gender, and Social Hierarchy in the Turn-of-the-Century Japanese Novel*. Stanford: Stanford University Press.

岩波茂雄 Iwanami, Shigeo. 1998. 「読書子に寄す——岩波文庫発刊に際して」 Dokushoshi ni Yosu: Iwanami Bunko Hakkan ni saishite. In 『茂雄遺文抄』 *Shigeo Ibunshō*, ed. 日本図書センター Nihon Tosho Sentā, 94–95. Tokyo: Nihon Tosho Sentā.

Jacobowitz, Seth. 2015. *Writing Technology in Meiji Japan: A Media History of Modern Japanese Literature and Visual Culture*. Cambridge, MA: Harvard University Asia Center.

Kasza, Gregory J. 1988. *The State and Mass Media in Japan, 1918–1945*. Berkeley: University of California Press.

Low, Morris. 2012. Physical Anthropology in Japan: The Ainu and the Search for the Origins of the Japanese. *Current Anthropology* 53 (S5): S57–S68.

Lukminaite, Simona. 2016. Imagining the Modern Japanese Woman through Literature: Iwamoto Yoshiharu's Ideas. *Ennen ja nyt*, November 18. http://www.ennenjanyt.net/2016/11/imagining-the-modern-japanese-woman-through-literature-iwamoto-yoshiharus-ideas/

Mack, Edward. 2010. *Manufacturing Modern Japanese Literature: Publishing, Prizes, and the Ascription of Literary Value*. Durham: Duke University Press.

Mackie, Vera. 1995. Liberation and Light: The Language of Opposition in Imperial Japan. *East Asian History* 9: 121–142.

前田愛 Maeda, Ai. 1973. 『近代読者の成立』 *Kindai Dokusha no Seiritsu*. Tokyo: Yūseidō.

Mehl, Margaret. 2017. *History and the State in Nineteenth-Century Japan: The World, the Nation and the Search for a Modern Past*. 2nd ed. Copenhagen: Sound Book Press.

Miller, J. Scott. 2001. *Adaptations of Western Literature in Meiji Japan*. New York: Palgrave.

宮下志朗 Miyashita, Shirō. 2008. 『本を読むデモクラシー ── "読者大衆"の出現』 *Hon wo yomu Demokurashī: Dokusha Taishū no Shutsugen*. Tokyo: Tōsui Shobō.

文部省 Monbushō (Japanese Ministry of Education). 1967. 『わが国教育の歩み』 *Waga Kuni Kyōiku no Ayumi*. Tokyo: Meiji Tosho Shuppan.

森鴎外 Mori, Ōgai. 1971–75. 『鴎外全集』 *Ōgai Zenshū*. 38 vols. Tokyo: Iwanami Shoten.

永嶺重敏 Nagamine, Shigetoshi. 2004. 『〈読書国民〉の誕生──明治30年代の活字メディアと読書文化』 *"Dokusho Kokumin" no Tanjō: Meiji 30-nendai no Katsuji Media to Dokusho Bunka*. Tokyo: Nihon Editāsukūru Shuppanbu.

夏目漱石 Natsume, Sōseki. 1972. 『こゝろ』 *Kokoro*. Tokyo: Nihon Kindai Bungakukan with Holp Shuppan.

———. 1976. 『吾輩は猫である』 *Wagahai wa Neko de aru*. Tokyo: Nihon Kindai Bungakukan with Holp Shuppan.

———. 1993–99. 『漱石全集』 *Sōseki Zenshū*. 29 vols. Tokyo: Iwanami Shoten.

『日本古典全集』 *Nihon Koten Zenshū*. 266 vols. Tokyo: Nihon Koten Zenshū Kankōkai, 1925–44.

Ōkuma, Shigenobu. 1909. *Fifty Years of New Japan*. 2 vols. Ed. Marcus B. Huish. London: Smith, Elder & Co.

Patessio, Mara. 2010. Readers and Writers: Japanese Women and Magazines in the Late Nineteenth Century. In *The Female as Subject: Reading and Writing in Early Modern Japan*, ed. P.F. Kornicki, Mara Patessio, and G.G. Rowley, 191–213. Ann Arbor: Center for Japanese Studies, University of Michigan.

Rubin, Jay. 1979. Sōseki on Individualism, 'Watakushi no Kojinshugi'. *Monumenta Nipponica* 34 (1): 21–48.

———. 1984. *Injurious to Public Morals: Writers and the Meiji State*. Seattle: University of Washington Press.

Rubinger, Richard. 2000 Summer. Who Can't Read and Write? Illiteracy in Meiji Japan. *Monumenta Nipponica* 55 (2): 163–198.

佐藤卓己 Satō, Takumi. 2002. 『「キング」の時代――国民大衆雑誌の公共性』 *Kingu no Jidai: Kokumin Taishū Zasshi no Kōkyōsei*. Tokyo: Iwanami Shoten.

Shirane, Haruo, and Tomi Suzuki, eds. 2000. *Inventing the Classics: Modernity, National Identity, and Japanese Literature*. Stanford: Stanford University Press.

Silverberg, Miriam. 2009. *Erotic Grotesque Nonsense: The Mass Culture of Japanese Modern Times*. Berkeley: University of California Press.

Starrs, Roy. 1998. Writing the National Narrative: Changing Attitudes Toward Nation-Building Among Japanese Writers, 1900–1930. In *Japan's Competing Modernities: Issues in Culture and Democracy, 1900–1930*, ed. Sharon A. Minichiello, 206–227. Honolulu: University of Hawai'i Press.

Suzuki, Tomi. 1996. *Narrating the Self: Fictions of Japanese Modernity*. Stanford: Stanford University Press.

Suzuki, Michiko. 2010. *Becoming Modern Women: Love and Female Identity in Prewar Japanese Literature and Culture*. Stanford: Stanford University Press.

Tanaka, Yukiko. 2000. *Women Writers of Meiji and Taisho Japan: Their Lives, Works and Critical Reception, 1868–1926*. Jefferson: McFarland.

谷崎潤一郎 Tanizaki, Jun'ichirō. 1981–83. 『谷崎潤一郎全集』 *Tanizaki Jun'ichirō Zenshū*. 30 vols. Tokyo: Chūō Kōronsha.

竹内洋 Takeuchi, Yō. 2003. 『教養主義の没落――変わりゆくエリート学生文化』 *Kyōyōshugi no Botsuraku: Kawariyuku Erīto Gakusei Bunka*. Tokyo: Chūō Kōron Shinsha.

Treat, John Wittier. 2018. *The Rise and Fall of Modern Japanese Literature*. Chicago: University of Chicago Press.

Vlastos, Stephen, ed. 1998. *Mirror of Modernity: Invented Traditions of Modern Japan*. Berkeley: University of California Press.

山田俊幸 Yamada, Yoshiyuki. 2000. 「橋口五葉と津田清風の漱石本――アール・ヌーヴォーからプリミティズムへ」 *Hashiguchi Goyō to Tsuda Seifū no Sōseki-hon: Āru Nūvō kara Purimitizumu e*. 『漱石研究』 *Sōseki Kenkyū* 13: 166–175.

与謝野晶子 Yosano, Akiko. 1979–81. 『定本与謝野晶子全集』 *Teihon Yosano Akiko Zenshū*. 20 vols. Tokyo: Kōdansha.

CHAPTER 11

"Books for Men": Pornography and Literary Modernity in Late Nineteenth-Century Brazil

Leonardo P. Mendes

1 Introduction

In Brazilian Studies, conceptions of modernity and "the modern" remain under dispute. When the influential critic José Veríssimo (1857–1916) published his *History of Brazilian Literature* in 1916, he used the word "Modernism" to describe post-1870 literature such as the realist novel and scientific naturalism, but the label did not stick. In the mid-twentieth century, the term "Modernism" was successfully repurposed to define the artistic *avant-garde* movements of the early twentieth century and their culmination in the 1922 "Week of Modern Art" in São Paulo. In guidebooks such as Alfredo Bosi's *Concise History of Brazilian Literature* (1970), the term "Modernism" refers to the art and literature produced around and after 1920, up to the mid-twentieth century. The period before 1920 is anachronistically called "pre-modernism," implying a time before "the modern" that was, by definition, subordinate to what came after. Traditional Brazilian historiography adopts a teleological perspective that regards post-1920 "modernist" literature as the peak of an evolution-

L. P. Mendes (✉)
Rio de Janeiro State University, Rio de Janeiro, Brazil
e-mail: leonardomendes@utexas.edu

© The Author(s) 2020   205
R. Aliakbari (ed.), *Comparative Print Culture*, New Directions in
Book History, https://doi.org/10.1007/978-3-030-36891-3_11

ary process of the national literary system, of which "pre-modernism" was just a preliminary stage. From that endpoint, it retrospectively rearranges the literature that came before to fit that model.

Despite the successful association of modernity with twentieth-century art and literature to the detriment of the previous century, it is nowadays commonly accepted that there were outbursts of modernity in the writings of nineteenth-century canonical writers such as José de Alencar (1829–1877), Machado de Assis (1839–1908), and Aluísio Azevedo (1857–1913), among others, who were engaged in practicing and developing an indisputably modern genre: the novel. They imitated, translated, and transformed the European model of the realist or bourgeois novel, as they each embarked on the modern quest of exploring and defining the national character. These authors envisaged and promoted a national mass reading culture grounded in the European novel as acclimated to Brazil. However, according to traditional historiography, they failed. Books were expensive and sold poorly, and many authors believed that the reading public was small and uninterested in their work (Sodré 1964). For example, Aluísio Azevedo famously complained about the need to write for periodicals in order to make ends meet (Mérian 2013). From the traditional point of view, the realist novel reached a limited readership. If we can speak of modernity then, it was a failed experiment.

In this chapter, I will argue for an alternative Brazilian nineteenth-century literary modernity grounded not in European and domestic novelism and realism, but in popular erotic prints.[1] In the last decades of the century, while elite authors lamented their lack of readers, publisher Pedro Quaresma (1863–1921), of the People's Bookstore in Rio de Janeiro, was selling several thousand copies of locally produced pornographic paperbacks and "sensation novels," at prices comparable to those of tram tickets (El Far 2004). On the margins of elite circles, conservatories, publishers and periodicals was a dynamic market of popular erotic prints, with an abundant selection of titles, formats, genres and prices, implying thou-

---

[1] In "The People's Entertainments: Translation, Popular Fiction, and the *Nahdah* in Egypt" (2006), Samah Selim argues that the dominant methodology in Arabic literary history "has arrived at a modern novelistic canon that represents the fruits of a *particular* version of modernity, to the exclusion of all others" (38). In a similar manner as proposed here, she examines Arabic popular fiction from the late nineteenth and early twentieth centuries as a discarded body of works that offers another textual site of "the modern," one that builds on established modes of popular narrative such as melodrama and cared nothing for origins and genealogies.

11 "BOOKS FOR MEN": PORNOGRAPHY AND LITERARY MODERNITY... 207

sands of readers eager for material. This body of work was ignored, and even fought against, because it eluded the nationalist conceptualization of subjectivity and classical definitions of literature as austere and pedagogical. This chapter examines how European humanist, libertine, and naturalist literatures were repurposed and used to develop pornographic material for popular consumption, and how such literature did more than the European bourgeois novel to shape the contours of an emerging modern reading culture in late nineteenth-century Brazil.

2 Context: The Pornographic Book Market in Late Nineteenth-Century Brazil

After 1870, a new space for the circulation of pornographic literature gradually emerged in Brazil. It is tempting to conclude that this shift was related to the decline of the monarchy, its ideologies, and cultural products, leading to the abolition of slavery in 1888 and the overthrow of Emperor Pedro II (1825–1891) in 1889. In an environment of remarkable freedom of the press, the number and formats of periodicals multiplied (Barbosa 2010; Mello 2007). Immigration surged, especially from Portugal, which in the 1890s sent an average of 20,000 people to Brazil annually. Their preferred destinations were Rio de Janeiro and São Paulo, where industrialization was incipient (Lobo 2001). In major cities, bookstores would sell lewd brochures, which were often illustrated. Writers cautiously commented on obscene literature in notes and chronicles while still being surprised by their openness. Although licentious works had circulated in Brazil since colonial times (Villalta 2012), it was only at the end of the nineteenth century that they were openly and legally commercialized in the transatlantic book market and in the country's major cities bookstores and newspaper offices (Mendes 2017b).

New publishers, such as the People's and the Modern Bookstores in Rio de Janeiro, started to operate openly in the licentious book market, offering an alternative to the traditional Laemmert and Garnier Bookstores (Hallewell 1985). Where the latter two were located on Ouvidor Street, the city's most elegant district, the others operated on alternate streets nearby that were closer to popular commerce. In São Paulo, the Teixeira Bookshop started publishing and selling pornography in the 1880s, as printers became more widespread (Deaecto 2011). In the 1890s, sensing the profitability of the new market and aiming at a more sophisticated reader, Laemmert started to publish licentious literature as well. In other cultural centers such as Porto Alegre in the south and Belém do Pará, Maranhão and Recife in the north, bookstores sold books printed in Rio de Janeiro and São Paulo as well as other licentious material imported from Europe. For a small fee, books could be sent by mail to all valid addresses in Brazil, taking advantage of navigation routes and cabotage trade along the coast and railway systems in Bahia, Rio de Janeiro, São Paulo, Curitiba and Porto Alegre (Barbosa 2010).

As a result of the increase in numbers, formats, and visibility, by the end of the century pornographic books were classified and advertised under a recognizable label. Bookstores used appealing expressions such as "Joyful Reading," "Happy Books," "Bachelor's Library" or most commonly, "Books (or Reading) for Men" as euphemisms for pornography, marking the works as licentious (El Far 2004). The variations highlighted the secrecy, fun, and edgy sexuality associated with the volumes. The descriptor "books for men" was meant as a joke, although it is safe to assume that some women would be put off by the branding. Those who dared had to be more discreet than male students and husbands. There were books for all tastes and budgets, from cheap realist brochures to pricy hardcovers printed in better-quality paper. By the end of the century, both men and women read "books for men" in secret, but now there was a place for pornography in bookstores, in bourgeois sociability, in *gabinetes de leitura* [Reading Rooms] around the country and in the chests and drawers of family houses.

Conservative periodicals such as the Catholic *The Apostle*, run by the Rio de Janeiro Prelacy, were the main mouthpieces of discontent with the dissemination of erotic print works. These publications viewed the phenomenon as a disease and described it as a "great epidemic" (April 24, 1896). Their anxiety can be best understood when we consider the titles of apocryphal low-priced brochures listed in one of the People's Bookstore's advertisements: *Prowess of a Clitoris, How to Treat Women as They Deserve, Jumpy Tales that Send a Chill Down the Spine, Electric Readings, Love and Sensuality, Screams of the Flesh, The Secret History of All Orgies, Incendiary Mussels, Gabriela or The Courtesan from Colonial Times, The Adventurous Women or The History of Famous Courtesans, Memoirs of an Insatiable Woman, The Interim Lover: Gorgeous Scenes that Take Place in the Garden, in the Bedroom and Finally in the Kitchen, Julia de Milo: Portrait of a Dishonest Woman* "and other works that help increase the appetite with some chili pepper, suitable for rust removal in cold weather" (*Gazeta de Notícias*, May 5, 1885). The list was long and included unpublishable titles that could only be revealed in private at the store.

These tantalizing anonymous brochures, of which so far none has been found, cost as low as 200 *réis*, at a time when a tram ticket cost 100 *réis*, the same price of the daily editions of 30,000 to 40,000 copies of mass-circulating newspapers such as *Gazeta de Notícias* and *Jornal do Brasil* (Barbosa 2010). One thousand *réis* would buy a cheap lunch in down-town Rio de Janeiro or pay for one admission fee to the *Musée Parisien*, a wax museum in which one could admire a life-size sculpture of Émile Zola (1840–1902) and other celebrities (Mendes 2018). A new copy of Aluísio Azevedo's successful naturalist novel *The Man* (1887) was worth 3000 *réis*, the average price of a 300-page volume and equivalent more or less to the amount a skilled worker such as a blacksmith or a woodworker would receive for a day's work. If he could read or knew someone who could, there were plenty of cheap brochures available, often illustrated.

The "books for men" phenomenon indicated an emerging modern print culture that challenged traditional conceptions of nationality, author-ship, time, and genre. Besides the anonymous low-priced brochures, the label included a large variety of titles and genres, old and new, including humanist and libertine literatures from the sixteenth, seventeenth, and eighteenth centuries, contemporary naturalist and decadent fiction from France, Portugal, and Brazil, anticlerical pornography, fantasies about the unruly sexual habits of the Ancients, history books about prostitution, narratives of famous prostitutes, manuals of sexual advice, and contempo-rary pornography written in Portuguese. These were successful editorial projects, and some had clandestine editions selling several thousand copies over the years, with the best-selling titles remaining in catalog until the beginning of the twentieth century (El Far 2004). Publishing and selling pornography were lucrative businesses. In Rio de Janeiro's daily *A Notícia* (November 20, 1895), critic Valentim Magalhães (1859–1903) told of a bookseller who confided to him that pornography alone kept him from closing the store.

3   Texts/Contexts in Comparison: Re-Tooling of Humanism, Libertinism, and Naturalism as an Alternative to European and Domestic Novelism and Realism

Until the early nineteenth century, pornography was linked to political satire and social commentary. Despite writing obscene books, eighteenth-century libertine writers saw their work as a denunciation of obscurantist thinking and political oppression (Kearny 1982). By the mid-nineteenth century, the overlap between the sexual and political spheres had begun to crumble (Kendrick 1987). Confrontational politics abandoned the expression of sexual ideas. New definitions of obscenity emerged based on evolving descriptions of bourgeois citizenship, which claimed the right to privacy and consumerism (Sigel 2005). Sexual discourse gradually gained autonomy, coming to exist as *an end in itself*, as a consumer product. This autonomy was built in parallel to laws intended to control pornography in some European states. Until the nineteenth century, pornographic books were expensive and traditionally reserved for aristocratic libraries or circuits of great social prestige. Around 1850, the "gentlemanly enclosure" had been breached (Kendrick 1987, 27). The emergence of a legal framework to control pornography was a direct result of the dissemination of cheap erotic printed works (Hunt 1999).

In Brazil, the body of literature that writers and publishers considered pornographic was well known and established by the late nineteenth century. Since they sprang from humanist and libertine literatures, all writers from those traditions were classified as such, including Giovanni Boccaccio (1313–1375), François Rabelais (1494–1553), Pietro Aretino (1492–1556), and Manuel du Bocage (1765–1805), but not the Marquis de Sade (1740–1814), whose works were rare in Brazilian nineteenth-century sources. "Books for men" also included the works of contemporary naturalist writers such as Portuguese Eça de Queiróz (1845–1900) and the most successful, Émile Zola, whose novels were widely perceived as pornography disguised as science (Mendes 2018). Some traits these works shared with naturalist fiction, such as anticlericalism, voyeurism/exhibitionism, sex as a social leveler, lesbianism, priapism, the prostitute as a paradigmatic character, and a calm and detached scientific style that avoided judgment, became trademarks of modern pornography.

Though they were clandestine, pornographic works were commercialized as light entertainment. Whatever was advertised as "books for men" appeared under a humorous heading. Pornography was associated with the satirical press and was advertised as an invigorating pastime. By titillating mind and body, these books provided the reader with a private moment of repose from the stressful, lonely life of the modern city. Bookstores promised that reading these texts would "activate the will" and rekindle the reader's inner fire. Making it clear the books were also meant to stimulate masturbation, one of the People's Bookstore's adverts (*Gazeta de Notícias*, July 13, 1885) advised the (male) reader to obtain "reinforced button pants" before opening the brochures. Sexual activity was typically framed within pre-industrial (and, for that matter, pre-Sadean) traditions such as Renaissance Humanism and early Libertinism, which were distant in time and afforded a dreamy, if not innocent, atmosphere without guilt or punishment (Mendes 2017a). Thus, the writings of Boccaccio and Rabelais were significant points of departure.

Easily available in bookstores and listed in library auctions, Boccaccio's novellas appeared in separate volumes with selections from the most obscene stories of Days VII, VIII, and IX of the *Decameron* (1353), so that the reader could experience an "immersion into life at its most real, a vicarious dip into the complete amorality of existence" (Barolini 1983, 529). It was these stories that secured Boccaccio's reputation as a licentious writer and served as inspiration for nineteenth-century Lusophone pornography. Implying they were capable of treating sexual impotency, in the Sunday edition of October 22, 1899 *Gazeta de Notícia*'s front-page columnist recommended Boccaccio's stories for "bachelors over forty." Following the pattern applied to "books for men," many agreed the *Decameron* was dangerous to women. By reading "the detailed and throbbing analyses of all vices and voluptuousness," writes the editorialist of Rio de Janeiro's daily *O Tempo* (December 22, 1891), a woman might feel inclined "to know and feel those divine pleasures, that set fire to the cold and deprave the pure." Such enticing admonitions worked as invitations to buy and read Boccaccio's books.

Along with Boccaccio's novellas, Rabelais' ubiquitous *Gargantua and Pantagruel* (1534) further articulated patterns of obscenity, censorship, and tolerance in literary culture. Throughout the nineteenth and early twentieth centuries, these writings pushed the limits of obscenity, with Rabelais cited as an exemplary figure of literary inadmissibility (Ladenson 2016). Conservative periodicals considered "Rabelaisian realism" mere pornography. Writing in *The Apostle* (July 13, 1883), the priest Ignácio Cândido da Costa declared the French writer a "pervert" and his work "the incarnation of the lascivious frenzy" typical of the Reformation period. Brazilian men of letters were aware of Boccaccio's and Rabelais' obscenity, but they did not call them "pornographic" because that would devalue them. Rejecting Catholic alarmism, Domício Gama (1862–1925), another co-founder of the Brazilian Academy of Letters, defined Rabelais' work as an "epic of youthful and exultant lasciviousness" in the February 4, 1890, *Gazeta de Notícias*. Like the *Decameron*, Rabelais' writing provided a cultured blueprint for pornography for the new market.

212   L. P. MENDES

The Rabelaisian matrix created a zone of ambivalence and liberation linked to the "lower body," which included sex, nudity, and the acts of bathing, eating, and going to the bathroom (Bakhtin 1984). It provided the foundation of obscene laughter and life-affirming physicality on which writers could build, adding characters, techniques, themes, and rhetorical patterns adapted and reworked from libertine literature.[2] Books such as the anonymous *Thérèse Philosophe* (1748), *Fanny Hill* (1748) by English writer John Cleland (1709–1789), and *Les aventures du Chevalier du Faublas* (1787–1790) by French writer Jean-Baptiste Louvet du Couvray (1764–1797), could easily be found in bookstores, in their original languages or in translation. Both nineteenth-century pornography and naturalist fiction were built upon libertinism, sharing themes, strategies, and narrative setups, such as anticlericalism, the character of the free-thinking woman, the centrality of the body and the Newtonian mechanical model of man and nature (Jacob 1999).

In the nineteenth century, "libertine" was synonymous with "obscene." In the Brazilian press and fiction at the end of the century, the libertine was a flirt and a lady-killer, but also a drunkard and a gambler. In the "books for men" context, the libertine novel was a fantasy of sexual and economic freedom without interdiction or guilt. Focused on pre-revolutionary French aristocracy, it spoke of a world closed upon itself. There, people lived apart from material problems and economic difficulties. They all disposed of their time freely. On the stages of the ballroom and the boudoir, libertine existence was a continuous act. In these books, theatricalization, travesties, play, adventure, and intrigue were more important than sex (Trousson 1996). However, libertine (or humanist) sexual energy was enough to "activate the reader's will," in a world with few representations of sexuality and the naked body and in which literature and print works were the main sources for information about sex.

3.1   Convent Evenings *by M. L. and Anticlerical Pornography*

One of the most successful "books for men" was *Convent Evenings*, published under the pseudonym M. L. The first and best-known edition, in three pocket volumes, was printed at the possibly fake *Typographia do*

---

[2] In her chapter in this collection, Judith Wilks similarly demonstrates the re-tooling of European literary models for the shaping of alternative articulations of literary and political modernities in Turkey and Azerbaijan.

Bairro Alto, in Lisbon. It had no address or date, but appeared around mid-century, when Portugal was extinguishing male religious orders, closing convents, and selling church property under a series of reforms aimed at weakening the power of the clergy (El Far 2004). Thus, *Convent Evenings* spoke nostalgically of the glorious days of convent life, when the image of the cloistered nun was a potent sexual fetish. The author considered the work dangerous enough to conceal his true identity under a pseudonym. From the beginning the book was known by its title, with the irrelevant authorship ignored in bookstore ads and comments in the press. Despite the elusive publisher and author, the last pages of the third volume listed the places at which the book could be purchased in Lisbon, Porto, and Coimbra, as well as at major bookstores in Rio de Janeiro (M. L. n.d.).

Anticlerical pornography told stories about the insatiable sexual appetites of priests and nuns. In a country in which the Catholic faith was embraced by the majority of believers, pornography with religious characters and settings was bound to be scandalous and commercially successful. Attacks on the Church's corruption through pornographic discourse, notably in the character of the "lascivious priest," could be found in Medieval *fabliaux* and Renaissance writers (Williams 1961) and the writings of the libertines, and by the nineteenth century was an erotic subgenre in its own right. The faithless priest was also a paradigmatic character in naturalist fiction, as in Eça de Queirós' *The Crime of Father Amaro* (1875), which was typically appropriated as anticlerical pornography (Mendes 2016). In these books, priests and nuns are mere activated bodies, while monasteries become the setting of festivities and orgies. Religious spaces, rituals, and objects are desacralized, undermining the legitimacy of the Church, hierarchies, and religious thought.

The success of *Convent Evenings* can be measured by the number of clandestine editions that circulated at the end of the century, with at least one published in Brazil. As early as 1862 a pirated edition had appeared in Rio de Janeiro, in a single volume published by bookseller Bernardo Xavier. It had no information about the year or printing location, which was against Brazilian law (El Far 2004). Loyal to its popular clientele, the People's Bookstore carried another edition in four volumes for the reasonable price of 4000 *réis* (*Gazeta de Notícias*, Oct. 14, 1889). The Cruz Coutinho Bookstore in Rio featured yet another in two illustrated volumes for 10,000 *réis* (*Gazeta de Notícias*, June 28, 1896). Though the original book had no illustrations, the expensive illustrated edition demonstrated that pictures could be inserted into clandestine publications of *Convent Evenings* and other licentious works, potentializing them as pornographic books, made to be read and seen (Abreu 2008). Available in many editions, formats and prices until the 1920s, *Convent Evenings* was constantly cited by writers, publishers and journalists as the paradigmatic "book for men."

The book belonged to a classical humanist sensibility from a pre-industrial imaginary. As in libertine literature, the style was gallant and cultured, with no foul language, and metaphors for sexual penetration such as that of a mouse entering a mousetrap. The book's obscene material is clearly inspired by the works of Rabelais and Boccaccio, repeating the *Decameron*'s basic structure: the "frame narrative," in which friends engage in zesty conversation, telling each other stories to pass the time and increase intimacy. A dozen nuns alternate in telling elaborate pornographic stories, often related to their own sexual experiences in convents and also adventures in secular contexts. *Convent Evenings* recaps entire plots from the *Decameron*, such as, from Day III, the tale of the young gardener who was (falsely) dumb, making him ideal for the nun's plans to have sex in secret. Often, after the stories, the nuns retire to their cells, in groups of two, three or four, and put into practice the sexual activity about which they had been narrating.

3.2   Voluptuousness: 14 Gallant Tales *by Rabelais and the New Pornography*

Another pornographic best-seller was *Voluptuousness: 14 Gallant Tales*, by Rabelais, the best-known pseudonym of Portuguese writer Alfredo Gallis (1859–1910). Gallis was famous in Portugal and Brazil for his licentious books (Moreira 2017) and offered a little-known alternative to France's dominance in the nineteenth-century market of pornographic literature (Santana 2004). As Rabelais, he published several volumes of licentious tales, such as *Aphrodisiacs, Cupid's Diatribes, Libertine women, Lust and Laughter, Venus Nights, Crimes of Love* and *Voluptuousness: 14 Gallant Tales*, his first and best-known work. Rabelais and *Voluptuousness* were routinely cited in the press as exemplary of the new pornography. In 1896, the celebrity of the "adored Rabelais" led the People's Bookstore to announce that it had acquired 6000 copies of *Crimes of Love*, of which 5000 had already been sold to booksellers in other states (*O Paiz*, Oct. 16, 1896). It was a "thick 400-page volume," with a spicy colored engraving of a sex scene on the cover, priced at 4000 *réis*. The following month, the People's Bookstore boasted having sold 300 copies of the "appetizing book" (*Gazeta de Notícias*, Nov. 21, 1896) in just one day.

The first edition of *Voluptuousness* appeared as a clandestine publication in 1886. It bore neither the author's nor the publisher's names, but designated São Paulo as the place of print. In the second edition, in 1893, published under a more liberalizing Penal Code in the early years of the Republic, the names of the author Rabelais and publishers Antônio Teixeira & Brother appeared on the front page, with a preface admitting that these were the author and publisher of the 1886 edition. The Portuguese brothers and booksellers Antônio Maria and José Joaquim Teixeira opened the Teixeira Bookstore in São Paulo in 1878. It sold all types of printed matter: practical manuals, school books, fiction, legal literature, and "books for men" (Pina 2015). Besides *Voluptuousness*, the Teixeira brothers published other best-sellers of the period, such as the naturalist novel *The Flesh* (1888), by Júlio Ribeiro (1845–1890), a *succès de scandale* that famously circulated as porn (Bulhões 2002).[3] Continuously available in bookstores in Brazil and Portugal until the beginning of the twentieth century, *Voluptuousness* cost between 2000 and 5000 *réis*. As proof of the book's success, a third edition appeared in 1906 at the city of Porto, in Portugal, published by the *Tipografia da Empresa Literária e Tipográfica*.

Confident that his pen name signaled the description of sexual activity, Gallis tested ways of telling stories with the sole purpose of "activating" the reader's mind and body. In the prologue, unlike libertine and naturalist writers, he admitted that these "gallant" stories were meant as sexual stimulation: "We don't write for scholars or moralists; we work for the carefree and lovers of spicy literary menus" (Rabelais 1893, 6). The book promised not only to reconnect the reader with his body, but also to promote physical and mental well-being through laughter, confirming the pattern of advertising "books for men" meant to "sweeten the annoyance of the sad and the melancholy of the discouraged." Reinforcing the bond with physical well-being and the stomach, the stories were "delicacies of

---

[3] In the late nineteenth century, pornographic discourse was an inescapable dimension of naturalist fiction. Naturalist works were routinely advertised as "books for men" in bookstore ads and treated as licentious literature in comments in the press, even by the authors themselves, as a way of boosting sales. In Brazil, Figueiredo Pimentel's (1869–1914) novel *O aborto* (1893) best illustrates that interface (Mendes 2016).

easy digestion and delicate flavor, those that please while eating, without leaving any unpleasant taste in the mouth." In order to take advantage of everything the book had to offer, the reader was invited to "put aside criticism and austerity as ugly things that do not fit here. Light a cigar of pure Havana tobacco and drink a glass of liqueur. Be alone at home. Keep the robe wide open for whatever comes" (Rabelais 1893, 9).

In *Voluptuousness*, Rabelais offered a mosaic of past and present pornographic traditions. The stories explore various styles and sexual combinations, including homoerotic love. There are the lesbian nuns in "Luiza," surely inspired by *Convent Evenings*. In "Ligurino," Rabelais revisits the orgies of ancient Rome to describe oral and anal sex between men. In "Wedding Night," he teases the reader with the fantasy of attending a young couple's first night, with the narrative explaining and describing how and what to do on the first night, including the importance of foreplay with oral sex. Libertine characteristics are everywhere, from the word "gallant" in the subtitle to the voyeurism of stories such as "In the Act," which presents a classic libertine storyline: through a keyhole, a young man observes two girls kissing, until he cannot resist, invades the room and has a *ménage à trois* with them. Some tales are set in contemporary Lisbon, with bodies sighted on the streets and desired, while sexual activity itself is narrated in erudite language with echoes of Parnassian and decadent writings. The vagina was "the sacred temple promised by Allah to his chosen ones" (Rabelais 1893, 96). Set against the backdrop of the modern city, these tales offered fantasies of feminine availability, masculine assault, and explicit sex, with which many Lusophone readers could identify.

3.3   Album of Caliban *and Polished Pornography*

Album of Caliban was the best-known among a series of licentious books produced in the 1890s and 1900s by a group of young Brazilian writers on the rise: Olavo Bilac (1864–1918), Coelho Neto (1864–1834), Pedro Rabelo (1868–1905), and Guimarães Passos (1969–1909). They had close ties with elite writers and thus became co-founders of the Brazilian Academy of Letters in 1897. Sensing that the new market was a promising space for earning stable income, they wrote obscene poetry and short stories, published under pseudonyms as was the traditions. Bilac used the names Puck and Bob; Guimarães Passos was Puff; Pedro Rabelo was Pierrot and Coelho Neto was Caliban, the most popular and prolific of them. These pen names were publicly known, and their Shakespearean reverberations were debated in the press. Their writings were journalistic material, tested in periodicals before being published in books. Therefore, they had to write palatable descriptions of sexual activity, if not for conservative periodicals such as the *The Apostle* (which unsurprisingly condemned the initiative), then at least for their peers in the elite literary community.

Throughout the 1890s, Puff, Bob, Puck, Pierrot, and Caliban published licentious poems, anecdotes, and short stories in several periodicals in Rio de Janeiro and the states, but especially in the column "The Pup" in Rio de Janeiro's *Gazeta de Notícias*. It was one of the most popular and innovative newspapers in the late century, renowned for hiring celebrity writers such as Machado de Assis, Olavo Bilac, and Coelho Neto (Sodré 1983). In August 1896, when it turned 21, the periodical claimed the license to dare more, having reached the legal age to do so, and created "The Pup" as a daily section on the front page dedicated exclusively to satire and adult content (Simões Júnior 2007). It lasted until May 1897 and achieved tremendous success, helping boost the paper's sales and normalize pornography in print. Caliban had his own subsection called "Album of Caliban," where he published brief obscene tales. The "album" metaphor suggested a collection of spicy pictures to be looked through during lonely hours. "The Pup" brought together the licentious writings of all these authors in one place, helped give these works an organic identity, and paved the way for the publication in book format.

The books appeared between 1897 and 1905, and were mostly published by the traditional bookstore Laemmert. Established in Rio de Janeiro in 1838 by the German brothers Eduardo and Henrique Laemmert, the bookstore was one of the most successful in nineteenth-century Brazil (Machado 2009). It consolidated its reputation around 1844 with the yearly publication of *Almanak Laemmert*, a catalog with information about industrial and commercial businesses in Rio de Janeiro Province, attracting clientele and becoming well known for its diverse dictionaries, grammars, and technical manuals (Hallewell 1985). By the 1890s, the bookstore had branches in São Paulo and Recife in the north, increasing its ability to distribute and sell books. After the death of Garnier's proprietor Baptiste-Louis Garnier in 1893, they ventured into the publication of literature, publishing translations of French works, naturalist fiction such as Figueiredo Pimentel's *A Scoundrel* (1895), and licentious literature for the new market. This move was a recognition that there was a place for erotic literature even in Ouvidor Street bookstores.

In 1897, Laemmert published *Pup's Stuff*, a volume of Pierrot's obscene poems, and *Bell Peppers*, featuring Puff's and Puck's erotic poetry, both sold in the popular price range of 2000 *réis*. Between 1897 and 1898, they published *Album of Caliban* in installments of six pocket-size brochures of 50 pages each for 1500 *réis*, totaling a volume of 300 pages if bound together. The serial publication was advantageous for the bookstore, as it raised the book's final price to 9000 *réis*, but also enabled the purchase of one or two leaflets if one was short of money. *Casa Mont'Alverne*, a stationery in downtown Rio de Janeiro that occasionally printed literary works, published Bob's obscene writings in the volume *Tales for Rogues* in 1897, priced at 2000 *réis*. Finally, Laemmert published two new collections of Pierrot's "happy" poems and tales: *Tales with Chilly Pepper* in 1902, and *Happy Tales: Stories for the Gloomy* in 1905, both priced at 2000 *réis*. These books collected pieces previously published in periodicals with new material.

Like other licentious writers of the period, Puff, Bob, Puck, Pierrot, and Caliban reworked Rabelaisian and libertine characters, plots, and settings. They rejected naturalist vocabulary and style, which were considered too crude to circulate in mainstream periodicals. Each 50-page volume of *Album of Caliban* featured an epigraph of Rabelais' verses from the opening of *Gargantua*, in French: "Mieulx est de ris que de larmes escrire/Pour ce que rire le proper de l'homme." This confirmed their affiliation with an erudite secular tradition that favored sex, laughter, and physical well being. To attain that, writers relied on "adultery tales" (Frantz 1989), a comic genre descended from the medieval *fabliaux* that appeared in Boccaccio's *novellas* and Chaucer's *The Canterbury Tales* (1387). The plots of these tales revolve around three characters: the naive husband, the bored wife, and the lascivious priest. Omnipresent in a patriarchal society in which marriages were hard to break, the infidelity of spouses offered a rich source of Rabelaisian plots with which many readers could identify. The model allowed for infinite variations of spicy anecdotes that could be told among friends or even at a Sunday family lunch.

Another typical *fabliau* plot reworked by Caliban and the writers of "The Pup" was the innocent (or not so) girl seduced by the priest during communion (Ladenson 2016). Since the sixteenth century, the Church had concerns about the sexual intimacy between penitents and priests in the confessional (Haliczer 1996). In England, Protestants accused Catholic priests of using the confessional to seduce innocent young girls (Peakman 2003). The place was eroticized by stories of adulteries, sex out of wedlock and forbidden loves. The writers resorted to the confessional as a space in which erotic stories circulated in that society. Caliban's tale "Penance" and Bob's "Sin" are variations of the same plot, in which the punishment applied by the confessor infers sexual activity taking place. In the two tales, upon learning from a friend that her penance was to wash her hands twice a week in the chapel's sink, the other fears she will have to take a daily general bath in the same place. The repetition of the identical plot confirms that writers shared a common repertoire of themes and symbols derived from humanist and libertine European literatures.

Although some stories in "The Pup" were located in contemporary Rio de Janeiro, considerations about place and time are often irrelevant in pornography, in which it is always time for bed and location is either a distraction or a limitation (Marcus 2008). Thus, the descriptions of spaces typically evoke an idyllic state of communion with nature, the ideal landscape or *locus amoenus*, from classical rhetoric. This element was explored in medieval troubadour poetry and appears in Boccaccio's *Decameron*, in which the Florentines, distraught by the plague, find a place—the novellas themselves—that bad news could not reach and from which they could organize a return to society (Barolini 1983). As reworked in nineteenth-century pornography, the agreeable landscape similarly provided the reader with a relaxing setting in which he could "develop the nerves" and recharge his will. Stories habitually take place in bucolic surroundings or in timeless villages by the sea; people are out in the open and the sun is always shining. In Caliban's "Hygienic Food," girlfriends talk about their sexual preferences in a "garden hut protected by thick foliage" on a "lovely warm August afternoon" (Caliban 1897, v. 2, 14).

The *Album of Caliban* was successful enough to instigate the appearance of clandestine editions before and after Laemmert's sixth volume was off the press (Machado 2011). One of them, in one volume, listed New York City as its place of origin, no date, and an ironic "Mature Press" as publisher. Like other clandestine editions of famous licentious works, it included nude pictures inserted between texts to potentialize it as a pornographic book. The pictures had no connection to Caliban's tales and told their own stories, appealing to the Gothic imaginary of sequestered women in dungeons or the fantasy of the Turkish harem. Coelho Neto was aware of the clandestine editions and regarded them as signs of the work's success. Laemmert Bookstore clearly viewed its publication as a superior product, printed on better-quality paper than *Pup's Stuff* and *Bell Peppers*. Coelho Neto was already renowned for the refined quality of his writing and his peers in the elite literary community enjoyed Caliban's tales, despite considering them minor works due to their humor and carnality. His reputation and good connections helped sell the idea of a superior form of erotic literature written in a loftier style, ideally bound in hardcover to be placed in a gentleman's library.

4 Conclusions

The "books for men" phenomenon helped shape an emerging modern print and reading culture in late nineteenth-century Brazil that has been overlooked by traditional historiography. As Samah Selim argues with regard to Middle Eastern Studies, the literature of the late nineteenth and early twentieth centuries "has been almost exclusively constructed around the genealogy of a narrow, elite political, and intellectual culture" (2006, 36). In a relatively similar manner, because they bypassed the construction of a properly national novelistic canon and challenged classical definitions of literature as educational, "books for men" were ignored, attacked, or even suppressed, eventually becoming bibliographical rarities. Nonetheless, considering the wide *popularity* of printed erotica, this chapter, in outlining modern literariness, has sidelined the Romantic and elitist conventions celebrating the centrality of authorship. Instead of emanating from the individual imagination of the writer, the erotic plots and libertine configurations came from a common reservoir of narratives, old and new, that were circulating in print. The description of sexual activity outweighed considerations about location and the national character. Moreover, as an alternative to European novels, "books for men" featured spicy anecdotes, picaresque tales, "frame narratives," and decadent short stories. Instead of the austere and hostile world pictured in the realist novel, "books for men" offered a literature of pleasure and abundance and a fantasy of erotic connection with matter. There were no economic difficulties and no crisis of the disillusioned bourgeois self. Commercialized as light entertainment, "books for men" proposed an escape from reality, while the European realist novel was about engaging with national reality. Examining the retooling of humanism, libertinism, and naturalism as an alternative to European and domestic novelism and realism, this chapter has sought to not only challenge elitist mappings of modernity as grounded in the European bourgeois novel acclimated to Brazil, but also to introduce an alternative that indicated a different articulation of "the modern," more conducive to popular consumption than to elitist literary engagements, and thus closer to comedy than to tragedy.

Works Cited

Abreu, Márcia. 2008. Sob o olhar de Priapo: narrativas e imagens em romances licenciosos setecentistas. In *Imagens na história*, ed. Alcides Ramos, Rosangela Patriota, and Sandra Pesavento, 344–373. São Paulo: Hucitec.

Bakhtin, Michael. 1984. *Rabelais and His World*. Bloomington: Indiana University Press.

Barbosa, Marialva. 2010. *História cultural da imprensa: Brasil, 1800–1900*. Rio de Janeiro: Mauad X.

Barolini, Teodolinda. 1983. The Wheel of the *Decameron*. *Romance Philology* 36 (4): 521–539.

Bulhões, Marcelo. 2002. Leituras de um livro obsceno. In *A carne*, ed. Júlio Ribeiro, 9–59. Ateliê Editorial: São Paulo.

Caliban. 1897–98. *Álbum de Caliban*. 6 vols. Rio de Janeiro: Laemmert.

Darnton, Robert. 1998. *Os best-sellers proibidos da França revolucionária*. São Paulo: Cia das Letras.

Deaecto, Marisa Midore. 2011. *O império dos livros: instituições e práticas de leitura na São Paulo oitocentista*. São Paulo: Edusp.

El Far, Alessandra. 2004. *Páginas de sensação: Literatura popular e pornográfica no Rio de Janeiro (1870–1924)*. São Paulo: Cia das Letras.

Frantz, David O. 1989. *Festum Voluptatis: A Study of Renaissance Erotica*. Columbus: Ohio State University Press.

Haliczer, Stephen. 1996. *Sexuality in the Confessional: A Sacrament Profaned*. Oxford: Oxford University Press.

Hallewell, Laurence. 1985. *O livro no Brasil (sua história)*. São Paulo: EDUSP.

Hunt, Lynn. 1999. Obscenidade e as origens da modernidade, 1500–1800. In *A invenção da pornografia: obscenidade e as origens da modernidade*, ed. Lynn Hunt, 9–46. São Paulo: Editora Hedra.

Jacob, Margaret. 1999. O mundo materialista da pornografia. In *A invenção da pornografia: obscenidade e as origens da modernidade*, ed. Lynn Hunt, 169–215. São Paulo: Editora Hedra.

Júnior, Simões. 2007. *Álvaro. A sátira no parnaso: estudo da poesia satírica de Olavo Bilac em periódicos de 1894 a 1904*. São Paulo: Editora UNESP.

Kearny, Patrick. 1982. *A History of Erotic Literature*. Hong Kong: Paragon.

Kendrick, Walter. 1987. *The Secret Museum: Pornography in Modern Culture*. New York: Viking.

Ladenson, Elizabeth. 2016. Literature and Sex. In *The Cambridge Companion to French Literature*, ed. John D. Lyons, 222–240. Cambridge: Cambridge University Press.

Leão, Andréa. 2013. *Brasil em imaginação: livros, impressos e leituras infantis (1890–1915)*. Fortaleza: INESP/UFC.

222 L. P. MENDES

Lobo, Eulália. 2001. *Imigração portuguesa no Brasil*. São Paulo: Hucitec.

M. L. n.d. *Os serões do convento*. 3 vols. Lisboa: Typograhia do Bairro Alto.

Machado, Ubiratan. 2009. *Pequeno guia histórico das livrarias brasileiras*. São Paulo: Ateliê Editorial.

———. 2011. *Coelho Neto*. Rio de Janeiro: Academia Brasileira de Letras.

Marcus, Stephen. 2008. *The Other Victorians: A Study of Sexuality and Pornography in Mid-Nineteenth-Century England*. New York: Routledge.

Mello, Maria Tereza Chaves de. 2007. *A república consentida: cultura democrática e científica do final do Império*. Rio de Janeiro: Editora FGV.

Mendes, Leonardo. 2016. Livros para Homens: sucessos pornográficos no Brasil no final do século XIX. *Cadernos do IL* 53: 173–191.

———. 2017a. *Álbum de Caliban*: Coelho Neto e a literatura pornográfica na Primeira República. *O eixo e a roda* 26 (3): 205–228.

———. 2017b. The Bachelor's Library: Pornographic Books on the Brazil-Europe Circuit in the Late Nineteenth Century. In *The Transatlantic Circulation of Novels Betweem Europe and Brazil, 1789–1914*, ed. Márcia Abreu, 79–100. London: Palgrave.

———. 2018. Zola as Pornographic Point of Reference in Late Nineteenth-Century Brazil. *Excavatio XXX*. n.p.

Moreira, Aline. 2017. Alfredo Gallis, o ponógrafo esquecido. *Graphos* 19 (2): 7–20.

Peakman, Julie. 2003. *Mighty Lewd Books: The Development of Pornography in Eighteenth-Century England*. London: Palgrave Macmillan.

Pina, Paulo Simões de Almeida. 2015. *Uma história de saltimbancos: os irmãos Teixeira, o comércio e a edição de livros em São Paulo, entre 1876 e 1929*. Master's Thesis in History, São Paulo, USP.

Rabelais. 1893. *Volúpias: 14 contos galantes*. São Paulo: Livraria Teixeira.

Santana, Maria Helena. 2004. Pornografia no fim do século: os romances de Alfredo Gallis. *Portuguese Literary and Cultural Studies* 12: 235–248.

Selim, Samah. 2006. The People's Entertainments: Translation, Popular Fiction, and the *Nahdah* in Egypt. In *Other Renaissances: A New Approach to World Literature*, ed. Brenda Deen Schildgen and Gang Zhou, 35–58. New York: Palgrave Macmillan.

Sigel, Lisa. 2005. Issues and Problems in the History of Pornography. In *International Exposure: Perspectives on Modern European Pornography, 1800–2000*, ed. Lisa Sigel, 1–26. New Brunswick: Rutgers University Press.

Sodré, Nelson Werneck. 1964. *História da literatura brasileira*. Rio de Janeiro: Civilização Brasileira.

———. 1983. *História da Imprensa no Brasil*. São Paulo: Martins Fontes.

Stoops, Jamie. 2015. Class and Gender Dynamics of the Pornographic Trade in Late Nineteenth-Century Britain. *The Historical Journal* 58 (1): 137–156.

Trousson, Raymond. 1996. Romance e libertinagem no século XVIII na França. In *Libertinos libertários*, ed. Adauto Novaes, 163–183. São Paulo: Cia das Letras.

Villalta, Luiz Carlos. 2012. Leituras libertinas. *Revista do Arquivo Público Mineiro* 48: 76–99.

Williams, Clem C., Jr. 1961. *The Genre and Art of the Old French Fabliaux: A Preface to the Study of Chaucer's Tales of the Fabliau Type*. PhD diss., Yale University, New Haven.

CHAPTER 12

Print Culture and the Reassertion of Indigenous Nationhood in Early-Mid-Twentieth-Century Canada

Brendan Frederick R. Edwards

1 Introduction

The discussion that follows seeks to contextualize an important portion of the history of Indigenous writing in Canada between 1915 and 1960, asking the reader to think not only about the *content* of writing, but also the *act* of writing in and of itself and the circumstances of the printing, circulation, and consumption of Indigenous writing—in other words, to think historically about *who* has been doing the writing, for *what purpose*, and whose voices have made it into print and widespread distribution. While settler colonial authors have historically dominated Canadian print culture, in this chapter I will argue for the significance of alternative designations of nationhood brought about by the (realized and aspirational) participation of Indigenous writers in Canadian print culture in the early and mid-twentieth century.

B. F. R. Edwards (✉)
The Royal Ontario Museum, Canada, Toronto, ON, Canada
e-mail: brendane@rom.on.ca

© The Author(s) 2020
R. Aliakbari (ed.), *Comparative Print Culture*, New Directions in
Book History, https://doi.org/10.1007/978-3-030-36891-3_12

225

226 B. F. R. EDWARDS

2 CON(TEXT)S IN COMPARISON

The vehicle of expression for European and settler-Canadian understandings, preconceptions, and inventions relating to the new world was print culture: the world of printed books and periodicals. Alphabetic literacy and print were the primary means by which Europeans took possession of the new world and placed it firmly within their known universe. Print culture provided a public vehicle which gave the new world official standing and made its discovery an "historical" event (Turner 1995, 58). Alongside the technology of gunpowder, and the unprecedented spread of European disease, print culture was a significant tool of colonial control in North America.

There have generally been two (mis)conceptions of North American Indigenous people since the time of Columbus and Gutenberg's invention of the printing press: the "Noble Savage," including the Indian Princess, and the "bloodthirsty" villain, including the intoxicated Indian and easy squaw. These images of the good and bad Indigenous person have been so strong and deeply held by Euro-American cultures to have persisted virtually unchanged since 1493.[1] Very soon after Columbus' "discovery," as information about the new world was dispersed and became more widely known in Europe, Indigenous peoples became permanent fixtures in the literary and imaginative works of Old World writers and popular storytellers.

Both the romantic and savage images of North American Indigenous peoples were widespread in nineteenth- and early twentieth-century Euro-American and settler-Canadian literature. Together with the duality of romantic and savage was the recurrent notion that Indigenous peoples were rapidly disappearing. As a literary device, the idea of a vanishing race before the onslaught of "civilization" inspired feelings of nostalgia, pity, and tragedy. The tragedy of disappearing Indigenous cultures, especially portrayed by the last living member of a tribe, thus became a staple of North American literature. The most famous of this genre was, of course, James Fenimore Cooper's *The Last of the Mohicans*, originally published in 1826, and still considered a classic by contemporary audiences and scholars.[2]

---

[1] For discussion on the popular image of North American Indigenous people in Western literature, art, and philosophy, see Berkhofer (1978, 71–111).

[2] Cooper's classic novel has been republished innumerable times, translated into several languages, and has inspired countless theatre, television, film, and comic book renditions. In

Thus, realistic, everyday Indigenous peoples were eliminated in the eyes and minds of settler North Americans by the printing press, the stroke of a pen, and the turn of the page. Widespread literacy and publishing by a non-Indigenous populace effectively erased Indigenous reality for a Western audience. A distinctly Canadian literature that worked to achieve this effect included works by missionaries such as John Maclean, John McDougall, and Egerton Ryerson Young. Their most influential books included Maclean's *The Hero of the Saskatchewan* (1891) and *The Indians of Canada* (1889), McDougall's *Indian Wigwams and Northern Campfires* (1895), and Young's *By Canoe and Dog-Train among the Cree and Salteaux Indians* (1890) and *Stories from Indian Wigwams and Northern Camp-Fires* (1893).[3] Increasingly pushed to the public and social back-burner, Indigenous peoples were seen by many Euro-Canadians as the caricatured representations in popular fiction and non-fiction. In history textbooks, continuing to the late twentieth century, Indigenous peoples were mentioned within a paragraph or two at the beginning of the first chapter, and then they vanished. In English Canada, settler children, like their American counterparts, likely learned to count, at least in part, by singing the nursery rhyme "Ten Little Indians." Written in 1868 as "Ten Little Injuns" by American songwriter Septimus Winner, the song counts down, featuring "injuns" dying by different means "until there were none" (see Hirschfelder and Molin n.d.; Jennings 2012; Jacobs 2017). As historian Jane Griffith (2015) has noted, "Ten Little Indians" was featured in songbooks and poetry textbooks authorized by Canadian provinces for curricular inclusion throughout the 1940s, 1950s, and 1960s (188).

While settler North Americans used print culture as a tool of cultural erasure against Indigenous peoples, religious missionaries were simultaneously introducing books and print culture to Indigenous peoples in Canada. It is thus important to consider the motivations and effects of introducing Western book literacy and print culture into Indigenous cultures in which orality and variant forms of literacy already existed and had served the people well for many generations. Syllabic and hieroglyphic

film alone there have been at least 17 productions, the most famous being that directed by Michael Mann in 1992, starring Daniel Day-Lewis. Martin Baker and Roger Sabin (1995) refer to *The Last of the Mohicans* as a "book that everyone knows but that few have read." Nonetheless, its inspirational and influencing qualities (right or wrong) apparently know no bounds.

[3] On the influence of missionary writers in early Canada, see Francis (1992, 44–60).

228   B. F. R. EDWARDS

writing forms developed by missionaries for the Nēhiyaw and Mi'kmaq, for example, were based on earlier forms of Indigenous writing and literacy. Christian missionaries such as Chrestien LeClercq and James Evans adapted these writing systems to serve religious and cultural purposes. Other Indigenous groups traditionally employed further methods of writing and knowledge preservation. The Haudenosaunee, for example, used wampum belts to record important events, Plains nations used winter counts, and the Ojibwe recorded information with birch bark scrolls, pictographs, and petroglyphs. Although rooted in oral culture, numerous Indigenous groups in Canada showed characteristics of what might be called *alternative literacies*[4] and engaged in scribal culture before Euro-Canadian missionaries introduced the alphabet and print culture.

The earliest uses and collections of books intended for an Indigenous readership were assembled by Christian missionaries. Missionaries sought to use books and literacy as a means of "civilizing" and converting Indigenous peoples to the Christian faiths.[5] The first full-length book printed in what is now Canada in an Indigenous language is likely Jean Baptiste de La Brosse's primer and prayer book, *Nehiro-iriniui aiamihe massinahigan* (1767), published in Québec in the Innu-alum language (see Banks 1983, ix). The eighteenth century saw only a handful of seminal works printed in Indigenous languages in Canada; however, the nineteenth century saw an explosion of such publications, as Moravians, Wesleyans, and Methodists joined Anglican and Roman Catholic missionaries in their translation and publishing efforts, resulting in thousands of books printed in Indigenous languages (Banks 1983, x). Beyond religious literature, Canada did not witness the publication of any translations of fiction or other popular literature into Indigenous languages until well into the twentieth century.

The late nineteenth and early twentieth centuries saw a great expansion in terms of missionary and government involvement in the formal education of Indigenous peoples. With the idea in mind of building and settling a nation from sea to sea, the British and Dominion governments actively sought to sign treaties with First Peoples. Provision of education was

[4] This term is borrowed from Elizabeth Boone and Walter Mignolo's *Writing Without Words* (1994), which relates to the Indigenous cultures of the Andes and Mesoamerica.

[5] I discuss the use of books and establishment of libraries among Indigenous peoples in Canada as tools of civilizing, conversion, and assimilation by missionaries and government representatives at length in my 2005 book *Paper Talk*.

usually a central aspect of the treaties, and the government encouraged missionaries to provide teachers, supplies, and initiative to school Indigenous peoples. Some Indigenous leaders accommodated religious education for practical reasons; others, such as Chief Shawahnahness of St. Clair River, wanted their people to acquire literacy skills but not religion. In 1833, Shawahnahness noted that his people had already agreed never to abandon their traditional religious beliefs, but added "we agree to send our children to school that they may learn to read, put words on paper, and count, so that the white traders might not cheat them" (qtd. in J.R. Miller 1996, 77–79).

Despite Indigenous interests in acquiring Western literacy skills, gaining access to relevant reading material was often difficult. The choice of books available to Indigenous peoples in their own languages at the time was entirely evangelical in nature and presented largely in the Roman alphabet. In addition, the nature of the education provided at the missionary and government-run schools was poor, and without adequate schooling, few Indigenous peoples took an interest in reading printed matter. Although many Indigenous children were sent by their parents to schools to learn "the whiteman's magic art of writing" (Kennedy 1972, 54–55), the schooling they received was generally not well suited to this kind of learning. Mike Mountain Horse, a day school student in the north-west in the late 1890s, recalled, "I do not remember any book learning acquired there" (1979, 15). With their focus more firmly rooted in religious, mechanical, and agricultural training suited to assimilate, the reading abilities of most graduates were questionable at best. Low-quality education did not produce many highly skilled readers in any language.

Alongside the likes of missionaries and popular writers such as James Fenimore Cooper, one of Canada's most compelling mythmakers in furthering misconceptions of Indigenous peoples was Duncan Campbell Scott (1862–1947), a respected poet and writer who was, critically, also a chief administrator of the federal government's Department of Indian Affairs, which was responsible for the creation and administration of government policy related to Indigenous peoples. Duncan Campbell Scott, now notoriously associated with his administration of Indian Affairs, was, during his lifetime, widely celebrated as one of Canada's Confederation Poets.[6] Scott's literary reputation has been solid since at least 1900, with

---

[6] For more on Duncan Campbell Scott as an administrator of Indian Affairs, see Titley (1986).

230   B. F. R. EDWARDS

his work appearing in virtually all major anthologies of Canadian poetry.[7] His tenure as Deputy Superintendent of Indian Affairs was turbulent, characterized by a paternal and narrow approach to administering affairs relating to Indigenous health, education, and welfare. Unironically, perhaps, much of his poetry was related to "Indians." Drawing on his experience as an administrator in the field, Scott expressed sensibilities as a poet saddened by the perceived waning of ancient Indigenous culture, or the "vanishing Indian." Yet in his administrative work, Scott actively sought to assimilate Indigenous peoples into the Canadian mainstream, effectively quickening the pace of the demise he felt was so imminent.[8]

Scott's reputation as a writer did nothing to help the aspiring literary careers of early twentieth-century Indigenous writers. Evidence shows that he very nearly single-handedly quashed the aspirations of aspiring Indigenous writers such as Edward Ahenakew (Nēhiyawēwin, 1885–1961) and Indian Affairs employee Charles A. Cooke (Thawennensere) (Kanien'kehá:ka, 1870–1958). Cooke attempted to start an "Indian National Library" within the Department of Indian Affairs in 1904, envisioning a collection of rare books and reports which could be accessed not only by departmental officials, but also by members of the public and Indigenous peoples themselves. Although Cooke found widespread support for this endeavour,[9] Scott stopped the idea dead in its tracks because he saw no value in the proposal.[10] While Scott can be credited with securing

[7] For more on Scott's literary achievement, see: Dragland (1974, 1994), Johnston (1983), R.L. McDougall (2008).

[8] For discussion of Scott's Indian poetry specifically, see Bentley (2006), Dragland (1994), Lynch (1982), Salem-Wiseman (1996), Weis (1986). For further discussion of Scott the administrator versus Scott the poet, see also Abley (2013), Neu and Therrie (2003), Smith (2014, 113–150).

[9] In correspondence available at Library and Archives Canada, in RG 10, Volume 3081, File 270,000–2 pt. 2A, there are at least 15 letters in glowing support of Cooke's idea to establish an Indian National Library. Several of the letters are in very poor condition and are thus unreadable. All those included, however, appear to express positive support. Cooke himself quotes from 12 of these in a letter to Frank Pedley, Deputy Superintendent General.

[10] It is important to note that the Canadian Federal Government's 1996 Royal Commission on Aboriginal Peoples recommended that a "National Aboriginal Documentation Centre" be established to "research, collect, preserve and disseminate information related to residential schools, relocations and other aspects of Aboriginal historical experience." Similarly, libraries, archives, and museums as cultural memory institutions feature prominently in the calls to action of the final report of the Truth and Reconciliation Commission of Canada (2015). Cooke's proposed Indian National Library was therefore more than 90 years ahead of its time. See recommendation 3.5.36 in the *Report of the Royal Commission on Aboriginal*

the legacy of the Department of Indian Affairs' historical activities by overseeing the management of the department's archives and establishing the department library in 1893 (Russell 1984, 70), he opposed Cooke's idea that the library be expanded to include Indigenous perspectives or be allowed to circulate to an Indigenous audience. Scott dismissed Cooke's ideas regarding his vision of an Indian National Library: "There is certainly an idea at the bottom of this scheme of his which is worth considering, but ... it has no great practical utility in its present form. There are two features which should not be adopted as part of an official scheme; I do not think the Indians ought to contribute, and I do not think the library should be circulating."[11] Cooke's "Indian National Library" would have followed up on his successful, but short-lived, venture, *Onkweonwe*, a Kanien'kehá:ka language newspaper (circa 1900–01).[12] As stated in an article published in May 1901 in the *Sudbury Journal, Onkweonwe* began "some time ago ... [as] a semi-monthly magazine." Finding success, Cooke "decided to turn it into a newspaper, the first of its kind in Canada and the second in America" (*Sudbury Journal* 1901, 1).[13] Although it was short lived, *Onkweonwe* was notable for its solicitations of contributions from Kanien'kehá:ka people from throughout the provinces of Québec and Ontario, and New York state, and it was the first Indigenous language newspaper written, compiled, and published solely by an Indigenous person in Canada, and just the second in North America.[14] The only known surviving copy of *Onkweonwe* is volume 1, number 1 (October 25, 1900), housed at Library and Archives Canada.

Peoples: Volume 3: Gathering Strength (1996, 538–539); and *Canada's Residential Schools: The Final Report of the Truth and Reconciliation Commission of Canada*, Volume 6 (2016, 223–241).

[11] Correspondence from Duncan Campbell Scott to the Hon. Clifford Sifton, Minister of the Interior, 29 January 1904, Indian Affairs Record Group 10 (RG 10), Volume 3081, File 270000-1, Reel C-11321, Library and Archives Canada, Ottawa, Ontario.

[12] The act of self-publishing and the use of the periodical form—which is by nature, ephemeral—in articulating both an alternative vision of modernity and to cross established cultural boundaries is notable, and parallels the experience of other underrepresented and marginalized groups discussed in several chapters within this volume. See the chapters by Hélène Le Dantec-Lowry, Arti Minocha, Shuk Man Leung, Corinne Sandwith, and Victoria Kuttainen and Jilly Lippmann.

[13] Similarly worded, if not identical, articles appeared in other North American newspapers, such as *The Cook County Herald* and the *Red River Prospector*.

[14] For a longer discussion of Charles A. Cooke's scholarly, literary, and performative endeavours, see: Edwards (2010).

232   B. F. R. EDWARDS

Furthermore, in 1922, Edward Ahenakew, with the help of academic and literary acquaintances, submitted a manuscript to Ryerson Press featuring stories he had compiled through conversations with Chief Thunderchild. Noted cultural nationalist and publisher Lorne Pierce, then chief editor at Ryerson Press, considered Ahenakew's manuscript to be of considerable interest and value. Pierce believed that more work needed to be published in relation to the Indigenous peoples of Canada "to establish the contribution of non-writing people to Canadian culture" (Campbell 2013, xx). Correspondence between Pierce and Ahenakew indicates that, for a time at least, Ryerson Press saw Ahenakew's work as worthy of publication; One of Ahenakew's letters to Paul Wallace, a professor of English at Lebanon Valley College and Ahenakew's longtime tutor and friend, mentions that Pierce was "very much interested in me and my work." Ahenakew quotes Pierce in this same letter as saying "I sincerely hope we may be able to find some way of publishing your ms. with the corrections you suggest."[15] Unfortunately for Ahenakew and other Indigenous authors of the day, Ryerson Press was in financial difficulties in the early 1920s. Under these circumstances, Pierce sought financial subvention to publish Ahenakew's work. Not surprisingly, Pierce approached the Department of Indian Affairs for financial assistance, since Duncan Campbell Scott had been an intermittent correspondent with Pierce on literary matters for several years (May n.d.). In his response to Pierce's request for financial assistance, Scott declined with little comment, simply stating, "I regret very much that we would have no funds to meet your suggestion with reference to Mr. Ahenakew's manuscript, much as I would like to assist."[16]

Scott's precise reason for neglecting to support Ryerson Press in publishing Ahenakew aside, he was known for being staunchly conservative. Scott's friend and contemporary, the professor and critic E.K. Brown (1951), wrote of him that he believed in the government's goal of assimilation of Indigenous peoples, and he believed that "by education and encouragement the Indians were to cease being interesting exotic relics" (xxvi). Scott was certain that there was no place for the Indigenous peoples

[15] Correspondence from Edward Ahenakew to Paul Wallace, 2 February 1923, B W15p, Box 1, Paul A. W. Wallace Papers, American Philosophical Society, Philadelphia.

[16] Correspondence from Duncan Campbell Scott to Lorne Pierce, 16 October 1924, Box 1, File 11, Item 14, Lorne and Edith Pierce Collection, Queen's University Archives, Kingston, Ontario.

in modern and progressive twentieth-century Canada. Therefore, he believed it necessary for Indigenous people to collectively abandon their cultural traditions and accept the customs, religion, and values of settler-Canadian society to survive. The literary efforts of aspiring Indigenous writers such as Ahenakew and Cooke, who sought to preserve and maintain the traditions of their people within the Western literary tradition, were thus unacceptable within the realm of Scott's Indian Affairs ideology. As literary historian Robert L. McDougall (2008) has aptly stated, "Scott's literary representations of First Nations peoples in his poetry and fiction has generated considerable critical controversy. In poems such as his 1894 sonnet, 'The Onondaga Madonna,' Scott presents his Indigenous subjects as noble, but 'doomed'.... Many late-20th- and early-21st-century writers...have noted the dark irony of Scott's poetic sorrow for dying cultures that his own Department of Indian Affairs was actively eradicating, mainly through the residential school."

The Ahenakew manuscript under consideration by Ryerson Press was a collection of stories that he had collected from Thunderchild (Peyasiw-Awasis) (Nēhiyawēwin, 1849–1927), and others that Ahenakew had written himself, loosely entitled "Old Keyam." Keyam was a fictional character created by Ahenakew who was both "pained and angry" and "humorous and satirical" (Miller 2010, 254). The character of Keyam is partly autobiographical, and this persona acted as a literary device for Ahenakew to express comment on a range of topics, including settler-Canadian insensitivity towards Indigenous peoples, the lethargy of Indigenous peoples about their own fates, and political satire. Old Keyam was Ahenakew's effort at writing "as things appear to the Indian himself."[17] Ahenakew was successful in publishing some of the Thunderchild stories as "Cree Trickster Tales" in 1929 in the *Journal of American Folklore.*[18] However, the bulk of his writing, including "Old Keyam," would remain unpublished until after his death.[19]

[17] Correspondence from Edward Ahenakew to Paul Wallace, 5 September 1923, B W15p, Box 1, Paul A.W. Wallace Papers, American Philosophical Society, Philadelphia.

[18] Three of these stories were later reprinted in *Saskatchewan Harvest: A Golden Jubilee Selection of Song and Story* (1955).

[19] During his lifetime, Ahenakew was successful in updating the Cree-English part of *A Dictionary of the Cree Language* with Archdeacon R. Faries (1938). He also translated some works into Cree syllabics for the Society for Promoting Christian Knowledge, including A. Leigh's *Cree New Testament Stories* (1936) and Caroline M. Duncan Jones's *Everybody's Prayer* (1933?).

Ahenakew only became well known as a writer posthumously when Ruth Buck[20] edited a selection of his manuscripts of Cree stories and published them as *Voices of the Plains Cree* with McClelland and Stewart in 1973. The extant of Ahenakew's personal papers, which have been preserved at the Provincial Archives of Saskatchewan in Regina, demonstrate that for a significant part of his life, he imagined himself as a writer. Among his papers are notebooks filled with poetry and a clear attempt at a full-length novel. "Black Hawk," in its original handwritten form, is more than 120 handwritten pages long, filling five scribblers, organized in clear chapters. Composed between 1912 and 1916, it is written in a romantic style that suggests that Ahenakew aspired to write in the spirit of E. Pauline Johnson. The full extent of Ahenakew's writing cannot be fully known, as the papers that today exist at the Provincial Archives of Saskatchewan were only saved several years after Ahenakew's death, and there are gaps due to large portions missing. What is clear, however, is that writing, both professionally in his role as an Anglican Minister and creatively, was a regular activity for Ahenakew.

When one examines Ahenakew's original papers at the Provincial Archives of Saskatchewan, the nature and condition of the manuscripts themselves strongly suggest that the gaps evident in the "Black Hawk" manuscript indicate an incomplete draft. The original scribblers in which "Black Hawk" was written are in surprisingly decent shape considering their age and the fact that they did not find their way into the Archives until after Ahenakew's death. Parts of the novel, such as a chapter titled "Hawk Goes to Boarding School," appear to be unfinished, rather than missing or damaged because of the ravages of time. What we know of other aspects of Ahenakew's life suggest that his demanding duties as an Anglican cleric and chronic poverty likely made it difficult for him to devote a lot of time and energy to writing.

At around the same time that Ahenakew was engaged in writing Old Keyam and Black Hawk, he began self-publishing the *Cree Monthly Bulletin* (*Nehiyaw okiskinohtahikowin*), a newsletter which he used to promote Christianity among the Nēhiyawēwin, in 1922. The newsletter was printed in set type in Cree syllabics, and was issued from the St. Barnabas Indian School at Onion Lake, Saskatchewan. The *Cree Monthly Bulletin* at some point became the *Cree Monthly Guide*, which was also issued in

---

[20] For more on Ruth Buck, see Matheson (1960); see also my article "Ruth Buck and the Publication of Edward Ahenakew's Voices of the Plains Cree."

syllabics, featuring editorials and articles on spiritual matters and lessons in catechism. Fortunately, several issues of the *Cree Monthly Guide* have been preserved in the papers of Robert Archibald Logan at the Provincial Archives of Saskatchewan. Logan was immensely interested in learning the Nēhiyawēwin language, and he wrote to Ahenakew about subscribing to the *Cree Monthly Guide*, and asked questions and advice of Ahenakew regarding various translations, dialects, and pronunciations. Logan's relationship with Ahenakew was important to his own research and writing on issues relating to the Cree language.[21]

From the cache of *Cree Monthly Guide* issues that survive, we can get some sense of the nature of Ahenakew's efforts in self-publishing. Amongst these issues, ranging from 1941 to 1954, we can see evidence of the wide range of topics that the monthly guide featured.[22] Mainly published in Cree syllabics, articles included relevant and contemporary discussion about religion and religious news and reflection, Indigenous news from around Canada (e.g., in regards to other Indigenous publications, such as the *Native Voice* in British Columbia, the rise in the Indigenous population, or changes in the *Indian Act*), political and election discussion, news from pupils and ex-pupils, community reports, and stories about individuals, including Henry Budd (c. 1812–75, celebrated as the first Indigenous person ordained by the Anglican Church in North America), and members of the British monarchy. The clear majority of the content and commentary originated from Ahenakew's pen, and reflected his views and

[21] See Correspondence between Edward Ahenakew and Robert Logan, 1942–1959, File 4, R-214, Robert Archibald Logan Papers, Provincial Archives of Saskatchewan, Regina; and Newsletter, Cree Monthly Guide, 1941–1954, File 14, R-214, Robert Archibald Logan Papers, Provincial Archives of Saskatchewan, Regina. Logan published some material on the Cree language as well, including *The Books of Kapuwamit* (1968); *Cree-English Dictionary and Remarks on the Cree Language* (1964); *Cree Language Notes* (1958a); and *The Cree Language as It Appears to Me* (1958b). He also curiously wrote a foreword to volume six of Reider T. Sherwin's nonsensical *The Viking and the Red Man: The Old Norse Origin of the Algonquin Language* (New York: Funk & Wagnalls, 1940–1957); and an article in *Beaver* magazine on the Cree language: "The Precise Speakers" (1951). See also Robert A. Logan Fonds, MS-2-580, Dalhousie University Archives and Special Collections, Halifax, Nova Scotia.

[22] Single issues of the *Cree Monthly Guide* are also available at Library and Archives Canada, Special Collections at the University of Saskatchewan Library, and the Glenbow Museum Library and Archives; three issues from the 1920s and 30s are housed in the Archives and Special Collections of the University of Manitoba Library, and six issues from between 1942 and 1960 are housed in the General Synod Archives, Anglican Church of Canada.

opinions. But Ahenakew did not work alone on the *Cree Monthly Guide*. Mimeographing, for example, was taken care of by someone else, who was presumably also Cree, as Ahenakew stated in a letter to Logan: "The Christmas number of the Cree Guide will be a little late this time as the man who mimeographs for me has been out trapping & hunting and will, I hope be back tonight & will be able to do the work next week."[23]

The *Cree Monthly Guide* was also occasionally published in English. Ahenakew explained in the September 1926 edition his reasons for issuing an English edition: because he wished to reach "the many ex-pupils of our Schools who cannot read the Syllabic but who are able to read English. These are not always in a position to secure English papers for themselves and are therefore out of touch with events and influences which would be for their welfare" (*Cree Monthly Guide* 1926, 1).[24] Ahenakew's second purpose was to induce "white people ... to subscribe and by this means an intelligent interest would be aroused in them in things that pertain to the Church's work among the natives of this land" (*Cree Monthly Guide* 1926, 1).

An initial reading of the body of Ahenakew's work might suggest to some that he was merely toeing the line of his non-Indigenous Church of England superiors, citing the need to "civilize" Indigenous peoples, but Ahenakew's active involvement in organizations such as the League of Indians (an early pan-Indigenous organization devoted to forming an Indigenous presence and voice on a national scale) suggests his motives were deeper.[25] In his introduction to "Old Keyam," Ahenakew encourages his Indigenous readers, and points out to non-Indigenous readers that as contemporary First Peoples, "we must face the challenge of our day, not as white men, but as good Indians" (Ahenakew 1995, 51). Ahenakew's published articles in organs such as the *Canadian Churchman* and the *Western Producer Magazine* suggest that at least part of his motivation in

---

[23] Correspondence from Edward Ahenakew to Robert Logan, 19 December 1953, File 4, R-214.1, Robert Archibald Logan Papers, Provincial Archives of Saskatchewan, Regina.

[24] *The Cree Monthly Guide* 11, no. 9 (September, 1926): 1 (in MSS C550/1/31.3, Morton Manuscripts Collection, Special Collections Department, University of Saskatchewan Library, Saskatoon, Saskatchewan, Canada).

[25] Ahenakew's apparent motives in self-publishing the *Cree Monthly Guide* reflect some of the objectives outlined in Hélène Le Dantec-Lowry's chapter in this volume on nineteenth-century African-American participation in print culture.

writing was to educate a non-Indigenous audience about the traditions, beliefs, and current plight of his people.[26]

Ahenakew and Cooke are but two examples of Indigenous literary endeavours and writing in Canada that fall roughly within the period after the death of the widely popular mixed-heritage Kanien'kehá:ka writer and performer, E. Pauline Johnson (Tekahionwake, 1861–1913), and before the emergence of contemporary Indigenous writing in the 1960s and 1970s. Others include—but are almost certainly not limited to—Andrew Paull (Skwxwú7mesh, 1892–1959), Bernice Loft Winslow (Dawendine) (Kanien'kehá:ka/Gayogohó:no', 1902–1997), K'HHalserten Sepass (Sto:lo, c. 1840s-1943), Deskaheh (Gayogohó:no', 1873–1925), and Dan Kennedy (Nakota, 1877–1973). Contemporary Ojibwe writer Armand Garnet Ruffo (1998) has referred to this period as the "dark days" (212); scholar Penny Petrone (1990) called it a "barren period" (95); and historian Cecilia Morgan (2005) says this time was the "nadir of Native-white relations" (70) in Canada. Widely read contemporary Indigenous writer and academic Thomas King (1994) notes that "there appears to be a gap of some fifty-odd years in which we do not see Natives writing" (357–58) after E. Pauline Johnson. All agree that the impact of the federal government's residential schooling policy served to silence many Indigenous voices, and the climate in Canadian publishing at the time was largely not interested in writing by Canadians of non-European descent.

Indigenous populations at the time were also believed to be in steady decline—at least from the settler-Canadian perspective—with the notion that their populations would very soon be completely irrelevant to the larger Canadian society. Even during the time that E. Pauline Johnson was writing, few other Indigenous writers could capitalize on her popularity. This was mainly the result, again, of the government-mandated education system that was based on settler-Canadian cultural expectations and that prohibited Indigenous students from speaking their traditional languages. Petrone noted that only a few "isolated" educated Indigenous peoples existed during this period because the system of education to which First Peoples were subjected was not a literary one (1990, 71). Few learned

---

[26] See "Sixty-Five Years Ago" (1951); "Island Lake Indian Mission" (n.d.); "Geographical Conditions as They Affect the Indian Character" (1919a), "Indian Superstitions" (1919b). Copies of Ahenakew's *Canadian Churchman* articles are held at the Provincial Archives of Saskatchewan, Regina.

238   B. F. R. EDWARDS

more than manual labour skills or trades. With few exceptions, most Indigenous peoples did not acquire sufficient language or literacy skills in English or French to be inspired to write, and because they were prohibited and punished for speaking their own languages, they became isolated from their home communities when they completed school.[27] Keeping these education standards in mind, it is perhaps of little wonder that few Indigenous peoples in Canada wrote between 1860 and 1960.

In her lifetime, Johnson was well loved and widely respected. But for nearly 50 years following her death—the same period in which Edward Ahenakew was active, for example—Johnson's reputation was very nearly forgotten. As Margaret Fairley wrote in 1954, "There is a sharp contrast between the reputation of Pauline Johnson in her lifetime and her reputation now. Two or three of her poems are known through anthologies.... The prose works are hardly known at all.... Yet in her lifetime her work was loved by audiences of people of all classes right across Canada, and won high praise from the leading critics of the time" (43). Carole Gerson and Veronica Strong-Boag (2002) note that during her lifetime, Johnson was most often referred to as a "poetess," but in the decades following her death, she was usually devalued as a "princess," playing to popular stereotypes. Much of the blame for this, according to Gerson and Strong-Boag, was due to the literary Indian impostors Grey Owl and Buffalo Child Long Lance,[28] who had built up considerable reputations in print, were adored by settler-Canadian audiences only to be later exposed as frauds: "The stories of these two phoney Indians, both of whom had been remarkably successful in deceiving audiences eager for 'safe' representatives of oppressed peoples, did little to create confidence in the authenticity of Native authors and performers" (Gerson and Strong-Boag 2002, 125). Within such an environment, settler-Canadian readers and critics devalued Johnson's literary reputation, suspecting that she too might have been some kind of an impostor.

Indigenous literary endeavours and writing in the first half of the twentieth century thus suffered from a similar modernist devaluation. In the 50 years following Johnson's death, settler-Canadian audiences were either

---

[27] The living conditions and nature of studies in the schools are well-documented. See, for example, Barman et al. (1986), J.R. Miller (1996), Milloy (1999).

[28] For more on "Chief Buffalo Child Long Lance," see Smith (1999). Long Lance used print and publishing as one means of inventing himself as an Indian. In addition to his biography *Long Lance* (1928), he was active as a journalist with the *Calgary Herald* and was often published in other periodicals such as *Maclean's*.

distracted by the convenient romance and fulfilled stereotypical imagery of Grey Owl and Long Lance, or they were turned off by having been deceived by these same fake Indians. The environment for Indigenous writing and performance was therefore largely hostile towards authentic Indigenous people, who ironically did not fit perceived notions of "Indianness," thus explaining their essential erasure from the Canadian literary memory. The impact of generations of popular and widely read non-Indigenous writing about First Peoples that cast Indigenous peoples as noble savages, a vanishing race, or savage menaces, were viewed not as mere fiction, but as a historical and contemporary truth. In part, this is how dress-up Indian impostors such as Grey Owl and Buffalo Child Long Lance established their careers of deception, by building on existing stereotypes and embodying the romantic image.

3   Conclusions

Indigenous writers such as Johnson, Sepass, Ahenakew, Cooke, Paull, and others were implicitly answering and trying to correct the negative, offensive, and inaccurate representations of "Indians" depicted in the writings of Europeans and settler North Americans. Rather than merely demonstrating evidence of Indigenous assimilation of Western literacy and book culture, such writing (published and not published) followed what Indigenous scholar Robert Warrior (2005) has termed an "intellectual trade route" (181–87). Indigenous writers articulated and adopted Western forms to suit their own purposes of communication, knowledge transfer, and community, and brought new information and knowledge to Indigenous and non-Indigenous audiences alike using the same tools that had been used against them.[29] Although the medium of their message was rooted in Western traditions of literacy and print culture, the messages they sought to transmit were not messages of defeat.

Alphabetic literacy and print culture were tools of colonialism, allowing settler-newcomers to lay claim over Indigenous lands and resources and to issue and administer laws and policies affecting the lives of Indigenous peoples. Although rooted in oral and scribal cultures, Indigenous peoples

---

[29] Such interventions in print culture, as ways of inserting/asserting one's cultural perspective into that of the dominant culture, bear resemblance to themes discussed in Corinne Sandwith's chapter in this volume discussing female writers in the colonial South African press, and Arti Minocha's chapter on female authorship in colonial Lahore.

adapted and articulated alphabetic literacy and print culture to suit their own cultural, historical, and political needs. The works of aspiring early-twentieth century Indigenous writers such as Cooke, Ahenakew, and others demonstrated concerted efforts to create an intellectual space for Indigenous peoples in early twentieth-century Canada. In turn, the writing of English settler-Canadians established for the country a "fictive ethnicity" in which Indigenous people, for one, were decidedly pushed to the margins, characterized as existing firmly in the past, and denied any existence in the present or future of the country. Indigenous writing in the nineteenth and early twentieth centuries, as much as it could, attempted to discredit such assumptions, to modify and correct Canada's fictive ethnicity.

The history of literacy in Indigenous communities shows us that Indigenous people have been mostly receptive to Western notions of literacy and the printed word since missionaries first introduced the book as a means of communication early in the colonial relationship. Furthermore, Indigenous reasons for embracing the printed word have been motivated by a desire to articulate and use this Western tool of communication for their own social and political purposes.[30] Indigenous interests in the printed word, as this comparative examination of their production and circulation circumstances shows, have reflected pan-Canadian Indigenous concerns of effectively adjusting to the permanent reality of settler-Canadians while at the same time finding ways to maintain Indigenous histories, literariness, and knowledge as means of forming, or aspiring towards, print-based communal subjectivities that were alternative to Euro-Canadian colonial settler templates.

Works Cited

A Paper for the Mohawks: The New Weekly Will Be Printed in Their Own Tongue. *Sudbury Journal*, May 30, 1901: 1.

Abley, Mark. 2013. *Conversations with a Dead Man: The Legacy of Duncan Campbell Scott*. Madeira Park: Douglas & McIntyre.

Ahenakew, Edward. 1919a. Geographical Conditions as they Affect the Indian Character. *Canadian Churchman*.

———. 1919b. Indian Superstitions. *Canadian Churchman*, Aug 14.

---

[30] See Minocha's chapter in this volume, which explores how women in colonial Lahore mobilized print technologies to project new identities into transnational print publics.

———. 1929. Cree Trickster Tales. *Journal of American Folklore* 42: 309–353.

———. 1951. Sixty-Five Years Ago. *Western Producer Magazine*, January 11.

———. 1995. Introduction to Old Keyam. In *Voices of the Plains Cree*, ed. Ruth M. Buck, 51–52. Regina: Canadian Plains Research Center.

Ahenakew, Edward, and R. Faries. 1938. *A Dictionary of the Cree Language*. Toronto: General Synod of the Church of England in Canada.

———. n.d. Island Lake Indian Mission. *Canadian Churchman*.

Baker, Martin, and Roger Sabin. 1995. *The Lasting of the Mohicans: History of an American Myth*. Jackson: University Press of Mississippi.

Banks, Joyce M. 1983. *Books in Native Languages in the Rare Book Collections of the National Library of Canada*. Ottawa: National Library of Canada.

Barman, Jean, Yvonne Hébert, and Don McCaskill, eds. 1986. *Indian Education in Canada: Volume 1: The Legacy*. Vancouver: UBC Press.

Bentley, D.M.R. 2006. Shadows in the Soul: Racial Haunting in the Poetry of Duncan Campbell Scott. *University of Toronto Quarterly* 75 (2): 752–770.

Berkhofer, Robert F., Jr. 1978. *The White Man's Indian: Images of the American Indian from Columbus to Present*. New York: Alfred A. Knopf.

Boone, Elizabeth H., and Walter Mignolo. 1994. *Writing Without Words: Alternative Literacies in Mesoamerica and the Andes*. Durham: Duke University Press.

Brown, E.K. 1951. *Selected Poems of Duncan Campbell Scott*. Toronto: Ryerson Press.

Campbell, Sandra. 2013. *Both Hands: A Life of Lorne Pierce of Ryerson Press*. Montreal: McGill-Queen's Press.

Canada. Royal Commission on Aboriginal Peoples. 1996. *Report of the Royal Commission on Aboriginal Peoples: Volume 3: Gathering Strength*. Ottawa: Canada Communications Group.

Cooper, James Fenimore. 1826. *The Last of the Mohicans: A Narrative of 1757*. Philadelphia: H.C. Carey & I. Lea.

Dragland, Stan, ed. 1974. *Duncan Campbell Scott: A Book of Criticism*. Ottawa: Tecumseh Press.

———, ed. 1994. *Floating Voice: Duncan Campbell Scott and the Literature of Treaty 9*. Concord: Anansi.

Duncan Jones, Caroline M. 1933?. *Everybody's Prayer*. Trans. Edward Ahenakew. London: Society for Promoting Christian Knowledge.

Edward Ahenakew Papers, R-1, Provincial Archives of Saskatchewan, Regina.

Edwards, Brendan F.R. 2005. *Paper Talk: A History of Libraries, Print Culture, and Aboriginal Peoples in Canada Before 1960*. Lanham: Scarecrow Press.

———. 2009. Ruth Buck and the Publication of Edward Ahenakew's Voices of the Plains Cree. *Historical Perspectives on Canadian Publishing*. http://digitalcollec-tions.mcmaster.ca/hpcanpub/case-study/ruth-buck-and-publication-edward-ahenakew-s-voices-plains-cree. Accessed 17 Aug 2018.

242   B. F. R. EDWARDS

———. 2010 Spring. A Most Industrious and Far-Seeing Mohawk Scholar: Charles A. Cooke (Thawennensere), Civil Servant, Amateur Anthropologist, Performer, and Writer. *Ontario History* CII (1): 81–108.

Fairley, Margaret. 1954. Pauline Johnson. *New Frontiers* 3 (2, Summer): 43–45.

Francis, Daniel. 1992. *The Imaginary Indian: The Image of the Indian in Canadian Culture*. Vancouver: Arsenal Pulp Press.

Gerson, Carole, and Veronica Strong-Boag, eds. 2002. *E. Pauline Johnson, Tekahionwake: Collected Poems and Selected Prose*. Toronto: University of Toronto Press.

Greenblatt, Stephen J. 1991. *Marvellous Possessions: The Wonder of the New World*. Chicago: University of Chicago Press.

Griffith, Jane. 2015. One Little, Two Little, Three Canadians: The Indians of Canada Pavilion and Public Pedagogy, Expo 1967. *Journal of Canadian Studies* 49 (2): 171–204.

Hirschfelder, Arlene, and Paulette F. Molin. n.d. I Is for Ignoble: Stereotyping Native Americans. Jim Crow Museum of Racist Memorabilia, Ferris State University. https://ferris.edu/HTMLS/news/jimcrow/native/homepage.htm. Accessed 17 Aug 2018.

Indian Affairs Record Group 10 (RG 10), Library and Archives Canada, Ottawa.

Jacobs, Alex. 2017. Ten Little Indians: A Genocidal Nursery Rhyme. *Indian Country Today*, September 12. https://newsmaven.io/indiancountrytoday/archive/ten-little-indians-a-genocidal-nursery-rhyme-zdEJZ1XzDE-uez7zs42LEQ/. Accessed 17 Aug 2018.

Jennings, Julianne. 2012. The History of 'Ten Little Indians.' *Indian Country Today*, October 11. https://newsmaven.io/indiancountrytoday/archive/the-history-of-ten-little-indians-q1WdVbswNEu5Hat3KCQoAA/. Accessed 17 Aug 2018.

Johnston, Gordon. 1983. *Duncan Campbell Scott and His Works*. Downsview: ECW Press.

Kennedy, Dan. 1972. *Recollections of an Assiniboine Chief*, ed. James R. Stevens. Toronto: McClelland and Stewart.

King, Carlyle, ed. 1955. *Saskatchewan Harvest: A Golden Jubilee Selection of Song and Story*. Toronto: McClelland and Stewart.

King, Thomas. 1994. Native Literature in Canada. In *Dictionary of Native American Literature*, ed. Andrew Wiget, 357–358. New York: Garland.

Leigh, A. 1936. *Cree New Testament Stories*. Trans. Edward Ahenakew. London: Society for Promoting Christian Knowledge.

Logan, Robert A. 1951. The Precise Speakers. *The Beaver* 31 (1): 40–43.

———. 1958a. *Cree Language Notes*. Lake Charlotte: Loganda.

———. 1958b. *The Cree Language as it Appears to Me*. Lake Charlotte: Loganda.

———. 1964. *Cree-English Dictionary and Remarks on the Cree Language*. Duluth: R. A. Logan.

———. 1968. *The Books of Kapuwamit*. New York: Vantage Press.

Long Lance, Buffalo Child. 1928. *Long Lance*. New York: Cosmopolitan.

Lorne and Edith Pierce Collection, Queen's University Archives, Kingston, Ontario.

Lynch, Gerald. 1982. An Endless Flow: D.C. Scott's Indian Poems. *Studies in Canadian Literature* 7 (1): 27–54.

Maclean, John. 1889. *The Indians of Canada*. Toronto: William Briggs.

———. 1891. *The Hero of the Saskatchewan: Life Among the Ojibway and Cree Indians in Canada*. Barrie: Barrie Examiner Printing & Publishing House.

Matheson, Ruth Buck. 1960. The Matheson's of Saskatchewan Diocese. *Saskatchewan History* 13 (2): 41–62.

May, Robert G. n.d.. The Poet and the Publisher: Duncan Campbell Scott and Lorne Pierce. *Historical Perspectives on Canadian Publishing*. http://digitalcollections.mcmaster.ca/hpcanpub/case-study/poet-and-publisher-duncan-campbell-scott-and-lorne-pierce. Accessed 17 Aug 2018.

McDougall, John. 1895. *Indian Wigwams and Northern Campfires: A Criticism*. Toronto: William Briggs.

McDougall, Robert L. 2008. Duncan Campbell Scott. *The Canadian Encyclopedia*. https://www.thecanadianencyclopedia.ca/en/article/duncan-campbell-scott/. Accessed 17 Aug 2018.

Miller, J.R. 1996. *Shingwauk's Vision: A History of Native Residential Schools*. Toronto: University of Toronto Press.

Miller, David R. 2010. Edward Ahenakew's Tutelage by Paul Wallace: Reluctant Scholarship, Inadvertent Preservation. In *Gathering Places: Aboriginal and Fur Trade Histories*, ed. Laura Peers and Carolyn Podruchny, 249–273. Vancouver: University of British Columbia Press.

Milloy, John S. 1999. *"A National Crime": The Canadian Government and the Residential School System, 1879 to 1986*. Winnipeg: University of Manitoba Press.

Morgan, Cecilia. 2005. Performing for 'Imperial Eyes': Bernice Loft and Ethel Brant Monture, Ontario 1930s–60s. In *Contact Zones: Aboriginal and Settler Women in Canada's Colonial Past*, ed. Katie Pickles and Myra Rutherdale, 67–89. Vancouver: UBC Press.

Morton Manuscripts Collection, MSS C550/1/31.3, Special Collections Department, University of Saskatchewan Library, Saskatoon.

Mountain Horse, Mike. 1979. *My People the Bloods*, ed. Hugh A. Dempsey. Calgary: Glenbow-Alberta Institute & Blood Tribal Council.

Neu, Dean, and Richard Therrie. 2003. *Accounting for Genocide: Canada's Bureaucratic Assault on Aboriginal People*. Black Point: Fernwood.

Of Mohawk Indians: To Have Newspaper in Their Own Tongue. *The Cook County Herald*, June 29, 1901: 1.

Of Mohawk Indians: To Have Newspaper in Their Own Tongue. *Red River Prospector,* June 20, 1901: 3.

Paul A.W. Wallace Papers, American Philosophical Society, Philadelphia.

Petrone, Penny. 1990. *Native Literature in Canada: From the Oral Tradition to the Present*. Toronto: Oxford University Press.

Robert Archibald Logan Papers, R-214, Provincial Archives of Saskatchewan, Regina.

Ruffo, Armand Garnet. 1998. Out of the Silence – The Legacy of E. Pauline Johnson: An Inquiry into the Lost and Found Work of Dawendine – Bernice Loft Winslow. In *Literary Pluralities*, ed. Christl Verduyn, 211–223. Peterborough: Broadview Press.

Russell, Bill. (1984–85). The White Man's Paper Burden: Aspects of Records Keeping in the Department of Indian Affairs, 1860–1914. *Archivaria* 19 Winter: 50–72.

Salem-Wiseman, Lisa. 1996. 'Verily, the White Man's Ways Were the Best': Duncan Campbell Scott, Native Culture, and Assimilation. *Studies in Canadian Literature* 21 (1): 120–142.

Smith, Donald B. 1999. *Chief Buffalo Child Long Lance: The Glorious Impostor*. Red Deer: Red Deer Press.

Smith, Keith D., ed. 2014. *Strange Visitors: Documents in Indigenous-Settler Relations in Canada from 1876*. Toronto: University of Toronto Press.

Titley, E. Brian. 1986. *A Narrow Vision: Duncan Campbell Scott and the Administration of Indian Affairs in Canada*. Vancouver: University of British Columbia Press.

Truth and Reconciliation Commission of Canada. 2016. *Canada's Residential Schools: The Final Report of the Truth and Reconciliation Commission of Canada*. Vol. 6. Montreal/Kingston: McGill-Queen's University Press for the Truth and Reconciliation Commission.

Turner, Margaret E. 1995. *Imagining Culture: New World Narrative and the Writing of Canada*. Montreal/Kingston: McGill-Queen's University Press.

Warrior, Robert. 2005. *The People and the Word: Reading Native Nonfiction*. Minneapolis: University of Minnesota Press.

Weis, L.P. 1986. D.C. Scott's View of History and the Indians. *Canadian Literature* 111: 27–40.

Young, Egerton Ryerson. 1890. *By Canoe and Dog-Train Among the Cree and Salteaux Indians*. Toronto: William Briggs.

———. 1893. *Stories from Indian Wigwams and Northern Camp-Fires*. Toronto: William Briggs.

Index[1]

NUMBERS AND SYMBOLS

1930s, 85

A

The abolitionist movement, 129
The abolition of slavery (1865), 125
Advertising, 56, 197
Aesthetics, 14
Afghanistan, 7
African-American cookbooks, 11
African-American intervention, 1
African Americans, 123
African book histories, 5
African heritage, 136
African newspapers, 13
African women, 12
   women readers, 158
   women's written literature, 12, 146
Ağaoğlu, Ahmet, 70, 71, 75
Agency, 139
Age of Consent Act of 1891, 180

Aghayean, 67
Ahenakew, Edward, 17, 230,
   232–234, 236, 238, 239
Ahmaddiya movement, 168
Akçura, Yusuf, 71
Akutagawa, Ryūnosuke, 191
Alabama, 135
The Alarming News from Russia, 8, 107
Album of Caliban, 16
Ali, Hüseyinzade, 71
Allen, 176
All India Women's Conference
   (1926), 179
Alphabetical literacy, 17, 226
Alpomis, 77
Alterity, 11, 19
Alternate modern, 12
Alternate vision, 15
Alternative African modernity, 13
Alternative literacies, 228
Alternative literary modernities,
   1, 15, 19

[1] Note: Page numbers followed by 'n' refer to notes.

© The Author(s) 2020
R. Aliakbari (ed.), *Comparative Print Culture*, New Directions in
Book History, https://doi.org/10.1007/978-3-030-36891-3

245

246 INDEX

Alternative literary print modernization, 9
Alternative modernities, 10, 12, 16, 19, 130, 159
Alternative or dissenting African modernity, 146
Alternative print cultural practice, 159
Alternative print modernity, 16
Alternatives, 3, 11, 20, 118
The American Anti-Slavery Society, 125
American exemplars, 6
Anatolia, 64, 71, 74
Anderson, Benedict, 5, 167
Anglo-American academic models, 2
Anti-Black racism, 12
Anticlericalism, 212
Anticlerical pornography, 212–214
Antifascist struggle, 91
Anxiety, 189
Appleton, Nathan, 128
Arab, 4
Arabic, 4
Archaism, 3
Archival examination, 17
Area studies, 2
Argentina, 1, 83
Aristocracy, 212
Armenians, 63–65, 67, 67n7, 74, 75n16
Art, 49
Articulations of modernity, 187
Art Nouveau, 196
Arya Samaj, 168
Asahi Shinbun, 191
Asia, 4
Aşıks, 66
Assimilation, 17
Assimilation of Indigenous peoples, 232
Association of Hunan Students Studying Abroad in Japan, 112
Association of Jiangsu Students Studying Abroad, 112

Asturian insurrection, 91
Audiences, 5
Australia, 1, 42
The Australian Woman's Mirror, 5, 45
Authors, 14, 213
Authorship, 220
Avant-garde, 1, 83, 205
art and mass culture, 100
experimentation, 91
poetry, 84
Azerbaijan, 1, 62, 64, 64n5, 71, 75–79, 75n17
Azerbaijani folklore, 76
Azeri, 7, 68
Azeri folklore, 65
Azeri nationalist movement, 76
Azeri press, 77
Azeri Turkish, 78

B
Bābak-e Khorrami, 76
Baghirov, Mir Jafar, 77
Baku, 62, 77
Balkans, 7
Bandit, 61–79
Bandit-Minstrel, 67
The Bantu World, 12, 143
Başgöz, İlhan, 74
Baudelaire, Charles, 10
Beecher, Catharine E., 129n10
Beetham, Margaret, 44
Beijing, 112
Bengali, 14
Benjamin, Walter, 10
Bernice Loft Winslow, 237
Besant, Annie, 180
Bharat Stri Mahamandal, 179
Bibliography, 109
Black female essayists, 13
Black female writers, 12
"Black Hawk," 234
Black illiteracy, 138

INDEX   247

Blacks, 124
Black subjectivity, 11
Boccaccio, Giovanni, 211, 218
Bolivian-Paraguayan War, 96
Bolu, 62, 75n16
Book, 213
  culture, 4
  history, 2, 17
  for men, 214
Bookism, 17
Bookstore, 217
Boratav, Pertev Naili, 64n4, 66, 67n7, 73, 74, 74n14, 76
Boston, 126
Bourgeois, 1, 208
Bourgeois modernity, 12
Bourgeois self, 220
Boxer Rebellion, 113
Brazil, 1, 16, 208
Brazilian, 213, 216
Brazilian literary, 16
Brochures, 211
Brown, E.K., 232
Buck, Ruth, 234
Buenos Aires, 8, 94
Bushidō, 189
Butler, Josephine, 180

C

Cai Yuanpei, 115
Campbell, Tunis G., 11, 127
Canada, 1, 42
  fictive ethnicity, 240
Canadian print culture, 225
Canon, 198
Canonization, 1, 19
The Canterbury Tales, 218
Capitalism, 127
Carpenter, Mary, 177
Carter, David, 42
Catholic, 208

Caucasus, 64, 68, 74, 78, 79
Celali, 74, 75n16
Çelebi, Evliya, 75n16
Celebrity authors, 197
Central Asia, 63
Chance Encounters with Beautiful Women, 109
Charleston, South Carolina, 128
Chaudhurani, Sarala Debi, 178
Cheap brochures, 209
Cherniack, Susan, 28
Chia, Lucille, 28
China, 1
  partition, 107, 111
Chinese, 105
Chinese New Fiction, 8
Chinese public sphere, 107
Chodźko, Alexander, 64n5, 65–69, 79
Chrestien LeClercq, 228
Christian missionary writings, 13
Chronicle, 7, 83
Church, 213
Circulating Libraries, 16n5
Circulation, 5, 17, 48
Citizenship, 8
The Civil War, 125
Civil War Amendments, 139n21
Clandestine editions, 209
Clandestine publications, 214
Classicism, 2
Cleland, John, 212
Close textual readings, 19
Coimbra, 213
Cold War, 9
Collectivity, 19
Colonialism, 11
Colonial modernity, 3, 153
Comedy, 220
Commercial books, 125
Commercialized, 210, 220
Commercialized literature, 16
Commercial magazines, 5

248 INDEX

Commercial media, 10
Commercial presses, 170
Commercial print culture, 6
Communication, 9
Communist modernization, 7
Communist Party, 90
Comparatism, 18
Comparative, 4, 18
Comparative literature, 2
Comparative print culture, 1, 19
Comparativist, 13
Comparison, 5, 19
Confucian, 111
Conor, Liz, 43
Conservative periodicals, 208
Consumer, 210
Consumerism, 6
Contested modernity, 134
Contests, 13
Context, 11
Contextual examinations, 11
Contributor, 12
Cooke, Charles A., 17, 230, 237, 239
Cookbooks, 123, 125
Coolidge, 131
Cooper, James Fenimore, 226, 229
Co-opt, 189
Cosmopolitan centres of Europe, 46
Cosmopolitan Hinduani (Ram), 14
Cosmopolitanism, 100, 173, 182
Coterie journals, 191
Counter-colonialism, 6
Counter-colonial literary, 6, 17
A counter-narrative, 125
Covent Evenings, Voluptuousness: 14
    Gallant Tales, 16
Cree Monthly Bulletin, 234
Cree Monthly Guide, 235
Cree syllabics, 234, 235
Cuisine, 137
Cultural capital, 189
Cultural flows, 166
Cultures of print, 5, 11

D

Danger, 48
De Man, Paul, 13
de Saint-Exupéry, Antoine, 95
De Weerdt, Hilde, 28
Decameron, 214
Deconstruct, 19
Dede Korkut, 77
Department of Indian Affairs, 229,
    230, 232
Deskaheh, 237
Destan, 62, 64, 73, 74, 77n19, 78
Diaspora, 11
Discourse, 11
Dissemination, 16
Distinctive, 18
Distribution networks, 12
Distributors, 14
Divergent, 18
Diversification, 4
Domestics, 126
Dora Msomi, 13
The Dream of a New Year, 110, 115
Durkheim, Émile, 9
Dystopian, 114

E

Early print cultures, 16n5
East Asia, 10n3
East-West transculturation, 7
Economic class, 18
Economy, 11
Edition, 215
Editor, 12
Editorials, 8, 107, 209
Edo period, 16n5
Education, 12
Education of Indigenous peoples, 228
Egyptian, 4
Eisenstein, Elizabeth L., 3, 167
Ekrem, Recaizade Mahmut, 70, 72
Elitist, 220

INDEX 249

Ellen Pumla Ngozwana, 13
Endogenous modernization, 3, 6, 17
Enpon, 195
Entertainment, 49
Equal rights, 139
Erotica, 1
Eroticized, 218
Erotic literature, 16
Ersoy, Mehmet Ākif, 72
Euro-Canadian colonial settler
    literature, 17
Eurocentric, 5
Europe, 3, 208
European colonial contact, 17
European modernity, 9
European realist novel, 220
Evans, James, 228
Evolution, 19
Experts, 139
Exploitation, 96

F
Faiz, Faiz Ahmed, 13
Fasana-i Azad (Sarshar), 14
Felski, Rita, 41
Female-oriented alternative literary
    modernity, 6
Female-oriented public sphere, 146
Feminine/femininity, 12, 216
Ferrier, Carole, 42
Fetish, 213
Fiction, 16
Fiction Circle, 112
"Fictive ethnicity," 240
Film, 46
Fisher, Abby, 11, 134
A Flapper Tragedy: A Short Story of a
    Modern Young Miss, 55
Folk literature, 69
Folklore, 62
Folkloric motifs, 62, 74–75
Folk narratives, 69

Folk poetry, 64n5
Food, 125
Formats, 19, 214
Frames, 20
France, 214
Francis, C. S., 128
Free, 128
Free-thinking, 212
French, 7
French Enlightenment, 13
The Future of New China, 105, 109

G
Genç Kalemler, 71
Gendai Nihon Bungaku Zenshū (現代
    日本文学全集, Complete Works
    of Contemporary Japanese
    Literature), 199
Gender, 11, 13, 15, 18, 132, 146
Gender hierarchies, 6
Genres, 19
Georgian, 65, 74
Gerson, Carole, 42
Ghana, 5
Ghazal, 13
Glamour, 48
Globalization, 9
Global South, 2
Gökalp, Ziya, 70, 73, 75
Good wives, wise mothers, 193
Gore, Christopher, 129
Gothic, 219
Government-mandated education, 237
Grey Owl, 238
Grove, Shannon Jaleen, 53
Guazi, 114
Guides, 125

H
Habermas, Jürgen, 13, 107, 167
Haggard, H. Rider (Victorian writer), 5

250 INDEX

Hajibeyli (Hajibeyov), Uzeir, 7, 76
Haksthausen, Baron von, 67
Hammill, Faye, 43
Han, 114
Han Yu, 3, 27–35, 31n5, 31n6, 37
Hangzhou, 112
Havana, 216
Hegemonic modernity, 9, 12
Hegemony, 19
Higuchi Ichiyō, 15, 193
Hindus, 14
Hiratsuka Raichō, 15, 194
Historical contextualization, 17
Historicizes, 11, 16
Historiographies, 14
History of Books, 16n5
History of Indigenous writing in
    Canada, 225
Hobsbawm, Eric, 73n12, 79
The Home, 5, 45
Homogeneous, 5
Homogenization, 9
Homogenizing tendencies, 9
Hong Kong, 10n3
Hotel, 127
*Hotel Keepers, Head Waiters, and
    Housekeepers' Guide* (Campbell), 11
Household employees, 128
Housekeeping, 125
Housekeeping guides, 11, 123,
    126–134
*House Servant's Directory or, A
    Monitor for Private Families*
    (Roberts), 11
Humanist literatures, 16, 210, 214

I
Ideal femininity, 149
Idealization of bandits, 73
Identity-formation, 176
Idiom, 19
Illustrated Fiction, 112

Immigrants, 98, 127
India, 1
The Indian Ladies Magazine, 173
"Indian National Library," 230, 231
Indigenization, 117
Indigenized, 3
Indigenous Canadian literature, 17
Indigenous languages, 228
Indigenous nationhood, 1
Indigenous readership, 228
Individualism, 19
Inoue, Tetsujirō, 189
I-novels, 191
Intellectual dialectics, 5
Intelligentsia, 15
Interfusion, 16
International historical, 11
Intertextuality, 8, 107
Iqbal, Muhammad, 14
Irish women, 126
Iwanami Bunko (岩波文庫), 199
Iwanami Shigeo, 195
Iwanami Shoten, 15, 195

J
Japan, 1, 15, 185
Japanese, 15
Japanese publishing industry, 195
Javed Nama (Iqbal), 14
Javid, Hüseyin, 76, 77
Jiangsu Journal, 8, 107
Johannesburg, 12
Johnson, E. Pauline, 234, 237, 238
Journalism, 83
Journalists, 214
Justice, 126

K
Kaçak Kerem, 76
Kaçak Nabi, 76
Kaizōsha, 195

INDEX 251

Kanien'kehá:ka language, 231
Kaplan, Mehmet, 72
Karacadağı, Andalib, 64
Kemal, Namık, 70, 72
Kemal, Yaşar, 74
Kennedy, Dan, 237
Kerala, 4
King Solomon's Mines (Haggard), 5
Kitchener, Dr. William, 135n17
Kokoro, 196
Kommunist, 77
Köprülü, Fuad, 73
Korea, 16n5, 115
Koroğli-nāma/Koroğli-nâma, 65–67
Köroğlu, 7, 61–79
Köroğlu *destan*, 61, 62, 67n7, 69, 73–75, 77, 78
Köroğlu'nun Meydana Çıkışı, 74
Kyōyōshugi, 195

L
Labor division, 12
Lahore, 14, 166
Language, 2, 19
La rosa blindada, 91
The Last of the Mohicans, 226
Late nineteenth-century Brazil, 207
Latin America, 7, 83
Latin American avant-garde movements, 88
Le Meunier d'Angibault, 68
Lewd brochures, 207
Liang Qichao, 105
Liberalism, 15
Libertine literature, 16, 209, 216
Libertinism, 211
Licentious literature, 207, 217
Light entertainment, 220
Lisbon, 213
Literacy, 12, 227
Literariness, 13
Literary, 13

Literary canon formation, 16
Literary cultures, 4
Literary historiographies, 16
Literary history, 13
Literary modernity, 7, 13
Literary modernization, 14, 84
Literary print, 1
Literary print cultures, 8
Literary print modernity, 3, 17
Literary Production Circulating Libraries, and Private Publishing, 16n5
Literature, 207
Lithography, 4
Liu Kai, 27, 29, 31
Liu Yun, 30, 31, 34, 37
Liu Zongyuan, 3, 27–33, 31n5, 31n6, 31n7
Logan, 236
Longfellow, Henry Wadsworth, 68
Long Lance, Buffalo Child, 238
Longman, 176
Louvet du Couvray, Jean-Baptiste, 212

M
Mackie, Ellen Evelyn, 48
Macmillan, 176
Magazines specifically aimed at women, 193
Mahalle Kahvesi, 72
Mainstream periodicals, 218
Male reader, 210
Manas, 77
Manchuria, 112
Manuscripts, 4
The margins, 125
Market, 211
Marx, Karl, 9, 10
Masculine, 216
Masnavi, 14
Material-cultural transactions, 5
Matthews, Jill Julius, 43

252 INDEX

Mayfair, 5, 45
McDermott, Joseph, 28
McLuhan, Marshall, 5
Media, 19, 186
Medieval *fabliaux*, 213
Meiji period, 110, 186
Melancholy, 215
Metal movable typography, 16n5
Metaphors, 214
Mexican citizenship, 11
Mexico, 11
Mhudi (Plaatje), 5
Mickiewicz, Adam, 67
Middle class, 11
Middle Eastern Studies, 220
Military coup, 99
(Mis)conceptions of North American
    Indigenous people, 226
Missionaries, 17, 228
Mobility, 52
Modern, 9
Modern genre, 206
Modern Girl Around the World
    Research Group, 5, 43
Modern indigeneity, 17
Modernism, 14, 84, 205
Modernist, 14
Modernity, 1, 3, 9, 19, 76, 84, 123,
    182, 205
Modernization, 8, 132
Modernizing genre, 83
Modern literariness, 220
Modern national identities, 79
Modern reading culture, 207
Modern subjectivity, 174
Modern Turkish literature, 70
Modjeska, Drusilla, 42
Molotov, 77
Monthly Fiction, 112
More, Sir Thomas, 8, 105
Mori Ōgai, 15, 189
Mu Xiu, 27, 30, 31, 31n7

Multiple modernities, 9, 75n17, 133
Multiplicity, 10, 20
Multi-volume collections, 199
Munroe and Francis, 128, 129, 139
Munshi, Iskender Beg, 75n16
Mushegean, Ilyas, 64, 67
Muslims, 4, 14

N
Nagasaki, 112
Narrative, 216
Nation, 107
The National Council for Women in
    India, 179
National hero, 61–79
National identity, 62
Nationalism, 16, 70, 75, 79
Nationalist modernization, 7
Nationalist poet, 72
Nationalization, 19
National literary histories, 5
National literatures, 2, 42, 198
National polity, 18
National subjectivity, 17
Nation formation, 1
Nation-states, 15
Natsume Sōseki, 15, 189
Naturalist, 16
Naturalist novel, 209
Negotiations, 13
Neoclassical prose, 25, 35n10
Neoclassical standards, 33
Neoclassical style, 29, 33
Neo-classical work, 38
Neoclassicism, 33–37
Neo-Classicism, 28–33
New Fiction Journal, 105, 112
Newspapers, 83
New Woman, 43
The new woman, 15
New York, 126

Nihon Koten Zenshū (日本古典全集, Complete Works of Japanese Classics), 199
Nineteenth-century US society, 123, 124
Niya, Ra'is, 64n4, 65, 68, 73, 76
Non-cohesive, 15
Non-European print cultures, 2
North, 125
Novel, 14, 16, 206
Novelism, 16
Novelists, 14

O
Official discourse, 187
Old Keyam, 233, 236
Oneiric, 97
Onkweonwe, 231
Oral culture, 7
Oral heroic traditions, 61
Orality, 4, 169, 227
Oral narratives, 14
Orientalism, 70
Orientalist publications, 7
Ottoman, 7, 63, 68, 71, 73n13
Ouyang Xiu, 33–37, 33n8

P
Pan-African modernity, 11
Patagonia, 95
Paull, Andrew, 237, 239
Performative traditions, 170
Periodical culture, 44
Periodicalism, 1
Periodicalists, 6, 19
Periodicals, 1, 217
Periodization, 3
Peripheral modernity, 100
Persian, 66, 73n13
Perso-Arabic tradition, 14

Phahlane, Johannah G., 13
Philippine, 6
Piccinino, 68, 70
Pierce, Lorne, 232
Pirated edition, 213
Plaatje, Sol, 5
Plot, 14, 219
Pluralize, 11
Pocket volumes, 212
Poeticization, 8
Poetics, 14
Poetry, 83, 100
Political poetics, 9
Politicization, 139
Politics, 11
Politics of responsibility, 133
Popular/popularization/popularizing, 10, 16, 19, 117–118, 220
    epics, 77n19
    erotic prints, 206
    journalism, 1
    literary print, 1
    literature, 76
Pornographic, 216, 219
Pornographic paperbacks, 206
Pornography, 208, 217, 219
Porto, 213
Portugal, 214
Portuguese, 209
Post-colonial, 3, 7
Postcolonial book histories, 4
Postcoloniality, 17
Practice, 11
Prescriptive literature, 125
Preservation, 17
Press, 8, 106
Prices, 214
Print, 1, 124
Print culture, 2, 185, 226, 227, 239
Print modernities, 1, 4, 15
Print-cultural contexts, 19
Print-cultural modernity, 2

254 INDEX

Printed literary works, 218
Printed literature, 17
Printed matter, 215
Printed periodical culture, 13
Printers, 14
Problematizing monolithic
perceptions, 18
Professionalization of writing, 84
Professionals, 138
Progress, 126, 134
Protest, 139
Provincial Archives of Saskatchewan, 234
Provincialized cosmopolitanism, 179
Publication, 12, 215
Public intellectual, 171
Public opinion, 108–112
Public print culture, 12
The public print culture
in 1930s South Africa, 146
Public spheres, 4, 107
Publishers, 14, 128, 195, 213
Punjab, 4, 14

Q
Qatır Mehmet, 76
Qing dynasty, 8, 106, 108
Qing public sphere, 108
Qissas, 169

R
Rabelais, François, 211
Rabelaisian realism, 211
Race, 11, 132
Racial uplift, 130
Radloff, 66
Rakhmabai case, 180
Ram, Susila Tahl, 14
Raúl González Tuñón, 8
Readers, 12, 14, 19
Readership, 5, 16, 186

Reading cultures, 1
Realism, 14, 16
Realistic, 97
Re-appropriation, 6
Recast, 16
Recipes, 129
Reconfiguring, 15
Reconstitutions, 15
The Reconstruction, 133
Redirection, 19
Refashioned, 12
Reform organizations, 165
Reforms, 213
Religious missionaries, 227
Remediations, 7
Renaissance Humanism, 211
Renegotiated, 12
Reportage, 83
Reporter, 94
Reports on Publications, 168
Reproduction, 18
Republican era, 73
Repurposing, 7, 15
Rescripting, 15
Resist, 17
Resistance, 139
Respectability, 130
Retool/retooling, 8, 15, 19
Reviewers, 19
Revisionist, 11
Revolutionary periodicals, 117
Revue de l'Orient, 68
Revue Indépendante, 68
Reworked/reworking, 7, 212
Rhetorical patterns, 212
Rig Veda, 4
Rio de Janeiro, 16, 213, 218, 219
Robert Archibald Logan, 235
Roberts, Robert, 11, 127
Robin Hood, 7, 62, 63, 70,
73, 73n12
Roman alphabet, 229

Romances, 6
Romantic Age, 70
Romantic-Age Paris, 69, 79
Romantic conventions, 220
Romantic-era France, 71
Romanticism, 66, 69–71
Romantic movement, 10
Romantic nationalism, 71
Romantic vogue, 7
Rossie Khabela, 13
Rumi, 14
Russell, Malinda, 125n5
Russia, 111, 114
Russo-Japanese War, 113
Ryerson Press, 232, 233

S
Sacramento, 135
Said, Edward, 70
Sand, George, 67, 68, 70
San Francisco, 112, 135
Sanskrit, 14
São Paulo, 16
Sarshar, Ratan Nath, 14
Schaffer, Kay, 42
Scott, Duncan Campbell, 17, 229, 232
Seitō, 194
Self-designation, 6
Selfhoods, 17
Self-publishing, 125, 235
Selling, 209
Sepass, K'HHalserten, 237, 239
Serial/serialized, 109, 190
Servants, 126
Settler-Canadian, 17, 226, 240
Settler colonial, 5
Settler colonies, 42
Sexuality, 12
Seyāhat-nāme, 75n16
Seyfettin, Ömer, 71, 72
Shakespearean reverberations, 216

Shanghai, 107, 112
Sikhs, 14
Simmons, Amelia, 135n17
Şinasi, Ibrahim, 70, 72
Sindhi, 14
Singh Sabha, 168
Sisterhood, 173
Six Classics, 111
Slave narratives, 124
Slavery, 11
Slaves, 124
Smith, Michelle, 44
Social banditry, 70, 72, 73, 75
Social classes, 6
Socialist icon, 7
Socialists, 110
Social reform, 14
Social sciences, 9
Song dynasty, 3
The South, 124, 126
South Africa, 1
South America, 94
South Asia, 13
South Carolina, 133
Soviet era, 78
Soviet regime, 9
Spaces of meaning, 185
Spanish, 6
Special correspondents, 83
Specimens, 67, 68
Spink, 176
Spivak, Gayatri C., 2
Stalin, 77
Stereotypes, 17
Storyline, 216
Struggles for emancipation, 96
Study Abroad and Translation
    Magazine, 8, 107
Subgenre, 213
Subjecthood, 1
Subjectivity, 1
Surrealism, 87

256 INDEX

T
Tabriz, 63–65
Tagalog, 7
Tahmasıp, M.H., 64n5, 65, 76
Tamil, 14
Tang dynasty, 3
Tanizaki, Jun'ichirō, 192
Tasvir-i Efkār, 70
Tbilisi, 65
Tecer, Ahmet Kutsi, 73
Techniques, 212
"Ten Little Indians," 227
Thacker, 176
Thacker's Indian Directory, 176
Thematic analysis, 17
Thematic examinations, 11
Themes, 212
'The Third World,' 19
Togan, Zeki Velidi, 73
Tokyo, 112
Tomorrow's Partition, 114
Tradition, 19
Traditional antecedents, 13
Tragedy, 220
  of disappearing Indigenous
    cultures, 226
Transdisciplinary, 2
Transmediations, 7
Transnational dialectics, 19
Transnationalism, 17
Transnational media culture, 83
Transnational networks, 15
Transnational Print Networks, 165–182
Transnational print publics, 167
Transregional dialectics, 10n3, 19
Transregional networks, 15
Treaties, 228
Trubner, 176
*Trubner's American, European and
  Oriental Literary Records*, 177
Tuñón, Raúl González, 83
Turan Hüseyinzade, Ali, 75
Turcology, 70

Türkçe Şiirler, 71
Turkey, 1, 62, 70–79, 75n17
Turkic, 7, 62, 64, 74
Turkic folklore, 65
Turkic heroic traditions, 77, 77n19
Turkish, 219
Turkish national identity, 71
Turkish nationalism, 70
Türk Yurdu, 71, 72
Typography, 4

U
United States (US), 12, 123
Universalism, 10
Universality, 19
Unpublishable, 208
Unwin, 176
Urbanization, 13
Urdu, 13
US Secretary of War Edwin Stanton, 133
Utopia, 8, 105
Utopian, 105

V
Vanishing race, 226
Vernacularization, 19
Vernacular publishers, 6
Victoria League, 177
Visual culture, 46
Voices of the Plains Cree, 234
Volumes, 213

W
Wagahai wa Neko de aru (吾輩は猫で
  ある, I Am a Cat), 196
Wallace, Paul, 232
Waugh, Evelyn, 47
Weber, Max, 9, 10
West, 8, 138
Western book literacy, 227

Western Europe, 2, 11
The Western Home Monthly, 5, 45
Westernization, 10
Western literacy, 229, 239
Western literary tradition, 233
Western modern femininity, 13
Western modernity, 11
Western print genres, 159
What Mrs. Fisher Knows About Old Southern Cooking, Soups, Pickles, Preserves (Fisher), 12
Wheatley, Phillis (Phyllis), 12, 124
White dominance, 11
White female journalist, 12
White hegemony, 139
White Southern women, 137
Wiley, 131
Womanhood, 15, 19
The Woman's Page, 12, 146
Women, 10n3, 12
  periodicals, 170
  solidarity, 136
  writers, 143

The Women's Indian Association (1917), 179
Woodblock printing, 4, 186
Woodblocks, 25, 26, 29, 32, 37
Work ethic, 131
A World of Yellow Men, 115
Writers, 19

X
Xi Kun, 30

Y
Yalnız Efe, 72
Yang Yi, 30, 31, 34, 37
Yangtze River, 112
Year of Blood, 76, 77
Yeni Yol, 77
Yokohama, 112
Yosano, Akiko, 191
Yurdakul, Mehmet Emin, 7, 70–72, 74n14

Printed in the USA
CPSIA information can be obtained
at www.ICGtesting.com
LVHW011129150324
774517LV00039B/1557